WOMAN'S LORE

SARAH CLEGG has a PhD in the ancient history of
Mesopotamia from Cambridge University, and reads
Sumerian, Akkadian, Arabic, Greek and Latin. Her
fascination with Lamashtu began with her BA thesis at
Oxford and she has been researching these monsters and
their demonic tradition as a passion project ever since.
Clegg was selected as one of the 2020/21 cohort of the
London Library Emerging Writers Programme.
She lives in London and works in heritage publishing.

SARAH CLEGG

WOMAN'S LORE

4,000 years of Sirens, Serpents and Succubi

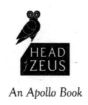

HEAD
ZEUS

An Apollo Book

First published in the UK in 2023 by Head of Zeus,
part of Bloomsbury Publishing Plc

9 7 5 3 1 2 4 6 8

A catalogue record for this book is available from the British Library.

ISBN (HB): 9781803280271
ISBN (XTPB): 9781804549650
ISBN (E): 9781803280257

Typeset by Adrian McLaughlin

Printed and bound in Great Britain by
CPI Group (UK) Ltd, Croydon CRO 4YY

Head of Zeus Ltd
First Floor East
5–8 Hardwick Street
London EC1R 4RG

WWW.HEADOFZEUS.COM

For my brother
because once, a long time ago,
he did the same for me.

Contents

To hear her whisper woman's lore so well,
and every note she spake entic'd him on

Keats, *Lamia*, 325–326

A Note on Capitalization and Pluralization

In all cases, the monsters discussed in this book have been given English plurals (Lamias as opposed to Lamiae, for example). In spanning numerous time-periods, languages and civilizations, the pluralizations of these names naturally vary wildly. Moreover, since these creatures are often under-attested in written sources, we don't always know their pluralizations for a given time period. The plural of the creature 'Gello' for example, was 'Gelloudes' in Byzantine sources, but should we back-apply this to Hellenistic Greece, where we don't have a surviving plural form of the word? For the sake of simplicity and clarity, English plurals are used instead.

Capitalization will also always be used for the demons under discussion. This is because they often shift from being a proper name of a single person, to a species of monsters, and back again. Lamia, for example, is both a much-wronged queen and a race of snake-tailed, seductive women. Often it's unclear which is meant in an individual source. To avoid confusion, capitalization will be maintained throughout.

Timeline

The key dates concerning our demons are in the left-hand column of the timeline below. To try to contextualize the 4,000 years of this tradition, the right-hand column contains important dates from history, such as the death of Tutankhamun and the beginning of the Crusades.

	*c.*3400–3300 BC – Earliest form of writing appears in Mesopotamia.
*c.*2000–1500 BC – First Lamashtu incantations and amulets.	*c.*1790 BC – Hammurapi becomes king.
*c.*1500–1000 BC – Writing of the first composite Lamashtu incantation in Ugarit, the likely Lamashtu text from Hattusa, and the Lamashtu text from Emar.	1323 BC – Death of Tutankhamun.
*c.*700–600 BC – First Pazuzu incantations and amulets.	631 BC – Death of Ashurbanipal.

*c.*700–600 BC – Egyptian Pazuzu statuette inscribed with the name 'Ssm son of Pdr'.

*c.*570 BC – Death of Sappho.

*c.*500–400 BC – Greek vase showing Lamia with a phallus produced.

*c.*480 BC – Vase showing the sirens as bird-bodied women surrounding Odysseus' ship produced.

*c.*450 BC – Crates writes his play describing Lamia with a 'staff'.

405 BC – First performance of Aristophanes' play *The Frogs*, which mentions Lamia's testicles.

306 BC – The concubine Lamia is captured at the Battle of Salamis by Demetrius.

*c.*300–200 BC – Likely period in which the poet Erinna was writing.

281 BC – Death of Duris of Samos, who wrote about Lamia.

609 BC – Fall of the Neo-Assyrian Empire.

586 BC – Sack of Jerusalem by Nebuchadnezzar II and the beginning of the Babylonian captivity.

509 BC – Creation of the Roman Republic.

499–449 BC Graeco–Persian Wars.

347 BC – Death of Plato.

323 BC – Death of Alexander the Great.

*c.*60 BC – Diodorus Siculus writes *Library of History*, including his rationalizing account of Lamia.

19 BC – Horace writes his *Ars Poetica*, mentioning Lamia devouring children.

AD *c.*115 – Death of Dio Chrysostom, who wrote about Lamia seducing and eating sailors.

AD *c.*120 – Date that Zenobius, the proverb compiler who preserved the fragment of Sappho relating to Gello's love of children, was teaching in Rome.

AD 172–200 – Period in which Apuleius wrote the *The Golden Ass*.

AD *c.*200 – Composition of Philostratus's *The Life of Apollonius of Tyana*.

AD 200–500 – Compilation of the Babylonian Talmud.

AD *c.*300 – Manufacture of the silver scroll inscribed with the charm story of the encounter between Artemis and the headache monster Antaura.

44 BC – Julius Caesar assassinated.

AD 75 – Writing of the last known cuneiform text.

AD 122 – Construction of Hadrian's Wall begins.

AD 224 – Sassanian conquest of Mesopotamia.

AD 324 – Constantine moves the capital of the Roman Empire to Constantinople.

AD 300–400 – Compilation of the *Cyranides*.

AD 300–400 – Earliest Mediterranean amulets produced that show Sisinis or Solomon impaling a woman with long, loose hair.

AD 397 – Death of Saint Ambrose.

AD 400–500 – Greek Palestinian amulets, which depict Sisinnios impaling a woman, often shown with a snake tail and described as 'Abyzou' produced.

AD 400–800 – First attestation of the Sisinnios story in Mesopotamia and Palestine.

AD 420 – Death of Jerome, translator of the Vulgate Bible.

AD 500–600 – The majority of the amulets depicting Sisinnios or Solomon impaling Abyzou produced.

AD 500–800 – Incantation bowls made and used.

AD 476 – Fall of Rome.

AD 570 – Birth of the Prophet Muhammed.

AD 600 – Death of Leander of
Seville, who wrote that all
women who were not nuns
were sirens.

AD *c*.700 – Composition of the
Liber Monstrorum, one of
the first texts to use the term
'mermaid'.
AD *c*.700–1000 – Composition
of the Alphabet of Ben Sira.
AD 749 – Death of John of
Damascus, the Christian
monk, priest and author,
who wrote dismissively
about the Gello.

AD *c*.806 – Death of Saint
Tarasios, who supposedly
held a trial for Gello-
possessed elderly women.

1072 – Death of Peter Damian,
who wrote angrily about
sirens and Lamias.
1074 – The Pope absolves
people of obedience to
bishops who allowed
married priests.

1165 – Creation of the mosaic
floor in Otranto Cathedral.

AD 636 – Muslim conquest of
Mesopotamia.
AD 661 – Foundation of the
Umayyad Caliphate.

AD 730–787 – First iconoclastic
period in the Byzantine
Empire.

AD 800 – Coronation of
Charlemagne as Emperor of
the Romans.

1095 – Beginning of the First
Crusade.

1153 – Death of the Byzantine
historian Anna Komnene.

c.1220 – Death of Gervase of Tilbury, author of *Otia Imperialia*.

c.1280 – Likely date of the composition of *The Treatise of the Left Emanation*.

1305 – Death of Moses de León, discoverer (or author) of the *Zohar*.

1308 – Yolande, the last surviving heir of the Lusignan family in Europe, sells the fief of Lusignan to Philip IV of France.

1391 – Composition of *Guerino the Wretch*.

1394 – Composition of *The Noble History of the House of Lusignan*.

1400–1500 – Earliest text relating the story of Melitene, Abyzou and Sisinnios in Greek.

1425 – Uccello finishes painting *Creation and the Fall*, including Lamia/Lilith amongst the animals.

1204 – Sack of Constantinople by crusader armies.

1215 – Signing of the *Magna Carta*.

1273 – End of the last major crusade in the Holy Land.

1299 – Founding of the Ottoman Empire by Osman I.

1346 – Beginning of the Black Death.

1400 – Death of Chaucer.

1453 – Ottoman Sultan Mehmed II sacks Constantinople.

1980 – Charles Stewart travels
to the Greek island of
Naxos.

1987 – Release of *Fatal
Attraction*.

1989 – Release of Disney's
The Little Mermaid.

1997 – First Lilith Fair.

2020 – Calida Rawles's
exhibition *A Dream for My
Lilith* opens.

1979 – Southall Black Sisters
formed.

Introduction

$\int$ et in ancient Greece, John Keats' 1819 poem *Lamia* tells the story of a beautiful snake-woman – the eponymous Lamia – who falls in love with a handsome charioteer, Lycius. Setting out to ensnare him, Lamia disguises her serpentine nature, seduces him with her 'woman's lore', and conjures incredible riches out of nowhere so they can live in luxury together. The besotted Lycius decides to marry her, but his mentor Apollonius comes to the wedding and exposes Lamia for the snake she is. Her true form revealed, she vanishes with a shriek, leaving Lycius to die of heartbreak without her. It's a strange little poem, which stands or falls on whether the reader enjoys the ambiguity at its heart: even though Lamia is deceptive, even though she is a literal monster, even though their relationship is described as one of 'sweet sin', the sympathies of the poet seem to lie with the lovers, and the reader is left feeling that Apollonius should have minded his own business, and that Lamia and Lycius could have lived together quite happily, if a little sinfully, had they just been left alone.*

Keats did not invent Lamia, or the story: he lifted it wholesale from Greek myths. The legend of the serpentine Lamia disguising

---

* When he wrote *Lamia* Keats was in the midst of his own romance with Fanny Brawne, whose mother was firmly against their relationship given the state of Keats' finances and health. Presumably this made Keats a little more sympathetic to the lovers, and a little less in favour of strident parental figures preventing marriages (however sensible their reasons for doing so).

her snake-form to seduce the handsome young charioteer, and being exposed at her wedding by Apollonius, is first attested in around AD 100, in Philostratus's *Life of Apollonius*. However, Keats's ambiguity is entirely absent in this earlier version – far from planning a happy life with her charioteer, Lamia admits she intended to eat him on their wedding night, and reveals she lures in attractive young men because their blood tastes the freshest.

Marriage was not the only method the ancient Lamia had for ensnaring her prey – another story describes her sitting by the sea with bare breasts and a serpentine tail, luring shipwrecked sailors to her with her beautiful face and chest before eating them alive. Lamia was so associated with seduction there was even an ancient Greek courtesan known by this name, but she was not just a danger to tasty young men – she also caused miscarriages, and murdered infants and their mothers. In most versions of the story this was because Lamia used to be a mortal woman who was beloved by Zeus and forced by an envious Hera to eat her own children. Turned monstrous by grief and guilt, Lamia went on to kill mothers and their babies out of uncontrollable jealousy that they had what she had lost.

Although Lamia is all but forgotten today, her legends are full of the echoes of more familiar myths. A scaly-tailed, bare-breasted seductress luring sailors to their doom has distinctly mermaid-esque undertones. A succubus with a habit of murdering infants and their mothers recalls the Jewish demon Lilith, the first wife of Adam. Fleeing the garden of Eden when she was refused equality with her husband, Lilith spent her time on the other side of the garden wall attacking children and pregnant women and seducing men. Lilith was also associated with snakes, and was frequently portrayed as the snake of Eden itself. In medieval art she appears as a hybrid monster with a serpent's tail instead of legs and the bare breasts and face of a beautiful woman, holding out the apple to Eve and looking indistinguishable from any mermaid or Lamia.

There are suggestions of other, lesser-known, monsters in Lamia as well: she looks a lot like Melusine, a beautiful snake-woman with a knack for marrying into the noble families of medieval Europe (and best known now as the Starbucks logo); she has similarities with the Byzantine Gello, a snake-tailed ghost of a girl who had died still a virgin, and who murdered young mothers and children out of jealousy. There are hints, too, of Abyzou, a child- and mother-killing monster who was defeated by King Solomon. Lamia even looks a little like a particular version of the prophetic Sibyl who lived in an earthly paradise in an Italian mountain, and tried to hide her snake tail from her lovers.

The similarities between these serpentine, child- and mother-killing succubi are no coincidence. Legends of all these creatures were bound up in each other, were part of a single tradition that has spanned almost the entirety of human history. The purpose of this book is to trace this tradition, to understand how it was passed down through the centuries, how it changed, and why it was so prolific and so widespread. To see where it began, we have to go back nearly four millennia.

The figure that stares out from a Mesopotamian amulet of the early first millennium BC (that is, around 800 BC) looks drastically different from any Lamia or mermaid. Carved into an oblong of grey stone is a demon with the head of a lioness, the talons of a bird, and a human torso. Although her head and feet are side-on, she has twisted her body so her bare, pendulous breasts are facing outwards, and on either side of her a wild pig and a jackal are standing on their hind legs, preparing to suckle on her teats. In each of her upraised hands, she clutches a snake. This is the Mesopotamian demoness Lamashtu – a monster attested in ancient Mesopotamian texts from as early as 2000 BC, who specialized in activities like choking babies on amniotic fluid and using her terrifyingly long fingers to reach inside women and drag out fetuses before their term.

We can trace a direct line of descent from this demon of the second millennium BC down to Lamia, Lilith and the mermaid, along with a multitude of other serpentine succubi. To get there we have to go via a snake-tailed ancestor of Richard the Lionheart, a child-eating wolf-monster of ancient Greece, a Roman spirit of headaches, the Queen of Sheba, a host of seductive vampires, and a rather sad species of virgin ghost called Lilitu. Some of the greatest literature and art has been inspired by these creatures, from Keats' poem to the best (and worst) of the Pre-Raphaelite paintings; from vivid collections of early Babylonian incantations to glittering medieval bestiaries and striking sets of Byzantine amulets; from the works of Hans Christian Andersen and Bram Stoker to the novels of Octavia Butler.

Spanning four thousand years, the demons described in this book represent one of the longest-surviving – and farthest-reaching – traditions of mankind, appearing in ancient Mesopotamia, in classical Greece and Rome, in Judaism, Christianity and (to some extent) Islam. They have touched four continents, picking up smatterings of different cultures and civilizations, tying themselves into other legends, constantly shifting and changing, but never so much that we cannot see and follow them through the millennia. They have proven so pervasive that in Jerusalem charms are still sold to ward off one of its most famous demons, Lilith; and as late as the 1980s inhabitants of the Greek islands were still working to drive away Lamia and Gello from mothers and their children. Even in cases where outright belief in these creatures has ebbed away, they remain – like the mermaid and Lilith – hugely important cultural touchstones.

But demons are never just demons, and stories are never just stories. As Sarah Iles Johnston (who studied Lamia and Gello in ancient Greece) put it, they are 'clay with which people mold images of their fears', a way of expressing our anxieties – and, hopefully, driving them away.

The demons examined in this book are no different, and the vast majority of fears that they reflect concern women. In creatures like the alluring, deadly Lamia and Lilith, not to mention the murderous mermaids, we can clearly see men using our monsters to confront their fears of seductive women,* and their own anxieties around sex. These monsters were used to define womanhood in the negative, and to brand as demonic any woman who behaved in a manner deemed insufficiently feminine. Many of them have been repurposed in the twentieth century as feminist and LGBTQ icons, so that Lilith, fleeing the Garden of Eden when denied equality, has found herself recast as the ultimate icon of women's liberation, and the mermaid, clearly gendered despite a complete absence of genitals, has become a trans symbol.

Perhaps more importantly, the child- and mother-killing aspects of these demons were a way for women to explore and understand the risks of pregnancy and labour, as well as the ever-present threat of infant mortality. In a world where a third of children would die before they reached adulthood (and women were almost solely responsible for childcare) and around 8 per cent of women would die in childbirth (and many more would

* Seductive behaviour, of course, could cover anything from turning up naked and actively trying to persuade a man to have sex, to existing while a man was nearby.

5

find their bodies permanently damaged by the experience), the charms and spells used to drive the demons away would have afforded women a small measure of control in terrifying circumstances. Incantations could be recited over sick and dying children and amulets could be placed round their necks; there were spells to help pregnancies go smoothly, and to drive demons away from the mother. The placebo effect may well have led to some real-world effects from these rituals, but just as important is the sense of agency they must have given women at such dangerous points in their lives. These aspects of the demons, and the spells that could be worked to keep them away from the childbed or a sickly infant, were passed down from woman to woman for thousands of years. They survived well into the twentieth century, almost unchanged over the millennia – a testament to the desperation of women attempting to survive one of the most dangerous things you could do in the premodern world: bearing a child.

So while this book is the story of a demonic tradition – a family tree of seductive, child-killing monsters – it is also the story of women and womanhood: of the dangers of childbirth; of attitudes to female sexuality; of women fighting for their rights. This is the true 'woman's lore' – not just a tool of seduction as in Keats's *Lamia*, but a tradition kept alive by women, that tells the story of women's lives, from 2000 BC to the present day.

There are two caveats to all of this. The first of these is that I will be using terms like demons and monsters fairly interchangeably to refer to the creatures described in this book. This is despite the fact that in, say, ancient Greece, the figures discussed here would certainly not have been thought of as 'daemons' (which was then a term that specifically referred to guiding spirits) or that in Mesopotamia Lamashtu is technically a goddess. There is simply not space to closely examine the specific supernatural belief systems of every period under discussion. 'Demons' or 'monsters', as they're used here, should be understood in the modern sense of malignant supernatural entities.

The second caveat is that every one of the following chapters could be a book in itself. There is so much to say about these creatures (who are often largely unknown in the modern day), so many stories to tell, that it felt almost impossible to stop writing about some of them. But the purpose of this book is to trace the history of the entire tradition, so the deepest dives into each individual demonic figure had to be put aside in order to understand the whole. If you want to read more about these creatures – and I'd strongly suggest you do; they're absolutely fascinating – do explore the selected bibliography.

I should also like to issue a trigger-warning. Inevitably, this book contains discussion of infant and maternal death. These issues affect a huge portion of the population. I've tried to steer away from detailed descriptions of births gone wrong and dying children, but there are plenty of people who would not want to read this book, or who are at a stage in their life where it could be extremely upsetting.

With these warnings borne in mind, we can turn to the very first member of this demonic family, the grand matriarch of them all: Lamashtu.

I

The Cradle of Civilization

The flat, arid plains of Mesopotamia – which roughly corresponds to modern Iraq, with a bit of Syria thrown in – are dotted with thousands of mounds. Some are so low as to be barely perceptible, others span many hectares and are hundreds of feet high – little mountain ranges grafted onto the surrounding plains. These mounds are entirely man-made, formed from the accumulated debris of millennia of inhabitation. The smallest of them mark sites of limited occupation, perhaps a minor village that lasted a handful of decades. The largest are the ruins of vast and ancient cities. Within these mounds you can find everything from libraries of clay tablets and palatial stone sculptures to the meanest ancient slums, but plunge a spade into one and you're all but guaranteed to come across two things: mudbrick and remains of dead infants.

The mudbrick should come as no surprise: it was the principal construction material of Mesopotamia. The proliferation of child remains, on the other hand, might initially feel stranger (not to mention sadder). Dig under a house floor, and you're bound to come across at least some, although since babies' bones are softer than those of adults, the skull will often have crumbled to dust, and even the leg and arm bones can flake away if you're not careful. Normally these little half-bodies are found in dirt-filled jars. The jars don't seem to have been specially made for the occasion: some are far too big for the job, others are on the small side. One of my most vivid memories, from time spent excavating at the ancient site of Tell Brak in Eastern Syria, is unearthing a baby packed into a lidded pot, about the size and shape of a Le Creuset casserole dish, its spine curved unnaturally so its little body could fit inside. It was one of three infant burials excavated in my small trench that season. This is a practice found in the ancient world well beyond Mesopotamia – child jar burials were common in ancient Greece and Rome as well. Even in areas of industry and manufacture, child skeletons turn up under the floors.

The sheer quantity of burials might seem shocking, but it's well in line with premodern mortality rates: prior to the development of modern medicine the chance of a child dying before adulthood is normally estimated at around 35 per cent. The other side of this tragedy is less evident in the archaeology – unlike infants, women's bodies blend into cemeteries with little to distinguish the circumstances of their death – but it's estimated that women had around an 8 per cent chance of dying in childbirth right up until the twentieth century, and we know that childbirth itself would have been an even more brutal, dangerous experience than it is today. Without advanced surgical tools, medicines and knowledge, for example, breech babies could not be safely delivered, infections post-pregnancy were rampant and usually untreatable, while haemorrhages and conditions like eclampsia (where high blood pressure causes seizures during pregnancy) would have caused numerous deaths. This doesn't even take into account the sorrows of miscarriage and infertility – even today around 1 in 4 pregnancies end in miscarriage, an experience that was taboo for all but the most recent generations of women.

There is little in the way of letters or literature to reflect the personal stories behind these grim statistics, but the horror, fear and pain that they inspired are revealed vividly in one collection of sources in ancient Mesopotamia: texts concerning demons, incantations and exorcism, especially those related to one particular figure, the terrible child- and mother-killing demoness Lamashtu. While she is little known today, for centuries she was the most powerful demoness in Mesopotamian tradition – a figure so formidable and important that her lore was passed down almost unchanged for over a millennium, inspiring fear over an enormous geographical area and at all levels of society, and standing preeminent above all other Mesopotamian monsters. This terrifying and fearsome creature was the foundational matriarch of the tradition that this book will trace, a vivid reflection of the lives of women and the horrors they faced before the advent of modern medicine.

There are dozens of texts that concern Lamashtu, scattered across the three thousand-odd years of ancient Mesopotamian history, but the most comprehensive surviving collection of them, and the best introduction to Lamashtu herself, comes from the Library of Ashurbanipal.

In 630 BC, the Neo-Assyrian empire was at its height. Stretching from the Zagros mountains of eastern Iraq through to Egypt and the Levant and up into Turkey, it was larger and more powerful than any empire the world had yet seen. Its capital, Nineveh, was a sprawling metropolis, dominated by a massive citadel rising at its easterly extent, circled by a tributary of the river Tigris, and perfectly placed to catch what little wind there was in the furiously hot summers. Atop this citadel was a chaotic assortment of temples and palaces, built of baked clay bricks, their entrances flanked by gigantic stone bull-men, and their corridors and rooms lined with six-foot-high stone friezes inscribed with the accomplishments of Assyria's kings.

The king in 630 BC, Ashurbanipal, had more than enough martial successes to fill all of his friezes, but he also had a hobby: he was a scholar.* In his palace – the Northwest Palace – he amassed one of the greatest libraries in the ancient world. It contained everything from incantations to omen decipherments to great epics. The Epic of Gilgamesh, one of the finest pieces of ancient Mesopotamian literature, was here, along with complete copies of such famous works as *Enuma Anu Enlil* (an astrological omen series), *Enuma Elish* (an epic of the god Marduk) and *Maqlu* (a set of rituals for removing negative magic), as well as many thousands of other treasures. All of these texts were inscribed with reed styluses on tablets made of clay, in a wedge-shaped writing known as cuneiform. The handwriting is beautifully standardized and precise, and many of the tablets have a

---

* Or at least, he tried to be. He wasn't very good at reading the Sumerian language, which is a bit like trying to be an intellectual in the Middle Ages and not reading Latin. We know the king struggled with the language because we have the letters he wrote to court scholars asking for their help with Sumerian words. If it feels unsporting to point out the academic failings of kings trying to better themselves, it's worth bearing in mind that Ashurbanipal did boast in an inscription that he had 'solved all of the mysteries' of 'all the tablets' so this is more like setting the record straight.

line at the end proclaiming that they belonged to the collection of Ashurbanipal.*

Even among these great works of literature, one set of incantations stands out – a gigantic 600-line text attested in three copies and consisting of fifteen incantations for driving away a particularly awful monster. The creature described in this text is a goddess, daughter of one of the most important deities in the Mesopotamian pantheon, the sky god Anu, but cast out of the divine company for expressing her desire to poison babies and small children. She has the wings of an eagle, the talons of a bird, the head of a lion or a dog, and the tongue and teeth of a donkey. She dresses in rags, and lives in swamps and other wild, desolate places. Nothing and no one seems to be safe from her – she strikes down young men and women and stalks livestock. Even walls become dirty when she leans on them. However, men and animals are fairly minor concerns for her – her principal interest is in mothers and their babies. She poses as a nursemaid and suckles children on her poisoned breast milk. She watches pregnant women, counting down the days until they give birth and then blocks their birth canal, or reaches inside them with her terrifying long fingers and drags out the baby prematurely. She clasps babies' bellies with her seven talon-like fingers and sickens them. She causes miscarriages and death in childbirth. In the Akkadian language, this horrific creature was called Lamashtu.

The text describes numerous ways of exorcising Lamashtu, most of which are long and complex (there's only one that takes less than three days). In one case, the exorcist makes figurines of

---

* Incidentally, this collection can only be described as a 'library' in the loosest sense – as a collection of written documents, as opposed to an institution that the public could use. It's unlikely that anyone but the king had access to the tablets.

Lamashtu and then destroys them: one is burned, one is buried at the city gate, and one is left in the wilderness beyond the cultivated farmland, along with provisions for her journey like a water bag, food, a comb and a spindle. Stones and plants in various combinations can be tied in a bag around the patient's neck, and depictions of Lamashtu can be drawn on the walls of her victim's room. One incantation advises the exorcist to make clay figurines of dogs and place them at the doors of the sick room. Wonderfully, clay models of dogs have actually been discovered buried under the floors of ancient Assyrian palaces, and most of them have cuneiform inscriptions written on the side, like 'expeller of evil' and 'catcher of the enemy', just in case there was any doubt that these were apotropaic tools associated with these kinds of rituals.

The tablets recording Lamashtu's incantations in the library of Ashurbanipal are called the Canonical Lamashtu Incantation Series by modern scholars, and represent the most complete surviving record of the demon, and the measures taken to protect against her. All three copies from the library (and an almost identical copy from a nearby temple) have survived more or less intact because of an inadvertent side effect of writing on clay: exposure to fire bakes the tablets, perfectly preserving them. When the Neo-Assyrian empire fell in 609 BC, only eighteen years after Ashurbanipal's death, Nineveh was sacked and the Northwest Palace and its library were burned to the ground. The tablets stayed where they fell, buried by the collapsed palace, until they were excavated over 2,000 years later by the archaeologist Hormuzd Rassam and carted off wholesale to the British Museum.

However, although the Neo-Assyrian empire may seem old enough by modern standards, by the time of Ashurbanipal's library and the Canonical Incantation Series Lamashtu was already ancient: spells had been worked against her for over a thousand years.

⁓

The god Anu begot her, the god Ea raised her,
The god Enlil gave her the face of a dog.
She has hardly any palms but long fingers,
And very long claws.
She enters the house through the door, she slithers in like
    a snake,
After slithering by the door socket, she saw the baby:
She grabbed him in the belly seven times.
Pull out your claws, loosen the grip of your arms,
Before a valiant exorcist with regard for Ea's craft
    overcomes you!
The door socket is wide for you, the doors are wide
    open!
Go and roam about in the wilderness!
I will fill your mouth with dust, your face with drifting
    sand,
Your eyes with tiny cress seeds,
I herewith conjure you by the curse of Ea:
Be gone![1]

This is one of the very oldest known incantations against Lamashtu, and dates to around 1800 BC. At this time, Assyria was a minor player on the political scene, a provincial backwater (albeit one with excellent trading networks) and centuries away from its empires. Even Babylon itself had only just risen to prominence under the rule of Hammurapi, the famous lawmaker-king. At fifteen lines, this little text is considerably shorter than the Canonical Lamashtu Series, but it packs in plenty of information. Lamashtu here is born and raised by gods, and important ones at that: Anu, the sky god, Enlil the god of the air and Ea, a trickster-ish god of freshwater and wisdom.* Together, they give Lamashtu a terrifyingly powerful pedigree and an impressive divine heritage. In fact, the word 'demon' isn't quite correct when applied to Lamashtu, although since it's the best description of her role, I'll continue to use it. She is, in fact, a goddess. The texts stress this even further by writing her name with a 'divine determinative', a star-shaped marker which indicates that the name which follows it is that of a god.

Most Mesopotamian gods are human in appearance, but this incantation describes Lamashtu as a hybrid animal monster: she has the head of the dog, coupled with snakey and slithery attributes. However, the main focus is on her hands, which are described as having clawed fingers so long that there is hardly any palm, an image so specific it feels genuinely creepy. Old Babylonian amulets depict Lamashtu in exactly the way she is described here – she normally has a dog's head, and she's often holding snakes, but it's the hands that get the most attention. Scratched into clay or beautifully carved on stone, her spikey, clawed fingers are shown longer than her face, sometimes longer than her torso. She often has seven of these hideously long fingers on each hand, a feature suggested in this incantation by the fact that she grabs her victim seven times. The emphasis on her hands makes sense, because despite her snakey-ness, and her dog head,

---

* The involvement of two of these gods in the birth and upbringing of a demoness is fairly easily understood: as will be discussed below, Anu is often designated the father to all demons, and Ea occasionally moonlights as a god of exorcism. Enlil, on the other hand, is a long way off his traditional role, and no incantation goes any further towards explaining his participation in giving a disgraced goddess the head of a dog.

her chosen method of doing harm is to plunge her hand into a child's abdomen.

This short, dense description is a means of identifying the demon, through her parentage, her appearance and her behaviour, a way of pinning her down and making sure that the incantation is correctly targeted. What follows next is a command, spoken directly to Lamashtu, insisting that she release the child she has seized. Threatened with the arrival of a skilled exorcist, she is told to roam in the steppe – a place that was viewed as a wilderness outside of civilization, and therefore the proper place for demons and ghosts. The speaker then issues the almost pettily vicious taunt that the demon's eyes will be filled with sand and cress seeds, and her mouth with dust. Finally, she is invoked by the god Ea, in his role as an exorcist, and ordered to be gone.

There are eight other surviving Lamashtu incantations which date from about the same time as this one.* These eight texts, some of which are far more fragmentary than the one above, give us bits and pieces of additional information about the demon. One expands on her estrangement from the other gods, detailing how her father Anu threw her out of their company because of her 'malicious ideas' and 'improper spirit'. Another expands a little on her iconography, giving her donkey's teeth as well as a dog's head, and a third describes in more detail her attacks on mothers, claiming that she 'counts the months of pregnant women; constantly blocking the doors' – that is, the birth canal – 'of women about to give birth'.

In these nine incantations, then, Lamashtu has a fixed

---

* None have any excavation context – they were either looted or dug up in such poorly performed and recorded excavations that dating them precisely is all but impossible. The dates here are based on the language and writing style.

iconography: the head of a dog, perhaps donkey's teeth, and an overall snake-like quality. She has a specific area of influence – babies and pregnant women. She even has a parentage and backstory. She is fairly coherent throughout the incantations – an impressive feat, given that these texts are from across Mesopotamia and some sort of geographical variation might be expected. Even more astonishing is how similar the Lamashtu of these earliest texts is to the Lamashtu described in the Canonical Incantation Series. It's not just that she murders babies and their mothers: in both, she has the teeth of a donkey, long fingers and claws, slips in by door sockets like a snake, and is banished to the wilderness. In both, she is cast out of heaven by her father, the god Anu. Some passages are reproduced almost verbatim – the Series, for example, contains the following lines, nearly identical to those from one of the Old Babylonian inscriptions above, from 1,000 years before:

She returns to the woman whose doors are blocked.
The daughter of Anu counts the pregnant women daily,
Keeps following behind those about to give birth.
She counts their months, marks the days on the wall.

Mesopotamian history and society over the millennium that separated the Series from the first recorded incantations was far from static: vast empires rose and fell, there were periods of peace and periods of near constant warfare, periods of internal focus and periods when Mesopotamia was part of a diplomatic network which included Egypt, Turkey, Europe and the Persian Gulf. Groups of immigrants came, were despised, and then integrated ready to hate the next incoming group. Literature, science, mathematics – all moved on in leaps and bounds.

That the Lamashtu incantations and rituals survived through

a millennium of upheavals; that they were passed down almost unchanged for centuries, shows their extraordinary importance, and highlights how vital they were as the principal method for defending women and children from the nightmares of infant and maternal mortality. Preserving a tradition for centuries might be difficult, but in this case how could it not be worthwhile?

Lamashtu seems fully formed in the Old Babylonian period, so it would be sensible to start looking for her origins in the written documents of the millennium of Mesopotamian history and culture prior to this. A small selection of incantations do survive from this time, and one demon name in particular stands out: Dimme.*

There are two principal languages which appear in the writing of ancient Mesopotamia: Akkadian (in various dialects) and Sumerian, a language that was certainly dead by the end of the third millennium, but which continued to be used as a scholarly language long afterwards, much like medieval Latin. In all Lamashtu texts, from the Old Babylonian period on, 'Dimme' is given as the Sumerian equivalent for the Akkadian 'Lamashtu'. Sometimes the name 'Dimme' is suggested as a translation of 'Lamashtu' in lists of Akkadian words with their Sumerian

* Technically this should be written DIM₂.ME. This is complicated, and fairly unimportant for an understanding of Lamashtu, but for those interested in the minutiae of the cuneiform writing system: there are numerous different ways of saying every cuneiform sign, and while these two signs have the names *dim2* and *me*, they can be pronounced in other ways too (the subscript '2' next to the 'dim' indicates that it's one of at least two signs that can be read as 'dim'). They're written in capitals to indicate that we aren't actually certain which of their many pronunciations should be used when applied to this demon. The latest evidence suggests that in this case, the signs should be read 'Kamadme', but this is still uncertain.

equivalents; sometimes it's given as one of the demoness's names. Occasionally, 'Dimme' is just used interchangeably with 'Lamashtu'. With the name 'Dimme' attested back into the third millennium BC, it might seem that we should seek the origins of Lamashtu here.

However, the third-millennium Dimme has nothing in common with the second-millennium Lamashtu. Instead, she is a shifting, amorphous creature with no fixed identity, iconography or area of influence. Dimme might even be a generic word for ghost in this period.* In fact, these creatures are so different that it seems likely the two names were only attached in the second millennium. It is clear that Lamashtu's fall from heaven, her obsession with harming women and babies, and her iconography are all new, or at least newly recorded, when she first appears in texts in the Old Babylonian period.

There is one possibility that would answer these difficulties. The early second millennium saw a massive influx into Meso-potamia of an immigrant group known as the Amorites. These immigrants were scorned by the settled Mesopotamians and derided as savages who barely knew how to eat bread, let alone live in a city. Apparently neither of these activities was par-ticularly difficult to master because within a few generations Amorites were integrated into Mesopotamian society, and rose to extremely prominent positions – Hammurapi himself is likely to have been an Amorite. In most cases immigrants were absorbed into Mesopotamian culture without any particular impact: Hammurapi behaved exactly like a normal Mesopotamian king,

* The evidence for this is that one list of Sumerian words with their Akkadian equivalents translates the Sumerian 'Dimme-bread' as 'ghost-bread' in Akkadian. Exactly what 'ghost bread' might be is never explained, although it was probably less a haunted loaf of sourdough and more a foodstuff offered to the dead.

and it's only his name that tells us otherwise (Hammurapi means 'the kinsman is the healer' in Amorite). Because of this, it's easy to underestimate any impact these immigrant groups might have had on the pre-existing Mesopotamian culture. However, the sudden appearance of an apparently new demon (and, as we shall see, one entirely unlike any 'normal' Mesopotamian demon of this time), in a period which is also noted for the influx of a new immigrant group, is interesting. Perhaps the Amorites brought Lamashtu with them. Perhaps she, like they, slipped into existing traditions, and was integrated into the Mesopotamian pantheon. If this were the case, her connection with the ancient demon name Dimme may have been an attempt to give her an appropriately Mesopotamian pedigree, rather than because Lamashtu had anything particularly in common with this vague, shifting creature.

An Amorite origin for Lamashtu is speculative, but however she was introduced to Mesopotamia, one thing is clear: she was seized upon instantly. She goes from entirely unattested in the third millennium to appearing in texts and on amulets across Mesopotamia in the early second. It suggests that she was grasped immediately by people who were desperate for the protection that spells against her could offer.

Lamashtu also spread beyond Mesopotamia itself. In Ugarit, a port city in what is now Syria, a slightly incompetent Akkadian scribe wrote down an error-filled set of incantations against her. In fact, this is the first example we have of what scholars call a 'compilation' Lamashtu text – a collection of multiple different incantations, and a precursor of the huge compilation represented by the Canonical Incantation Series – although given the quality of the scribe's work, it seems likely he was copying off someone else, as opposed to making it up for himself. There's even a broken text that suggests Lamashtu rituals were being copied in the libraries of Hattusa, the capital of the Hittite empire in modern Turkey. We have amulets to back up this range as well – Lamashtu amulets have been found in the Levant, and in the south-east of modern Turkey.

However, although these texts and amulets suggest a wide spread in Lamashtu beliefs, there isn't much evidence for any changes to her tradition as she travelled beyond Mesopotamia. At least in the case of the texts, some of this lack of change may be because Akkadian was the lingua franca of the Near East for much of the second millennium BC. Even the Egyptian kings (Tutankhamun included) used it to write letters to their Levantine vassals, despite the fact that neither party would have had Akkadian as a mother tongue. This means it's possible that the Lamashtu texts in Ugarit and Hattusa (which happen to date to the second millennium BC) represent the spread of Meso-potamian scribal culture: native scribes learning Akkadian by copying the rituals, for example, or Mesopotamia-born Akkadian speakers travelling with them. The texts may not say much about how Lamashtu was perceived by the local populations.

A single text from Emar, a city in northern Syria on the great bend of the Euphrates, is more exciting. Written by a scribe who apparently thought nothing of adding random cuneiform signs just for the fun of it, it is an absolute mess, riddled with errors and inconsistencies, and is painfully difficult to read.* However,

---

* Its original translator, Walter Farber, claimed 'I unhesitatingly call it the most difficult Akkadian text of reasonable preservation that I have ever tried to read', and, because all linguists are masochists, he added: 'I love this text.' (Walter Farber, *Lamaštu: An Edition of the Canonical Series of Lamaštu Incantations and Rituals and Related Texts from the Second and First Millennia B.C.* (Eisenbrauns, 2014), p.15.)

the mess is what makes it interesting. It means that its author probably was neither an Akkadian scribe, nor copying from an original Akkadian tablet. This suggests that there was an independent Lamashtu tradition in Emar, and that it wasn't wholly dependent on Akkadian scribal culture.

Lamashtu – and the protection offered by spells against her – was so important that belief in her had gone beyond the borders of Mesopotamia and into the wider Near East.

Belief in Lamashtu also pervaded all levels of Mesopotamian society. While rituals against the demon are well attested in temple and palace libraries like Ashurbanipal's and in homes of high-profile private individuals,* there is plenty of evidence for Lamashtu-belief from non-elite contexts as well.

We have one Lamashtu incantation which appears to record a far less scholarly tradition than that found in palace libraries. While most Lamashtu incantations are attested in at least two or three different copies, this incantation is attested in a single text, and no part of it appears in the Canonical Series. In fact, it is formatted differently from the Series, which is in 'poetic' lines (or at least the Mesopotamian equivalent). This, on this other hand, is prose, a clear sign that it came from a less scholarly background. It was written to be recited by the woman who is suffering herself, rather than by an attendant exorcist – another sign that it was used by people of less prestigious backgrounds than those who had access to palace and temple libraries. Found on a tablet composed of multiple other shorter texts, it reads:

---

* We have one set that belonged to a well-off family of Neo-Assyrian exorcists, who also had a hastily written abbreviation of the rituals, presumably for use when they were out on the job.

You make a figure of the Daughter of Anu [that is, of Lamashtu] from clay from a riverine meadow ... to the sun god Shamash, you speak thus:

Oh soother of distress, or releaser from sin: why are you creating distress for me, why do you not remove my sins ...

I was pregnant, but unable to bring my child to term; I gave birth but did not bring a child to life. May a woman who can grant success release me ... may I have a straightforward pregnancy ...

Go at sunset and put the figurine of the Daughter of Anu onto a boat and let it cross to the other bank of the river. Then you surround it with a magic circle and recite the following incantation:

Woe unto you if from now on you go toward _, the daughter of _ and enter the house where she lives.[2]

This is a haunting text, more so than any other incantation against Lamashtu. There is striking immediacy in the simple fact that it is in the first person – being spoken by a woman who is laying out the effects the monster has had on her. The direct sorrow in the simple statement 'I gave birth but did not bring a child to life' is one that can be felt across the millennia, and the plea 'may I have a straightforward pregnancy' is a prayer that might be echoed by any woman up to the present day.

However, despite the poignancy of the incantation, it does not suggest a Lamashtu who was much different from the demon attested in the Canonical Series. This similarity with the Canonical Series is echoed in another set of Lamashtu-sources that reflect less elite contexts than the Library of Ashurbanipal: amulets.

Most people in Mesopotamia were likely illiterate, and so were excluded from the textual tradition entirely, even when the incantation was written in prose and made to be recited without an exorcist. Amulets, on the other hand, often didn't require reading or writing of any form, and were accessible to a far greater range of individuals, meaning they can tell us even more about Lamashtu outside of temple and palace contexts. Altogether, there are some few hundred Lamashtu amulets, made of stone, metal and clay, and dating (just like the textual sources) from the Old Babylonian period down to the Persian period, in the second half of the first millennium BC. There are some staggeringly impressive examples – giant, beautiful affairs cast in bronze and covered in text – but a significant number seem to have belonged to the less well-off. These are the ones where the figure of Lamashtu is etched poorly and lightly, her shape and menace conveyed in a few hastily scratched lines, so she looks almost like a stick figure. Although the more costly amulets are often inscribed with excerpts of Lamashtu incantations, these cheap ones are frequently accompanied by a 'pseudo-inscription' – a collection of symbols half-heartedly imitating writing.

What might be surprising is that even the poorest-quality amulets conform almost exactly with the textual sources. One clay plaque is a perfect example of this. Probably intended to stand in a patient's room (rather than to be hung around their neck) it's an unashamedly ugly object: roughly rectangular and clumsily made, with the figure of Lamashtu lightly, almost hurriedly, inscribed on the surface. She stands side-on, her legs apart as if she is striding. Her head is either that of a lion or a dog and her tongue a snake's. Although she only has five fingers, they are long, thin, and spread aggressively. One the reverse is a pseudo-inscription. No matter how poorly and cheaply made this object is, it remains consistent with the textual tradition. The only difference is that the demon has the tongue of a snake, but while this is never directly referenced in the texts it feels picky to paint this as a true difference: in textual sources Lamashtu is frequently compared to snakes, and spends a lot of time poisoning her victims.

This similarity to the texts is to be found on all the Lamashtu amulets. Objects that were used to defend against her in rituals, such as spindles, combs or donkey's legs, are frequently depicted, and the appearance of the demon never strays beyond the limits suggested by the texts. Even rather complex and specific scenes from the incantations are sometimes shown, such as Lamashtu being tied to a tamarisk, or being sent away in a boat. It suggests that although the texts, by their very nature, come from elite contexts, they reflected with some degree of accuracy a tradition that was held in every level of society. This sort of cultural coherence is impressive, and speaks again to how valued Lamashtu was in Mesopotamian society as a whole. People worked hard to preserve their knowledge of her, to make sure that no matter how cheaply made an amulet might be, it was still accurate enough to ward her away.

Unlike Lamashtu, with her clear iconography, backstory and habits, Mesopotamian demons appear to the modern historian as a formless, indistinguishable lot. Normally, we're stuck with creatures like this:

The evil Udug, which is let loose in the street, seeks
  contact.
The evil Ala-demon, which is let loose in the street,
  envelops people.
The evil ghost, which is let loose in the street, turns a
  man into a corpse.
The evil Galla-demon, which is let loose in the street,
  snatches people away.
Neither male nor female, they flit about
Evil Udug, evil Ala, evil ghost, evil Galla-demon,
  Dimme,* Dima and Dimme-Lagab demons
They take the wife from the lap of her husband,
They remove the children from the lap of their father,
They take away the young maiden in the street[3]

These demons may have different names, but the evil they
cause is resoundingly generic and their specializations are so
poorly distinguished that they can work and be exorcized as
a unit. You will search these incantations in vain for any indication of what the demons look like: with a couple of exceptions
discussed below, they are never described, except perhaps as a
storm which blocks the street. In many cases, even their names
are left out and this group of seven demons is referred to simply
as 'the seven'. There aren't even any amuletic representations to
fill in the gaps – they don't seem to have any iconography at all.
  In only one way do they seem like Lamashtu: all demons are
the children of the sky god Anu. However, while Lamashtu's
parentage may be derived from a general idea that all demons
were created by Anu, only she is marked as divine herself, and

* This is the same Dimme demon who is occasionally connected with
Lamashtu.

only she is given any sort of backstory for how her father came to cast her out of divine company.

Lamashtu, then, stands preeminent, entirely apart from any other demonic force in Mesopotamia. She is without question the most important demon, the only one with an iconography, a backstory, a defined area of influence, with amulets and incantations made against her specifically. She is a real, concrete figure against all the shifting, unidentifiable monsters.

There are two other exceptions to this 'boring demons' rule, two creatures known as Lilitu and Pazuzu who have some degree of definition in their form and actions. Both are inextricably linked to Lamashtu.

In Mesopotamia the most powerful gods, the ones at the top (or moving to the top) of the pantheon, tended to cannibalize and absorb lesser divinities. When Marduk, the city god of Babylon, grew vastly in importance as Babylon itself rose to power, previously independent gods, like Assarluhi (the god of exorcism) gradually became just another facet of Marduk. This ability to absorb other figures is a clear indication of importance, of a focus on the primary creature that was so fixed a wholly separate being could become nothing more than a different aspect of their personality. Given everything we know about Lamashtu's supremacy among demons, it is perhaps unsurprising that she absorbed other creatures as well – in her case, the ghostly Lilitu.*

* A lot of places will tell you that the so-called 'Queen of the Night' relief in the British Museum is a representation of Lilitu, but this is unlikely to be the case. The clay plaque, which shows a naked, talon-footed woman flanked by owls, is far more likely to be a representation of the goddess Ishtar.

Lilitus (sometimes called Ardat-Lili) were the spirits of young girls who had died still virgins, before marriage and before children. Under cover of darkness, these winged ghosts visited living men to act out their thwarted passions, and were thought to be the cause of nocturnal discharge and wet dreams. Their names refer to the timing of their activities – the letters L Y L are the Akkadian root for 'night' (as they are in Arabic),* with Lilitu being a female variant on this ('t' at the end of Semitic words normally denotes femininity), and Ardat-Lili meaning literally 'handmaiden of the night'. Tragic, mournful spirits, the descriptions of Lilitu in incantations are more pitiful than terrifying. One typical example explains how:

The maiden [Lilitu] is a woman who never had intercourse
The maiden is a woman who was never deflowered
The maiden never experienced sex in her husband's lap.
The maiden never peeled off her clothes on her husband's lap.
The maiden for whom no nice-looking boy ever loosened her garment clasp.
The maiden who had no milk in her breasts, but only bitter liquid comes out.
The maiden who never fulfilled her sexuality nor satisfied her desires in a man's lap.

---

* Akkadian, like all Semitic languages, works using consonantal roots – combinations of (usually) three consonants that contain a generalized meaning. These consonants can then be used to form actual words by adding suffixes, prefixes and vowels. So, in the traditional example: the letters k t b in Arabic are the root for 'writing'. These can be used to form words like *kataba* (he wrote) *katib* (writer) *maktab* (letter) and *aktaba* (he dictated).

And on and on, until it becomes almost pathetic:

She is a woman who has never seen a city feast, nor ever raises her eyes, who never rejoiced with the other girls, who was snatched away from her spouse, who had no spouse, nor bore a son.[4]

These sorrowful spirits posed relatively little danger to the men they visited. At worst, they tended to be blamed for illnesses whose symptoms included continuous erections or masturbation, but generally the most a man could expect to worry about was a wet dream or two.*

There was a male equivalent to these ghosts, known as Lilu (which is the same name as Lilitu just without the feminine 't' ending); men who had died before they could marry, seeking to have their way with mortal women. These creatures visited women rather than men but there are fewer incantations concerned with these creatures and, as we'll see, while the legends

---

* There is one other occurrence of the Lil spirits in Mesopotamian sources – in the Sumerian story *Gilgamesh and the Underworld*. In this legend, the goddess Inanna had planted a tree, intending to use it for timber. Over time, however, it had become the home of a 'snake that knows no charm', an Anzu Bird (a mythical storm bird) and a 'ki-sikil-lil-la-ke'. Although this last term is never used to describe Lilitu in incantations, it roughly translates as 'woman, Lil demon', so they were likely equivalents. Inanna turns to her hero Gilgamesh for help, and he kills the snake while driving the Anzu bird into the mountains, and Lilitu to the wastelands (the place where demons and ghosts were meant to live, not in goddesses' lumber yards). It is an odd story, and Lilitu hardly matters at all – she's just something that is upsetting Inanna in a generic sort of way, bundled in with snakes and mystical birds: the passage as a whole tells us very little about the Lilitu demons themselves. (Andrew George, *The Epic of Gilgamesh. The Babylonian Epic Poem and Other Texts in Akkadian and Sumerian*, p.175–195).

of Lilitu would survive in one form or another for thousands of years, Lilu would fade away far sooner.

At first Lilitu, Ardat-Lili and Lilu might sound very different from the child-killing demoness Lamashtu, who was unlikely to inspire erections or try to find herself a husband (or a wife), but from the Old Babylonian period on, Lilitu and Lilu were connected frequently to Lamashtu and comparisons between them appear in the Canonical Lamashtu series. By the latest incantations, Lamashtu would have Lilitu's wings, and in one case is even called 'Ardat-Lili'. The cause of this jump from nocturnal sex to baby killing is rather obscure in the Mesopotamian sources, but it has been suggested that their actions are precipitated by envy. The ghosts murder infants (and their mothers) because they are filled with jealousy at living women who have children and husbands when they cannot: a motivation that we'll see repeated again throughout this book.

Perhaps Lilitu's sadness was also tied into Lamashtu's own. Despite being such a terrifying demonic force, Lamashtu can read like a tragic parody of a mother. In the incantations she is constantly placated with domestic items, like pots, spindles and combs; she is frequently shown breastfeeding, but it's dogs and pigs that she suckles instead of babies. She is often described as doing typically motherly things, like feeding infants and wrapping them in blankets – albeit in her case, her milk is poisoned, and any child touched by her is likely to die. There is a sense that perhaps Lamashtu does want to be a mother, and that having been robbed of that opportunity, she steals it from others. We'll see this idea given far greater prominence in Lamashtu's descendants, but even in the Mesopotamian sources Lamashtu, like Lilitu, can be read as a tragic figure as well as a malevolent one.

Eventually, Lamashtu and Lilitu became almost completely entwined, the one entirely absorbed into the other, to the extent that Lamashtu could be dispelled by a force who was originally only connected to Lilitu – the protector-demon Pazuzu.

One of the most remarkable Lamashtu amulets is a beautiful bronze plaque that dates to the Neo-Assyrian period (that is, about the same time as Ashurbanipal's library). Standing at thirteen centimetres high, it was likely intended to be set up in a patient's room – it is certainly too large and heavy to be worn. The level of craftsmanship displayed in its manufacture is astonishing, with even the tiniest details delicately picked out. The front of the plaque is divided into four rows that show, from top to bottom, divine symbols, protective figures, a patient whom Lamashtu has attacked being treated by healers,* and the defeat of Lamashtu herself. This final scene depicts the lion-headed demoness, clutching snakes in each hand and suckling dogs at her breasts, being driven into a boat. Forcing her on is a figure who looks almost more threatening than Lamashtu does – winged, claw-footed, with bulging eyes set deep in a snarling, leonine face, this is the demon Pazuzu. Pazuzu is depicted a second time on the amulet as well – as a fully carved, three-dimensional figure, he holds the entire plaque; his head, viciously grinning, peers over it; his claws clutch the top; while his winged, bird-footed body is shown curving down the reverse. It puts Pazuzu solidly in the room with the victim of Lamashtu – this is not just a scene on an amulet, but a conjuring.

* Slightly jarringly, the patient is not a woman or child but a bearded man. The incantations do suggest that Lamashtu could cause fever in men even if it wasn't her primary area of interest, so this isn't entirely surprising. It's also depressingly unsurprising that the most prestigious, expensive amulet to protect against a demon who typically hurt women and children was made for a man.

32

We have dozens of less remarkable anti-Lamashtu Pazuzu amulets – everything from snarling little bronze heads that were likely clutched by women in childbirth, to complete figurines that were probably free-standing in the room. It is clear that Pazuzu was a powerful force who could be summoned to counteract Lamashtu.

Pazuzu appears in our records from the Neo-Assyrian period onwards, with very little hint as to where he came from (there is some suggestion he might have bled over from Egyptian mythology, but the evidence for this is meagre). What is certain is that he had his own personality and sphere of interest that was entirely separate from Lamashtu. One of the inscriptions about him reads:

I am Pazuzu, son of Hanbu, king of the evil winds.
I ascended the mighty mountain that quaked.
The winds that I went against were headed towards the west.
One by one I broke their wings.[5]

There is a lot packed into these four lines, and much we don't understand from the surviving evidence. We don't know who Hanbu is, for example, or why he might be the father of a demon. The mythological reference – to Pazuzu climbing a mountain and breaking the wings of the winds – is not known in any more detail than is given here. A few other incantations indicate that Pazuzu, in his role as king of the evil winds, brought storms and droughts, but there isn't much to go on. What is clear is that he was a vicious and malignant force in his own right, with no obvious impetus for helping infants or their mothers, and, as such, an odd character to turn to for protection from Lamashtu. Most scholars believe that the explanation for his sudden pivot from destroyer to protector is the virgin Lilitu.

The word for wind in Sumerian is 'lil', and, like all good magical texts, Pazuzu incantations are written in Sumerian. This means that when Pazuzu claims to be 'king of the evil winds', he is actually declaring himself to be 'king of the evil *lil*'. It's easy to see the connection with the Lilitu ghosts, with Pazuzu functionally declaring himself as king of these spirits as well as the winds. As Lamashtu absorbed Lilitu, Pazuzu turned against Lamashtu as well, and a monster of the winds came to be a protective spirit first and foremost. There is some irony in the fact that Pazuzu is best known in modern times from his role as the antagonist demon in *The Exorcist*, where, entirely out of character, he spends the film viciously attacking a young child and her mother.

Lamashtu gives some insight into how terrible it must have been to live with the dangers of mass maternal and infant mortality: a way of feeling the aching sadness of all the women who died and suffered, of those tiny half-bodies huddled in the ruins of ancient Mesopotamian cities. However, even with the vast reduction in mortality rates brought about by modern medicine, the pain evident in the Lamashtu incantations is still identifiable, still chimes with the experiences of women today. The text of the prose incantation especially drives this home:

> I was pregnant, but unable to bring my child to term; I gave birth but did not bring a child to life. May a woman who can grant success release me ... may I have a straightforward pregnancy...

Here is the heartache of a miscarriage of a much-wanted child – a sorrow that is felt by women all over the world even now. The plea 'May I have a straightforward pregnancy' is the prayer of every pregnant woman, and every woman who hopes to have a child, whether today or in the ancient world. Lamashtu and her descendants are the echo of that heartache, and that prayer, uttered by women generation after generation, down through the millennia. The first place we will follow this echo to is ancient Greece, where a monster called the Lamia was carrying on Lamashtu's legacy.

2

Virgin Ghosts and Failed Mothers

n 306 BC, as the heirs of Alexander the Great fought over control of his empire, Ptolemy I's fleet was captured at the battle of Salamis by the young ruler of Macedon, Demetrius Poliorcetes. Aboard one of Ptolemy's ships was a courtesan by the name of Lamia, who was taken as a concubine by Demetrius. While we have little information regarding how she felt about this, we do know that she quickly became Demetrius' favourite – not, apparently, due to her looks (as Plutarch insists on repeating throughout his account of her life, she was 'already past her prime' when she was captured by Demetrius)[1], but because she was witty and 'prompt in repartee'.* Lamia was also (supposedly)

---

* We have some examples of this wit, especially relating to the case of Thonis, another courtesan. A man offered Thonis a small fortune to sleep

demanding and prone to extravagant whims, which were often indulged by a besotted Demetrius: we have multiple accounts of lavish feasts that he held in her honour, and according to Plutarch he even levied a substantial tax on his citizens to pay for her soap.* A curious anecdote about her has also survived, concerning a discussion between a group of Demetrius's representatives and a Macedonian officer called Lysimachus. During a lull in the conversation, Lysimachus began showing off the scars on his leg and back, souvenirs from a time he had fought a lion. Demetrius's men laughed, and claimed that their king, too, had scars on his neck from a 'dreadful wild beast' – Lamia.

This was not just a reference to Lamia's allegedly controlling nature, but also a pun – the king's lover shared her name with a mythical monster.† This monstrous Lamia was said to have been a beautiful queen of Libya who was loved by Zeus and forced by

---

with him, but after the deal was struck he dreamt he had sex with her, and, his desire sated, withdrew his offer. When Thonis took him to court, claiming that she was still owed payment, the judge ordered that the money be brought in and moved about in front of her so that she could only grasp its shadow, since 'a thing imagined is the shadow of reality'. Lamia felt this was unfair, pointing out that 'while the dream put an end to the man's passion, the shadow of the money did not set Thonis free of her desire for it'.

* As a captive of Demetrius, it's unlikely Lamia actually had much control over him, but ancient (male) authors certainly didn't see it this way. Demetrius deferred to her publicly, abused his citizens and claimed he was doing so for her, and acted as if he was indulging her – the fact that he was her captor and that she likely had very little say in this gets no consideration in the ancient sources.

† Demetrius' representatives to Lysimachus were not the only ones to make this joke – Demetrius' own father did as well, along with a man called Demochares of Soli, who called Demetrius 'the fable' because he had his own legendary beast. With this and the debate about Thonis, it was clearly a laugh a line in Demetrius' court.

an envious Hera to devour her own children. Driven mad by grief and guilt, Lamia turned into a demonic creature – serpentine, terrifying and vengeful. She spent her time slaughtering mothers and eating their children, furious that they had what she had lost, ripping open the wombs of pregnant women to devour the fetus inside. And if that sounds familiar, it's because this monster was the Greek and Roman equivalent of Lamashtu, a direct descendent of the Mesopotamian child- and mother-killing demon.

Given this, Lamia might seem like a strange name for a courtesan, but although Lamashtu had never made any pretence at sexiness, Lamia was not just a child-killer. She was also given to seducing handsome young men, concealing her monstrous features so as to appear a great beauty, before eating men alive once their guard was down. Her name was perfect for a prostitute who, according to Plutarch, had 'utterly vanquished' her royal lover.*

The mythical Lamia, like her Mesopotamian counterpart, still gives us deep insight into the tragedies of infant and maternal mortality, and the desperation with which women struggled against these horrors, but she has another side as well: she shows us how womanhood and femininity could be policed. In every way, the monstrous Lamia stood opposed to the Greek and Roman ideals of womanhood. Where a good woman should be a mother, Lamia murdered children and prevented pregnancies; where a woman should be a chaste wife, Lamia was unmarried and seductive. Where a woman should be beautiful, Lamia was

* It's not entirely clear whether the courtesan Lamia's name was a purposeful reference to the monster, or whether it was a coincidence (there was at least one man with this surname – Lucius Aelius Lamia – who was teased about it by Horace), but people were happy to draw the comparison either way. While we're at it, this monster was not in any way connected to the popular Arabic girls' name 'Lamia' which comes from the word for 'radiant' in the Arabic language.

hideous (albeit able to appear attractive when she needed to); where a woman should be submissive and meek to men, Lamia manipulated and murdered them. In some cases, Lamia is given testicles or a phallus, a way of emphasizing, in Greek and Roman eyes, how completely she was the antithesis of the supposed ideal of femininity.

The courtesan Lamia was breaking the standards of womanhood in similar (albeit less dramatic) ways – she, too, was the opposite of the chaste wife and mother. She was seductive, unmarried, argumentative, 'past her prime', dominating her man as opposed to being dominated by him, refusing to conform to the societal standards by which women were judged. The constant comparisons between the real-life Lamia and her mythical namesake make it clear that these characteristics did not just make the courtesan unconventional – in the eyes of some, they made her monstrous. And while comparisons between a woman and the monster who shared her name might seem fair enough, 'Lamia' would eventually become a more general insult, thrown at any woman who was deemed insufficiently feminine, a tool for literally demonizing those who dared to break with the 'ideal' of womanhood.

Before digging any deeper into her lore, it's important to consider how Lamia was related to Lamashtu (or even whether she was related at all). In the West we're used to thinking of 'civilization' as beginning in ancient Greece, with the thousands of years of Middle Eastern history – of writing, cities, great epics, complex and enormous trade networks, art, science, and mathematics – relegated to a faintly barbaric prelude. This perception is not helped by the fact that the contact points between East and West that tend to be emphasized (by both sides) are the wars, whether it's the conquests of Alexander the Great or the battle of Thermopylae. There are no Zack Snyder films or ancient epics about the time a nice Greek family migrated to Asia and slowly integrated with the local population, or the connections between a Roman businessman and his trading partner in Phoenicia, even though these sorts of relationships were just as characteristic of the thousands of years of contacts between the East and West as the moments of conflict.

But no matter what modern and ancient media might have you thinking, cultural crossover between Greece, Rome and the Middle East was inevitable – they traded with each other, lived with each other, immigrated and intermixed – and we have plenty of clear examples of cultural borrowing (with most of the influence passing from East to West). Greek and Roman statuary, literature and art all owed a debt to ancient Mesopotamia – even Greek gods are tied to the Mesopotamian pantheon: plenty of aspects of the goddess Aphrodite, for example, are derived from the Mesopotamian Ishtar (by way of the Phoenician Astarte).

It's not surprising that a demoness as important as Lamashtu crossed over too, and her appearance in Greece and Rome should be no more unexpected than her turning up in the Levant, or Anatolia. The connections between Lamashtu and Lamia are clear in Lamia's name,* in her habit of murdering infants and their mothers, in her associations with snakes; even the sagging breasts Lamia is sometimes portrayed with look distinctly Lamashtu-like. Her origin was also placed in the Middle East by the ancient Greeks themselves, who claimed she came from Libya. Each one of these attributes, taken by itself, is not enough

---

* The Greeks did have their own, rather clumsy, proposed etymology for 'Lamia' – they claimed it was related to their word for gullet, because Lamia ate her victims.

to demonstrate a connection, but looked at together the evidence seems clear. In fact, the most marked difference between Lamia and Lamashtu is the nature, and extent, of the sources that reference them.

Compared to the gigantic incantation series and extensive amulet collections relating to Lamashtu, Lamia-related sources from ancient Greece and Rome might, at first glance, look a little thin on the ground. We have no Lamia amulets, and the written sources amount to a handful of texts, the longest of which is barely more than a paragraph. Based on this, it might seem like Lamia wasn't a very important monster, certainly when compared with Lamashtu.

However, when Lamia does appear, it's often in contexts that suggest she was known more widely than it might initially seem. There seems to be an assumption on the part of writers that their audience were well aware of who Lamia was, and would understand passing references to her. It wasn't just the joking representatives of Demetrius who did this. Horace, for example, in his *Ars Poetica*, cautions that when telling a story 'you should not draw a live boy out of Lamia's belly' – that is, you must not make a plot too fantastical – and never thinks to explain who Lamia is or why she'd be eating children.*

Unfortunately, while these sorts of sources show that belief in (or at least, knowledge of) Lamia was widespread in ancient Greece and Rome, they make it much harder to understand her. Where knowledge is assumed, it isn't given, and we're left with a lot of gaps in our Lamia-lore. Especially frustrating is the fact that we can't tell whether belief in her was different between

---

* The cruel twist of this line is that having a dead child in her belly covers all aspects of Lamia – both that she eats children, and that the children she gives birth to die.

ancient Greece and ancient Rome (she appears in sources from both), or even how belief in her changed through time. However, there is still plenty that we can see – and most of it is related to snakes, eating children, and murdering mothers.

The most matter-of-fact description of Lamia comes from Durius of Samos – a tyrant of the city of Samos in the third century BC who moonlighted as a historian and literary critic in his spare time.* He writes:

> Lamia was a beautiful woman in Libya. Zeus had sex with her. Because of Hera's envy towards her she destroyed the children she bore. Consequently she became misshapen through grief, snatched other people's children and killed them.[2]

This is all pleasantly straightforward and clear, if a little stilted.† The only part Durius is vague on is exactly how Lamia was 'misshapen', but we don't have to look far to find out. Most accounts make Lamia at least partially serpentine, a monstrousness brought on by her horror at what she has lost (or what she has done). In one account she's called a 'snake' by her foes, in another she's given a serpent's tail instead of legs. There's even a story where she is a child-eating monster with a 'scaly gait' and

---

* Or, alternatively, a historian and literary critic who moonlighted as a tyrant – we're not quite sure how long he ruled Samos for, or even how he became ruler in the first place. In fact, we know so little about his reign that one modern classicist has described it simply as 'uneventful'.

† Dionysius of Halicarnassus, writing in 30 BC, described Durius' writing as something that 'no one can bear to read to the final flourish of the pen' because he put so little effort into his style, an observation made much harsher by the fact that it's broadly accurate.

a single snake growing from her forehead. This particular Lamia was not a once-beautiful queen – instead she was sent by Apollo to punish the Argives, for causing the death of Apollo's lover Psamathe and their child. Lamia here is described as:

> A monster conceived in the deepest part of the Acheron, in the Furies' unspeakable halls. The monster had the face and breast of a girl but from her head there rose a snake, hissing continuously, parting her ruddy forehead. Then this dread blight slid into rooms by night with a scaly gait, snatched newborn souls from the bosoms of their nurses, devoured them with bloody bite and grew fat on the grief of the land.[3]

A woman with a snake growing from her forehead might sound reminiscent of the snake-haired Medusa but, oddly enough, Medusa was never connected with Lamia. Lamia was, however, linked with another serpentine monster – in some stories she is the mother of Scylla, a creature with six snake-like heads growing out of her torso, who lived by the sea and menaced Odysseus, murdering six of his crewmembers (one for each of her snakes) as he sailed by.* Scylla is especially similar to the iteration of Lamia described by Dio Chrysostom, a philosopher writing in the first century AD. This Lamia is not a single monster with a backstory, but a species of creatures with the upper half of a beautiful woman and the tail of a snake. According to Dio Chrysostom, these creatures lived by the sea in Libya, waiting to tempt in

---

* How Lamia could be a mother to Scylla when she killed all of her children is unclear, and legends that have her as Scylla's mother don't address this. In other myths, Scylla's monstrosity is not inherited: Ovid describes how she was once a beautiful nymph (and daughter of the nymph Ceto), turned monstrous by a jealous Circe, who had fallen for Scylla's admirer, the sea god Glaucus.

shipwrecked sailors and eat them alive. All of this sea-going and sailor-devouring may be why Aristotle refers to Lamia as a type of shark – and it's important as well to notice how prominent the sea is in these Lamia legends. This oceanic facet of her myth would have a long afterlife: Lamia is the mother of our mermaids.

While snakey-ness and child-killing don't appear in every single iteration of the Lamia – the snake-women of Dio Chrysostom don't kill children, and Durius of Samos' description of a child-killer doesn't specifically mention snakes – they are by far her most prominent characteristics, and it's rare to find an account of her without one or the other. Where other characteristics do appear – where Lamia seems wolf-like rather than serpentine, or goat-legged rather than snake-tailed – it's often because she was blending with a host of other Greek and Roman monsters, who brought their myths to tangle into Lamia's own. Eventually, as with Lilitu and Lamashtu, these monsters became other aspects of Lamia, their names and legends interchangeable, a process we can already see beginning in antiquity.

In the *Life of Apollonius of Tyana*, written in the second century AD, the hero is confronted by Lamia, and identifies her as:

> One of the Empousa, who most people would call Lamia or Mormolykeia.[4]

Here are three names for one creature, but 'Empousa' and 'Mormolykeia' were not just alternative designations for Lamia.*

* The reason 'Lamia' has stuck as the term for this monster of this story despite these other names is that the author claims the story is commonly known as 'The Lamia of Corinth'.

They were (or at least, they could be) entirely separate monsters.

Of these two names here, the Empousa is the easiest to deal with, simply because we know the least about her. Crates of Mallus, a philosopher of the second century BC, mentions her in passing as having the ability to shapeshift, something that is supported in our second source for her – a comedy written by the ancient Greek playwright Aristophanes. In *The Frogs* a slave plays a practical joke on his master and pretends to see an Empousa. As his master cowers, too terrified to look himself, the slave claims to be watching the Empousa turn into a donkey, a beautiful woman, a bull and then a dog, while also assuring his master that in her true form she has one leg of brass and one leg of donkey dung.

The Empousa is certainly related to a modern Greek Lamia attested in the 1980s (AD), who was said to have a leg of brass and a donkey leg, and possibly even to the medieval tradition of beautiful women who concealed monstrous legs beneath their skirts. But the ancient sources concerning her are so limited that it's impossible to see where the crossover between Lamia and Empousa came, or why they blended into each other. Perhaps it was simply that both monsters could shapeshift, and could appear as beautiful women while hiding more bestial attributes. This is rather thin pickings, and we can be fairly certain we're missing huge portions of Empousa lore that might have given us a deeper understanding of her connection to Lamia. Thankfully, we have significantly more information concerning the other monster named in the *Life of Apollonius* – the Mormolykeia, or Mormo.

In the third century BC, the nineteen-year-old poet Erinna composed her masterwork – a 300-line hexameter poem called *The Distaff*. From the 50-odd lines that survive we can see that it was written as a memorial to her friend, Baucis, who had died young, almost immediately after her marriage. Erinna portrays this as a double grief – first losing her friend (and possibly her lover) to a man's bed, and then, almost immediately afterwards, to death. It's a heart-wrenching poem – Erinna's sorrow feels naked and real, torn between grief and anger, furious at her friend for abandoning her twice over in such quick succession but also heartbroken at her loss. Most of the surviving lines consist of Erinna reminiscing about her idyllic childhood with Baucis, and, among nostalgia for their old games,* she mentions:

> What terror the monster Mormo brought when we were
>   both little girls!
> On her head were massive ears, and she walked on
> four feet, and kept changing her face.[5]

It's clear from this that Mormo, like Empousa and Lamia, could shapeshift – she 'kept changing her face' – but Erinna implies that Mormo's primary form is of a quadruped with big ears. This is generally interpreted as a wolfish form, since Mormo is related to wolves elsewhere: often (as in *The Life of Apollonius*) her name is even extended to 'Mormolykeia', which means 'terrible wolf' (Mormo means simply 'terrible one'[†]).

---

* Including one game called Tortoise, something that has led to a set of delightful papers written by serious academics speculating on what, exactly, the game 'Tortoise' involved.
† This simple, sensible etymology suggests that Mormo, unlike Lamia, began her life as a Greek monster before blending with the Mesopotamian Lamia (unless, that is, she started out as a descriptive epithet for Lamia, and only later became a separate(ish) monster in her own right – but this is all messy enough without tangling everything any further).

We can also see from Erinna's poem that Mormo, like Lamia, was a child-snatcher. She was terrifying to Erinna and Baucis when they were 'little girls'. This child-killing is attested elsewhere as well: the Greek geographer Strabo claimed Mormo (and Lamia) were used as 'frightful' tales to discourage bad behaviour in children, and in Theocritus' *Idyll* (a collection of pastoral poems written in the fourth century BC), when a child starts whining that he can't go to a festival with his mother, the mother responds: 'I will not take you with me, child – Mormo, the horse, bites', at which point the child bursts into tears. It's confusing that Theocritus has Mormo as a horse, and not as a wolf, but perhaps this is another sign of her shapeshifting abilities, and while no other sources refer to her as a horse (and her later incarnations are all snake- and wolf-based), it's interesting that the description of Mormo in *The Distaff* could technically apply to a horse as well as a wolf. Perhaps Erinna was keeping the shape of her Mormo intentionally vague, allowing her to shapeshift in the poem as well.

There is no suggestion in any of these sources that Mormo has a specific, Lamia-like backstory, but we do have one late reference to Mormo that makes her a once-human woman, turned murderously demonic. This comes from a scholia (an explanatory comment written by a later scholar) to the work of Aristides, a Greek orator of the second century BC. Like most scholia it's painfully difficult to date, but it was likely Hellenistic or Byzantine. It reads:

[When Aristides writes about] 'The things that terrify children when they hear them' [he] refers to Mormo and Lamia ... Mormo was a Corinthian woman. She devoured her own children and then in the evening flew up into the sky for some reason. So now, when women want to scare their children, they shout 'Mormo!'[6]

This is a grim, odd little story – Mormo acts without any provocation, an ordinary Corinthian woman suddenly turning monstrous, the author's own comment that this was 'for some reason' an almost sarcastically lacklustre approach to understanding her motivations. However, the oddness is likely because the story is simply a retelling of Lamia's legend, with the specific details of Zeus' love and Hera's jealousy removed, leaving no reason for the shift from human woman to demon. Given that this variant of the story is never referenced outside of this single case, it's also unlikely that it was particularly well known. Perhaps it was even invented by the scholar who wrote it.

Despite the many similarities between Lamia and Mormo we have no sources that reference Mormo killing mothers as well as infants. However, there are hints in *The Distaff* that girls were not safe from her even when they reached adolescence. The death of Baucis is a tragedy not just because she was beloved by Erinna, but because she was young, and died on the cusp of adulthood, almost immediately after she was married. The suddenness of her death, the horror that it came so soon after her wedding, is emphasized in an epitaph that Erinna wrote for Baucis alongside the poem, which reads:

I am the tomb of Baucis, a young bride, and as you pass
the much-lamented gravestone you may say to Hades:
'Hades, you are malicious'. When you look, the beautiful
    letters
will tell of the most cruel fate of Baucis,
how her father-in-law lit the girl's funeral pyre

with the pine-torches over which Hymen sang.
And you, Hymen, changed the tuneful song of weddings
into the mournful sound of lamentations.[7]

We know of another Greek monster, who attacked and killed girls just like Baucis, murdering young women before (or just after) marriage – a monster who was also connected to Lamia and Mormo to the extent that their names would, in some circumstances, become synonymous. It's possible that when Erinna brought Mormo into her poem about a girl who died almost immediately after her wedding, she meant to recall a monster called the Gello.

In ancient Greece (and, to a lesser extent, Rome), there was a deep-seated interest in, and anxiety about, young girls like Baucis who died before they could marry or have children. We have dozens of epitaphs like the one Erinna wrote for Baucis – concise little laments, filled with longing for what might have been, and the lives these girls might have led:

This dust is Timas, struck down before she could wed. Persephone's dark bridal hall received her, when she died her girlfriends all sharpened blades and sheared their gorgeous hair.[8]

I never completed the rite of the bridal chamber and bed, nor did my body lie on the couch, nor was there an all-night knocking by the girls my age on the cedar doors.[9]

I, Lento, died a virgin. I was like a young flower at the time of high bloom when it first shows its petals. And at fifteen, when I was about to be united in marriage, I went to lie among the dead, in a long sleep.[10]*

Girls who died in this way – unfulfilled virgins on the brink of womanhood – were not just unlucky in life. In death they were denied entry to the underworld, forced to linger at the gates of Hades, or wander for eternity with the Furies. These girls (often called *aorai*, a word which means 'prematurely dead') were even used in magic, since they could move between the upper and lower worlds. Having been unable to fully live, they were likewise unable to fully die.

These virgin ghosts were sad, wistful creatures, but they could also be viciously dangerous – Gello in particular. Gello, like all *aorai*, was the ghost of a girl who had died before marriage and children. Much like Lamia, she could be portrayed as either a single creature or a whole race of virgin ghosts, and spent her afterlife murdering infants and their mothers out of jealousy. She was also blamed for the deaths of other young girls like her – and like Baucis. This is laid out by a proverb compiler called Zenobius, who lived in Rome in the second century AD and described Gello as:

---

* Incidentally, all Greek epitaphs are great fun to read. Cutting across most sections of society, they run from sweet ('I looked on 86 years before I died, and I leave my children's children under the sun') to fascinating ('I was not, and I came to be; I am not, and I don't care.') to boastful ('Though dead, I have a mind, and not a slight one, either.') to impressively dramatic ('I am dead by the most pitiful death, all because of my wife, a vile, false mate, may Zeus destroy her utterly. Her secret lover, who was disgracing my name, dragged me to a cliff and threw me off like a discus.'). All of these are taken from Richmond Lattimore, *Themes in Greek and Latin Epitaphs* (University of Illinois Press, 1962)).

a maiden, and because she died prematurely, the people of Lesbos say that her ghost haunts little children, and they also blame her for the deaths of those who die prematurely.[11]

Gello, then, was a prematurely dead girl causing the premature deaths of other girls; a hideous, warped form of reproduction, whereby instead of having the children she so wanted, Gello turned other hopeful young girls into thwarted, jealous monsters like herself.

The reason Zenobius was talking about Gello in the first place (and the reason he associated her with Lesbos) was because he was commenting on a fragment from an otherwise lost poem by Sappho, which reads 'More child-loving than Gello', a dark little turn of phrase that perfectly encapsulates Gello's nature – she steals children because she loves them, desperately, violently, possessively.

Although Gello is much more distinct from Lamia than Empousa and Mormo, it's easy to see how and why they ran together. In spells found in the *Cyranides* (a collection of magical lore, compiled in the fourth century AD, but likely using earlier material), Gello is described as 'a thing that strangles the infant and persecutes the woman in the childbed', a description that could easily apply to Lamia herself. One list of magical stones from the Hellenistic period advises that stones be hung around the necks of newborns to drive away *megaira* – 'she who is envious'. Without any further information, this could apply to either the furiously jealous Lamia or Gello. Perhaps it was kept intentionally vague so it could protect against both at once.

The connection between the two was often made entirely explicit: writing on Theocritus, a scholiast (who like all scholiasts is difficult to date, but was likely working in the Hellenistic or Byzantine eras) even describes Mormo, Lamia and Gello as one single being. This could explain how and why Mormo came to feature in Erinna's poem, with Baucis' death recalling the loss of girls like her to these jealous, monstrous killers, something for girls to be afraid of both as children and as budding women.

However, the connections between Gello and Lamia are often thought to run even deeper than their shared murderous envy of young women and their children – it has been suggested that Gello, like Lamia, had her origins in Mesopotamia, in the ghostly, jealous Lilitu.

With all the virginal, ghostly child-killing, the similarities between Gello and Lilitu are immediately striking, but the difference in their names would give anyone pause when connecting the two monsters – even the most creative linguist would have difficulty suggesting how 'Lilitu' could become 'Gello'. It is, however, possible that this name shift was caused by another Mesopotamian demon, called a 'Gallu'.

We know relatively little about Gallu demons, but they seem to have been responsible for taking human souls to the underworld. It's said of them in one myth that they:

Know no food, know no drink, eat no flour offering, drink no libation. They never enjoy the pleasures of marital embrace, never have any sweet children to kiss. They snatch the son from a man's knee. They make the bride leave the house of her father-in-law.[12]

If you squint, this does look a little Lilitu-like, with all the missing marital embraces and murdered brides and sons. If you really try, you could see a world in which the two demons were confused, especially by the ancient Greeks, who were often quite free and easy with Mesopotamian names.* It's also worth pointing out that in the Canonical Incantation Series of Lamashtu, the Gallu demon is mentioned, and that Gallu, like Lamashtu, is often connected to strangulation. A final point in favour of the Mesopotamian transmission is that the name 'Gello' has no sensible etymology in ancient Greek – it does contain 'gel', 'to grin', something which Greek monsters certainly did in a leering, hideous way, but which the virgin ghost is never described as doing herself.

On the other hand, there is the rather damning fact that Gallu in Mesopotamia was male and is never particularly associated with murdering mothers or their children.† Moreover, the Greek and Roman Gello lacks one of Lilitu's most prominent characteristics – she has no interest at all in men, and never seduces anyone. Even when she has blended with Lamia, to the extent that their names can, at times, be used interchangeably, all the sexual elements are Lamia's alone. However, whatever Gello's origins her eventual merging with Lamia would bring plenty of Mesopotamian influence of its own.‡

---

* The Greek-named 'Hanging Gardens of Babylon', for example, were not in Babylon, but in Nineveh – the Greeks got the two mixed up.
† Since the word 'Gallu' could also mean 'sheriff' in Sumerian, the demon is often translated in modern texts as the 'sheriff-demon' or 'policeman-demon', a name that could not be less suggestive of a seductive young girl.
‡ There was another child-stealing monster in ancient Greece and Rome – the strix, or striga, a screeching, shapeshifting bird monster, which would eventually go on to become the basis for the witch in western Europe (like the *strega* of Italy) and the revenants of eastern Europe (like the *strigoi* of Romania) – a fascinating story that is sadly beyond the scope of this book.

Just like Lamashtu and Lilitu, Lamia and Gello (and Empousa, and Mormo) give flashes of insight into the lives of women in antiquity. These creatures inhabited an almost entirely female world, and through them we can get glimpses of a side of history that's often obscured by important men and their important achievements, from a mother crossly threatening her child with a monster unless he behaves, to little girls playing games, and women cutting their hair in joint mourning for a friend. It's no surprise that two of our most significant sources for these monsters come from Erinna and Sappho, two of the greatest female poets of antiquity.

Lamia and Gello especially emphasize one of the most painful aspects of infertility and child-loss: overwhelming jealousy towards other women who are able to have children. This is especially evident in the account of Lamia recorded in Diodorus Siculus's enormous *Library of History* (an attempt at a universal history of the world, written in about 60 BC and filling an impressive 40 books):

> They say that this cave is where Queen Lamia was born, who was outstanding in her beauty. The passage of time thereafter rendered her appearance bestial, because of the wildness of her nature. For all the children that were born to her died. She was crushed by her suffering and came to envy the fertility of other women. So she commanded her men to snatch babies from their mothers' embraces and kill them at once. And so it is that still now in our own age the story about this woman is kept alive with children and her mere name is terrifying to them.[13]

This is a rationalizing account – an attempt to explain away the supernatural myth by giving it a supposed real-world grounding in history, and it's notable that while Diodorus left out the gods and snake monsters to make it more believable, he felt a woman crippled by jealousy after the loss of her children, and committing terrible acts because of it, was plausible. His Lamia is almost sympathetic – a woman 'crushed by suffering' at the deaths of her children and driven to terrible things.*

The jealousy displayed by Lamia (and Gello) is another aspect of the pain that women felt, and feel, when they lose their child, or struggle with infertility – another side of the pain of infant death, or the inability to have a much-wanted child. Even today, 'pregnancy envy' is an acknowledged side effect of child-loss, miscarriage, and infertility, to the extent that NHS and infertility counsellors report it as a common issue. Some women report that their jealousy is so overwhelming they cannot be around pregnant friends, or children – some have even said that they will cross the road when they see a pregnant woman, so painful is the envy it provokes. In a time when infant mortality was vastly above what it is today, when there were no IVF or infertility treatments, the jealousy of seeing women with living, healthy children after suffering a loss must have been a pain that many women knew, reflected in the envious, murderous impulses of Lamia and Gello.

It is also clear from these monsters that the loss of a child (or the inability to have one in the first place) was not thought of solely as a personal tragedy for a woman – it was a failure of womanhood. Lamia and Gello may be sympathetic, but they are monstrous nonetheless. Lamia is, fundamentally, a woman who is unable to keep her children alive, and while

* This level of empathy is not surprising coming from Diodorus – his accounts of slavery were so detailed and sensitive that Marx suggested they be read to fully understand the horrors of slave labour.

there might be understanding of the pain this causes her, she is nonetheless demonized for it. Gello, meanwhile, is tormented not just because she died young, but because she never married or had children. There is no suggestion that her lost life could have taken a different path – she is not driven to furious murder because, had she lived, she could have composed great poetry, or written works of philosophy, or become an athlete. The failure to marry or have children, or to keep existing children alive, turned Lamia and Gello from beautiful young women into monsters, demons who were entirely outside of civilized society. They had failed at being women, to such an extent that they were women no longer.

An inability to produce children was not the only way that these monsters 'failed' at the Greek and Roman ideal of womanhood. When they weren't killing mothers, young girls and children, they were also succubi, seductive, manipulative and murderous towards their male victims. Perhaps the story about Lamia that is best known today is the one that formed the subject of Keats' poem, and is first attested in Philostratus's *Life of Apollonius of Tyana*, written in around AD 200: one of Apollonius's pupils, Menippus, meets a lovely and apparently wealthy young lady, who lives in a beautiful mansion full of great riches and staffed by many servants. Menippus falls in love and plans to marry her but on the wedding day the wise Apollonius warns Menippus that he has been 'nursing a snake' and exposes the wife-to-be as a Lamia (and an Empousa, and a Mormo). Thus revealed, the beauty of the Lamia evaporates, along with her mansion, servants and possessions, all of which had been an illusion. The monster admits that she had been planning to eat her victim, since the blood of young men is 'fresh and pure', and flees.

Dio Chrysostom, a Greek philosopher and historian writing in the first century AD, also has Lamia as a literally man-eating seductress, albeit a more bestial one. He claimed that Lamias were a species of monsters that lived by the sea, near a passage that, once it is sailed into, could not be sailed out of. From the waist up, his Lamia were beautiful, naked women, but their bottom halves were snakes. They lured lost sailors to them with their beauty, and then sprang upon them and devoured them.

It's not entirely clear how or when this sexy side developed, and we're once again hampered in our understanding by the sparsity of the sources. It's notable that both texts which explicitly mention Lamia seducing and murdering her lovers are fairly late (both are from the ADs, rather than the BCs) and it's certainly possible that this seductiveness was a later addition to her personality. It's also the case that other Greek monsters had a tendency to become more attractive over time, so that Medusa went from being a grinning, hideous monster to a beautiful woman whose only monstrous feature was a head of snake hair, and it's possible Lamia suffered the same fate. On the other hand, Lamia had always been a great beauty, albeit one who was 'disfigured' by her grief, and the sources are so fragmentary that it would be no surprise at all if Lamia had been sexy for centuries before Dio Chrysostom described her seducing sailors. It also seems likely that she had a seductive side when she was being jokingly compared to the courtesan Lamia in 300 BC. But however, and whenever, Lamia started seducing young men, it's clear that this was viewed as another failure of womanhood – and a distinctly more serious one as well.

Rather than being turned monstrous through grief and guilt, after having striven desperately to be a good woman, the seductive Lamias revel in their monster-hood, and in breaking social norms. The Lamia in the stories of Dio Chrysostom and

Apollonius of Tyana might seem markedly different physically –
in the former Lamias are more like wild beasts, and in the latter
she is a very human monster. But both manipulate men with their
beauty, their power over them compounded when they eat their
victims alive. Both appear superficially lovely, but are disguising
hideous, bestial forms. Neither is sympathetic, or understandable,
like the Gello or the version of Lamia as an abused and guilt-
ridden queen. Neither has any interest at all in being a good
woman, even if they appear as one to ensnare their prey. They
have turned their backs utterly on the Greek and Roman ideas
of femininity.

This is further emphasized by the fact that Lamia is, in some
circumstances, given male sexual organs. In 450 BC, the comic
poet Crates described her as having a 'staff' (*skutale*),* and
Aristophanes describes an entirely separate monster as having
'Lamia's testicles'. There is even one (possible) image of Lamia
on a vase from the fifth century BC where she is shown with
sagging breasts and, just visible under a damaged portion of the
vase, an enormous phallus.† In every way, a woman who became
Lamia-like, who failed to have children, or behave seductively,
or dominated men as opposed to letting them dominate her,
was – in Greek and Roman eyes – at risk of losing her womanhood entirely.

---

* Crates also wrote an entire comedy called *Lamia*, which, depressingly,
does not survive.

† Not every depiction of hermaphroditism in ancient Greece and Rome
was negative – Hermaphroditus himself, the beautiful blend of nymph
and young boy, is shown as stunningly lovely, with both breasts and penis
displayed. But this is certainly not what these comic writers and vase
artists were going for when they gave Lamia her sagging breasts, testicles,
and grotesque, enormous phallus (a large phallus, in ancient Rome, was a
sign of barbarism, not sexual prowess).

Given this, it was perhaps inevitable that 'Lamia' would come to be used as a gendered insult in the ancient world, the equivalent of the modern 'bitch' (or perhaps 'witch'), a way of reprimanding women whose behaviour was deemed insufficiently feminine, of threatening them with demonization. There are two occasions of this preserved, both in Apuleius's *Golden Ass*, a Roman comic novel written in the second century AD. The overarching narrative of the play follows the protagonist, Lucius, who has been magically transformed into the donkey of the title, but it is full of numerous self-contained stories as well.

One of these tales concerns a man called Socrates and his lover, an apparently beautiful woman called Meroe, who is in fact a witch disguising her ugly, wrinkled appearance with magic. When Socrates, with the help of a friend, finally leaves her, she and two other women break into his house at night and drain his blood before ripping out his heart, stopping up the hole in his chest with a sponge. The next morning, Socrates initially seems unharmed, but when he bends to take a drink the sponge falls out and he dies. Throughout the story, Meroe (and the women who accompany her) are referred to as *saga* – 'wise women' or 'witches' – but at one point Socrates' friend, and the narrator of the story, calls them 'Lamias'.

It's possible that this term was meant to literally describe the monsters – Meroe, much like Lamia, is supernatural, seductive and deadly to the men who fall for her charms.* On the other

---

* It's likely as well that Apuleius knew these links were there, and was consciously drawing attention to them. When he describes Meroe's disguised, beautiful form as 'older, but still attractive', it's even possible he was intentionally linking her with the 'past her prime' courtesan Lamia, who had lived about 400 years before him.

hand, Meroe seems to be a human woman who can perform magic – a witch rather than a once-human demoness. She is seductive, monstrous, and magical, but she isn't an inherently supernatural being: there's an implication that any woman who learned the same spells could become like Meroe. It makes more sense if the term is being used as an insult, rather than a literal descriptor – an interpretation that's supported by the second time Apuleius uses the word 'Lamia' in *The Golden Ass*, in the legend of Cupid and Psyche.

In this story, Psyche (in proper fairy-tale fashion) is the youngest and most beautiful of three sisters. Cupid falls in love with her, marries her, and transports her away to an incredible palace, full of astonishing, magical riches. However, he only visits her in darkness and tells Psyche that if she ever sees his face he will be forced to leave her. Psyche is satisfied until her sisters visit and, in their jealousy at the magnificence of Psyche's new home, convince her that her husband is a monster. At their urging, Psyche contrives to see Cupid's face and, as promised, he flees, leaving his lover to suffer a series of trials before they can be happily reunited.

Just before Psyche gives in to her sisters' persuasions, Cupid tries (unsuccessfully) to extract a promise from her that she will not talk to her sisters again, saying:

So if those foul Lamias armed with their noxious thoughts return, as I know they will, you must hold no conversation with them.[14]

Apuleius makes hints at the comparison between the sisters and Lamia elsewhere as well: they 'breathe viperous venom', they (like Mormo) are 'she-wolves'. However, this is all metaphorical – the sisters (who end up dying after being tricked into flinging themselves off a cliff), are among the few non-supernatural characters in the story, and they certainly aren't child-eating, seductive snake monsters. Modern scholars puzzling over this passage have come to the conclusion that 'Lamia' is being used as a gendered insult: the sisters may not be supernatural beasts, but they are certainly insufficiently feminine – jealous, conniving, complaining about their lot in life and their relationships with their husbands.* They are, in other words, the opposite of good women, and this makes them monstrous and demonic to the extent that they can be called Lamias.

It is simplistic to say that there was one ideal of womanhood in ancient Greece and Rome. There were plenty of differences between and within these civilizations, and the role of women changed over time – even drawn in very broad strokes, the life of an ideal Athenian woman (kept at home, with very few rights to hold property or trade, and wearing clothing that covered her from head to toe) was very different from the life of an ideal (property-owning, estate-running, short-dress-wearing) Spartan woman. Besides, individual woman could be, and were, praised for their accomplishments in spheres that are often assumed to be male, so that Sappho and Erinna were acknowledged as great

---

* One sister is upset that her husband is old and weak and keeps her at home, another that her husband is ill and she feels like his doctor instead of his wife. These seem like perfectly valid things to complain about, but it's pretty clear that Apuleius doesn't want us to feel sympathy: these disappointing men are a pre-emptive punishment for the sisters and also highlight how inadequately feminine they are in the way they complain about them. Psyche is too good and sweet to be lumbered with a man 'older than father and balder than a pumpkin', and also too kindly and womanly to moan about her lot if she were.

poets and Hipparchia of Maroneia and Arete of Cyrene were revered as philosophers. Even in combat and sport, women excelled – Hydna of Scione, an accomplished diver, was praised as a hero for helping to defeat the Persian invasion at Salamis by swimming under their fleet and cutting the moorings of their ships. Women could exercise political power, too, albeit normally through their male relatives, and there are plenty of Roman and Greek women who became de facto rulers.

Despite this, there were still overriding ideas about what the ideal woman should be. Even the relatively free Spartan women were expected to marry, to have sex only with their husband, and to bear and raise children. Women were certainly not expected to be more powerful than men (although, of course, some were), nor to behave seductively (although, of course, some did). Lamia and her fellow monsters were part of the policing of these expectations, a warning for women who stepped out of line that they faced literal demonization, a reminder that a failure at womanhood would place you outside of society, with the snakes, wolves and monsters. This was not a role that Lamashtu had played, except in the way that she can, occasionally, feel like a tragic parody of motherhood, suckling her dogs and placated with spindles.

This idea of our monsters as seductive dangers to men would only gain momentum, while their relationship to childbirth and infant death was increasingly sidelined. Only a few centuries after Zenobius wrote about the Gello, belief in child- and mother-killing monsters would be ridiculed as something only for very young children or foolish old women.

3

Foolish Old Women

The biography of Saint Tarasios, an eighth-century patriarch of Constantinople and onetime secretary to the Emperor Constantine VI and Empress Irene, was written by Ignatios the Deacon in the early ninth century. It contains everything you might expect from the life of a Byzantine saint: there are plentiful commentaries on iconoclasm, lots of bits of imperial intrigue and more complex religious allegories than you can shake a stick at. Among all this, one odd little story stands out, concerning a time when Tarasios's father, George Patrikios, presided as a judge at the trial of a group of impoverished, elderly women. The women stood accused of murdering infants, but this case was different from most murder trials. It was claimed that the women had been possessed by the Gello, the jealous and malignant spirit of a girl who had died without children, and that this spirit had not only driven the women to kill, but had given them the power to turn into ghosts, so they could slide through the cracks of houses and under closed doors to pursue their victims.

George was well aware of the Church's views on this sort of thing: according to Church dogma, demons had no gender, making the existence of the female Gello demon an impossibility. Worse still was that the notion of independent demons challenged the omnipotence of God: the loss of a child was a punishment from God, caused by the sin of the parents. People whose children died were supposed to do penance, not blame the loss on a demon. The Church even went so far as to formulate rules against any belief in Gello at all. George had a further problem with the accusers' story: he was entirely confident that human bodies couldn't take on spirit form and slide their way through cracks or around closed doors. After all, even Christ had been forced to assume flesh and bones, because his spirit alone had neither. Only fools would believe in something as nonsensical as the Gello. George had no hesitation in ruling that the women – who could not have reached their infant victims without the supposed powers of the Gello – were innocent.

There were those who lacked George's wisdom and sense, including the emperor himself, Constantine V, who, according to Ignatios's telling, believed in the Gello. He only gave up the idea once George had sternly pointed out to him all the reasons that Gello-belief was plainly ridiculous. Just in case we could miss how Ignatios (and, presumably, George) felt about the Gello, the anecdote finishes with the statement that those who tell stories about the Gello 'as if they are true' have been 'deceived and beguiled'.[1]

This dismissal of our monsters by scholars and religious authorities might seem like something new in the Byzantine era, but there were signs of it in ancient Greece and Rome – Strabo, for example, claimed that belief in Mormo and Lamia was used to control the uneducated, while Plato decided that in his utopian Republic, stories about our monsters would no longer be told. The demons were also written off in more subtle ways by ancient authors – accounts abound that classify them as bugbears used to frighten children, placing them in the realm of silly children's fears rather than allowing them to be legitimately terrifying creatures. Even the rationalizing accounts, like the one written by the otherwise sympathetic Diodorus, contain within them the implicit suggestion that the monsters were certainly fictional, rather than real. This chimes well with what we know about ancient (male) thoughts on the horrors of childbirth and infant death – namely, that women should suffer in silence. Cicero and Plutarch both stated that women (and men) who lost their children should not show 'excessive' emotion, and get over it quickly. No wonder monsters that would help women through these trials were thought unimportant.

Ignatios was far from the only Byzantine scholar who followed his ancient forefathers in his dismissal of our demons. Michael Psellos, an eleventh-century scholar, wrote that belief in the Gello was something for 'common people';[2] Allatios, a later Greek writer, considered it an 'absurdity' which only 'very silly' people believed; the seventh-century monk and scholar St John of Damascus called Gello-belief 'nonsensical thinking'.[3] With Church law insisting that these monsters were 'a deception of the devil, and not to be believed',[4] it was clear that for the scholarly elite of Byzantium, Gellos were embarrassing (if slightly dangerous) fairy tales, rather than horrific, life-threatening forces. And while men might occasionally be accused of believing in the Gello, she was normally associated with women – particularly 'foolish old women', a turn of phrase used by everyone from the fourth-century church fathers John Chrysostom and Gregory of Nyssa to Balsamon, a twelfth-century canonist.[5]

In some ways these dismissals of our demonesses might seem legitimate: we can, after all, be fairly confident that there weren't snake-women flying around murdering children, nor virgin ghosts returning from the grave to kill young women. Perhaps the men who ridiculed Gello-believers were just logical, thoughtful individuals: philosophers, who understood the natural world better than the 'foolish old women' around them. However, this defence only holds up so far. As we'll see plenty of men – even educated, religious, revered ones – were quite happy to accept myths about seductive snake-women who wanted to murder sailors, or monsters disguised as beautiful women trying to trick innocent men into marrying them. It wasn't the existence of magical snake monsters that disturbed the cool logic of their minds – it was the existence of magical snake monsters who didn't focus their attentions on men. We can also see this, to a lesser extent, in ancient Greece and Rome – there are no slightly patronizing rationalizing accounts about the sexy version of Lamia.

However, while people like John Chrysostom and Ignatios might have preferred to write off our monsters as the province of gullible female fools, there are plenty of signs that belief in our demons was not as marginalized as these men would have us believe. Even within the story of George Patrikios, we can see that Gello-belief was both a living tradition and fairly widespread. The idea that women could be possessed by Gellos is an entirely new addition to the legend, and one that is perfectly in line with the new, Christian beliefs of the time: in Mesopotamia and ancient Greece and Rome, demonic possessions weren't really a thing. Christianity, on the other hand, was full of evil spirits taking over people's bodies, and the legend of Gello had incorporated this. Belief in her was also clearly common enough that the case could be brought to trial. And although there are plenty of reasons to be a little suspicious of Ignatios's story of the trial, and especially his account of Constantine V's role,* we can see these new beliefs, and their wide reach, reflected in our other Byzantine sources. New stories added to the old traditions spread far and wide, new ways of protecting against our monsters were formulated and practiced, and beautiful amulets were made of precious metals, speaking to belief among the wealthier classes. We even have other, more trustworthy stories of Gello-believing members of the imperial family – Nikephoros Kallistos Xanthopoulos, a thirteenth-century ecclesiastical historian, claimed (without any apparent agenda) that the empress herself believed in the Gello, and Mormo is mentioned in the *Alexiad*, a twelfth-century history written by the Byzantine princess Anna Komnene.

In defiance of all the mockery and derision of church scholarship, our demons were prevalent throughout Byzantine society. If foolish old women were the ones passing on belief in her, they had a cultural and societal reach that is undeniable.

---

* Primarily, this suspicion is because all the parties involved were heavily embroiled in the iconoclasm debate, and the iconophile Ignatios Deacon seems to have turned his account of the Gello trial into part of this. Like so many iconoclasm debating points this was a complex mess, but, briefly explained: one of the arguments of iconoclasts was that Christ couldn't be depicted, because while it was possible to make an image of a flesh and blood body, no image could ever capture Christ's divinity. Iconophiles, meanwhile, claimed that while Christ was divine, his body was just a normal body, and so could be depicted just fine. When Ignatios had George Patriokas argue that human bodies could not become spirits – whether because of Gello possession or because the body in question belonged to the son of God – he was restating this iconophile position.

Portraying Constantine V, a famous iconoclast emperor, as a Gello-believer was an attempt to mock both him and the entire idea of iconoclasm: in fact, what we're seeing in the story isn't a wise man rejecting Gellos – it's an entire theological argument being scorned as something so ridiculous that its followers would believe in Gellos. So little was thought of Gello-belief that it could be used to make fun of something else.

Byzantine sources primarily relate to Gello, rather than Lamia, Mormo or Empousa. This isn't necessarily because beliefs in other monsters fell away – Lamia, Mormo and Empousa do still pop up occasionally. More to the point, all of these monsters appear in the folk stories of twentieth-century Greece, making it very unlikely that they disappeared entirely in late antiquity. Their (relative) absence in the Byzantine sources could just be a quirk of survival, but it may also be because our demons were often referred to by nicknames in this period, something that can disguise exactly which monster they were correlated with, or, alternatively, allow them to be correlated with the entire set. This idea, that one demon could cover all of them, is made more likely still as Lamia and Gello blended to a far greater extent than they ever had in ancient Greece or Rome, with Gello taking on Lamia's snake tail and her affinity for the ocean. An amulet against a serpentine, child-snatching woman referred to obliquely as 'the oceanic one' could protect you against an attack from both monsters. Either way, while the majority of this chapter will focus on the Gello, we should always bear in mind that the traditions of her sister monsters continued, albeit slightly out of sight of the sources.

The sources are extremely informative on Gello. While there are plenty of additions to the mythology of the monster in the Byzantine period, she was, fundamentally, still a jealous ghost who murdered children and young women. According to St John of Damascus, for example, Gellos came at night to strangle children, flying through the air and slipping under doors, unimpeded by locks or bars. The eleventh-century Michael Psellos, meanwhile, claimed that Gellos were thought to suck the blood and vital fluids of children, that even a child who was saved from Gello would waste away after being touched by her, and that Gellos would murder young women as well as infants. Interestingly, he also equated Gellos with the Jewish demon Lilith – a perceptive comparison, as we'll see in the next chapter.*

Possessing people was a new skill for our monsters, an adaptation to the new religion of Christianity, but once someone was possessed they behaved just as a Gello of ancient Greece might: murdering children and young girls. It's notable that on the occasions where they possessed people, their preferred hosts were old women – this isn't just evident in the trial of George Patriokas, but also appears in a story told by Nikephoros Kallistos Xanthopoulos, where old women bringing a baby from the bedroom are said to be Gellos. It's never explained in the ancient sources why old women were the preferred targets of possession for young, girlish ghosts but modern commentators have pointed out that Gello's furious jealousy at never having a husband or a child herself could be applied to aged spinsters as well as prematurely deceased young girls, and that perhaps this affinity led to the connection.

One of the main changes to Gello was her increasing similarity to Lamia, whose snakey tail and connection to the sea became a fundamental part of Gello-lore. These new serpentine, watery additions are best illustrated by a new tradition of amulets and stories used to defend against our monsters.

There are a few dozen Byzantine-era amulets which relate to

---

* Less impressively, Psellos also claimed that he could not find anything about the Gello in classical Greek sources, despite the fact that the line from Sappho, discussed in the last chapter, was definitely known to the Byzantines.

our demons. A typical example can be found in the Ashmolean
Museum, lying in a little case in the centre of the Byzantine gallery
with a handful of other odd charms and coins. Made from a
thin and uneven circle of silver with bent and fraying edges, it
is not, in itself, a particularly attractive little object. The figures
and writing on it are more utilitarian than skilful, and the large
number of lightly incised symbols crammed into a small space
make it look more like a silver doodle pad than anything else.
The majority of the images – pentagrams, snakes, rings, palm
branches – are crowded onto the reverse of the amulet, while
the obverse is left (relatively) clear, to make room for a single
scene which depicts a haloed figure on horseback, surrounded by
symbols of Orthodox Christianity and using a spear to impale
a female figure in a long robe, while an angel with outspread
wings looks on. Written around the edge of this is an inscription
in Greek: 'Abyzou Anabardalea, Sisinis pursues you, the Angel
Araph...'[6] after which the writing becomes illegible. Angel
Araph, then, is presumably the angel; Sisinis is our knight; while
Abyzou and/or Anabardalea is our female monster.*

Made of bronze, silver and gold, all the amulets in this
tradition are decorated with a variety of symbols. Snakes appear
frequently, and the evil eye, a symbol meant to drive away envy,
also appears (in one case with the word 'envy' written above it,
just in case there was any confusion), perhaps because of these
amulets' connections to the jealous Gello. Most of these amulets
also contain little charms against the wandering womb, and all

---

* The angel Araph may well be a cross-pollination from the tradition in
which King Solomon is said to defeat our demons. In a rather obscure
Islamic tradition, Solomon has a genie helper known as Alaph, and the
angel Araph on these amulets may be a Christian version of this. Or it
might just be a case of two names that sound a bit similar.

depict the scene of a rider on horseback impaling a prone woman, or, in some cases, a woman with the tail of a snake. The earliest of these amulets date from around AD 500, and come from Palestine, although there are plenty more dating to throughout the Middle Ages, and found across the territory of the empire. There is also a very similar scene on a Coptic fresco from Egypt, which again shows a woman with loose clothing and wild hair being impaled by a rider. In the top right-hand corner of this image is another woman with a serpentine tail, identified as the 'daughter of Alabasdria', a name that is normally supposed to be a variant of Anabardalea. Where an inscription is included (and preserved, and legible), it tends to identify the rider as Sisinios or Sisinis, or some variant name with a lot of S and N sounds in it, while the monstrous woman is called Abyzou or Anabardalea.

Abyzou is attested in another source as well – a magical text called 'The Testament of Solomon'. The Testament as we have it is likely medieval, but elements of it date to significantly earlier periods. It tells the story of how the archangel Michael gave King Solomon a ring that allowed him to control demons, which Solomon then used to build his temple.* Some of the demons that Solomon encounters aren't recorded in any other sources, but one sounds very familiar: Obizuth – a variant of the name Abyzou. The Testament describes her as a being whose body is in darkness, the only visible part of her a gleaming face, surrounded by dishevelled hair. When Solomon demands to know who she is, she reveals her name and tells him that she wanders the world looking for women about to give birth, and infants to strangle. Just in case there could be any doubt that Obizuth is connected

---

* The tradition of King Solomon having control over demons is extremely common in Christian, Jewish and Islamic thought and dates back to at least the second century BC.

with Abyzou, in some rare cases the spear-carrying rider of the amulets is identified as Solomon instead of Sisinios.

A serpentine woman, connected with envy, who hunts down pregnant women and murders children certainly sounds like our monsters. But the names 'Abyzou' and 'Anabardalea' would make anyone hesitate in connecting the demon of the amulets and the Testament to Gello or Lamia, while Sisinios sounds like someone entirely new (even though he was, in fact, an old friend in disguise). So how do we know that the figures depicted in these images are our demons, and not completely different serpentine child-killers? For that, we need to look at the stories that likely reflect the tradition of the amulets.

There are numerous Greek manuscripts that relate a story concerning Gello and a woman called Melitene. Although there are plenty of variants, the story tends to run as follows:

A woman by the name of Melitene had given birth to seven children, each one of whom had been snatched away and devoured by Gello. When she conceived again, in order to protect her unborn child, she built herself a fortified tower, and provisioned it with enough food and water to last twenty-five years. There she gave birth in peace.

Melitene's two brothers, the saints Sisinnios and Sisynodoros, came to visit their sister. They arrived at the gates of her tower, and shouted out to her, begging to be let in. She refused, so afraid was she that the Gello would take her newborn son, but her brothers convinced her that as saints she could have nothing to fear from them. However, as Melitene opened the gates, the Gello turned into a fly and entered the throat of Sisinnios's horse. In the middle of the night, the Gello rose from her hiding place, ate Melitene's son, and escaped the tower, fleeing to the ocean.

The brothers pursued the monster through the night, finally seizing her on the shore of the sea. She shapeshifted to try to escape them, but they held her fast, eventually forcing her to return their nephew, and to reveal to them her names, which, when written on an amulet or spoken aloud, would protect any woman and her children from the Gello.

This story exists in numerous versions. In some, Gello becomes a spider and hides on one of the brothers' spears. In others she turns into a mouse and hides in their saddlebags. On one occasion she disguises herself as a hair in one of the brothers' beards. The names she gives change as well, as do the forms she shifts into to try and escape, and while the brother's names tend to have a lot of Ss and Ns in them, they aren't constant from one telling to the next.

The addition of Gello's names renders the tale as half story and half charm: when the story is told, the repetition of the names, and Gello's promise that she will not be able to enter where they are proclaimed, serve to drive her away. Some of the names are nonsense words, but others describe characteristics of her personality. One is Pataxarea, meaning 'she who strikes' in Greek. Another is Paedopniktria, meaning 'child strangler'. She also has dragon-like names, including Chromodracaena, stressing her serpentine links (something also indicated by the fact that she takes on the form of a dragon when she tries to escape the brothers). Two of the most commonly included names for Gello in these charm stories stand out in relation to the amulets and the Testament of Solomon: Anabardalea and Abyzou. Here is the monster that is hidden by a nickname on the amulets, revealed as our Gello.

The name Anabardalea is likely to be based on the Hebrew word for copper, 'barzel'. The clue to understanding why our monsters have a metal name might be found in the fortified tower that Melitene builds for herself and her unborn child, which is often described as being in Chalcopratia, a part of Constantinople named after the brass workshops it was famous for. This choice of sanctuary suggests that metals could be used to repel these monsters (perhaps this was always the case, at least to some extent – it's notable that the ancient Mesopotamian Pazuzu heads and statuettes were always made from metal). Naming the demons after these metals was a way of reducing their power, of giving them a nickname that related to something which could drive them away, and we'll see plenty more metal names like this in the next chapter.

Abyzou, meanwhile, is related to the Greek word *abyssou*: the bottomless deep, or the depths of the sea (for which we have our word 'abyss').* This is not the only watery term in Gello's name lists – 'Pelagia' – Greek for 'sea' – also turns up frequently.

---

* This will be a lengthy footnote, but it has to be said and there's no reason to have it in the main text. One of the seminal articles on our monsters and all their myriad iterations, from Liliths and Lamashtus to mermaids, was written by A. A. Barb in the 1960s. His article is fascinating, and a deeply enjoyable read even now, but it does contain a fundamental error, which has been repeated in later scholarship on our demons under the Byzantines. Barb believed that these demons could be connected to 'Apzu', the god of freshwater in ancient Mesopotamian legend, that this connection began in the Mesopotamian period, and that the name 'Abyzou' in the Byzantine charms was directly related to this. His evidence for this is as follows (and bear with me here, because it's a bit convoluted): in ancient Mesopotamia the god Apzu is often partnered with Tiamat, the goddess of salt water. In one epic, this divine pair are fighting the god Marduk, and Tiamat creates an army of monsters to do battle at her side. Barb suggested that Tiamat and Apzu might have become muddled, with this Tiamat-Apzu taking on the role of 'mother of demons' through her creation of the monster army. Then, according to Barb, this murderous mother-of-demons persona, with the name of Apzu, became connected with the child- and mother-killing demonesses Lamashtu and Lilitu, eventually becoming just another name

These ocean-themed names tell us clearly that the connection between our monsters and water which we first saw in ancient Greece was still there in force in the Byzantine period. As with the snake tail, the connection to the sea was mainly related to Lamia in ancient Greece, where she was linked with the oceanic Scylla, where Aristotle called her a shark, and where Dio Chrysostom had her living by the sea devouring sailors. By the Byzantine period this aspect of Lamia had fully transferred onto Gello as well. This isn't just evident in the name lists: it's clear in the Melitene story itself, where Gello is chased back to the sea by her foes. In one variant the brothers are even told to hurry because Gello is getting close to the water, implying that should she reach it, they would never be able to catch her.

---

for these monsters by the Byzantine era. Barb proposed this as a reason not only for the name Abyzou being associated with the child-killing monsters, but also as a reason for their links with water, which, in his telling, went back to ancient Mesopotamia.

If you're thinking this all sounds like a bit of a stretch (and a very tangled stretch at that), it's because it is. Being 'mother of demons' is not a part of Tiamat's identity: she spends ten lines making an army of monsters in one fairly late myth. And while, as we'll see, being a mother of demons was a feature of later iterations of Lilith, it certainly wasn't a concern for Lamashtu, Lilitu, Gello or Lamia. There's also no evidence that Tiamat and Apzu ever blended together, and the names Apzu and Tiamat aren't ever linked to Lamashtu or Lilitu in the Mesopotamian sources: it's only in the Byzantine period that the name Abyzou is connected to our demons. Far more likely is that an association between our monsters and the sea came about in ancient Greece – the first time these links are attested – and was carried over into Byzantine beliefs as well. By this stage, the Sumerian word 'Apzu', which meant 'fresh water' as well as referring to the god, had been adopted into the Greek to mean 'depths of the sea' or just 'the deep', and was attached to the sea-going Gello, along with other oceanic names like Pelagia.

We are going to encounter the Sisinios vs Gello story (or at least ones very like it) a lot in the next few chapters, spreading from late antiquity to the Middle Ages and even to the twentieth century, and covering a geographical range from Greece to Romania, into Egypt and Ethiopia, through Mesopotamia and Iran and up into Russia. The story would attach itself to other familiar demons in our tradition – especially the monstrous Lilith – and give us new additions as well, like the child-devouring Al demon of Turkmenistan and Russia.

Despite their wide geographical and chronological reach, these stories contain some elements that are always (or almost always) the same, and that we can see in these Greek versions as well. The monster is a child-snatcher; she is connected to the sea (or at least to water); she changes her shape to get at her victims; she can be driven away by metal, and she is pursued to the ocean or a river by a protector figure with a name that uses the letters S and N prominently. This figure eventually extracts from her a promise not to harm children wherever her names, or the names of the protector figure, are spoken. With similarities that are so specific, there can be no doubt that these stories are all from the same tradition, and the question of where they originated has been asked for at least a century.

The first textual sources for this legend come from Mesopotamia and Palestine and date to between the fifth and seventh centuries AD, while the earliest attestation of these stories in Greece comes from much later: the first manuscript for the Melitene story dates to the 1400s. By the timeline of the written sources alone, these look like Middle Eastern tales that spread west to Greece. However, these were likely oral traditions, meaning that the first surviving written source doesn't necessarily correspond to the first time the tales were told. And, if we look outside the texts, we can see this tradition appears in Byzantine sources at around the same time as those first Mesopotamian ones.

Even on the earliest Byzantine amulets we can see most of the elements of the Melitene story. The very oldest amulets show us a female, snake-tailed monster, named Abyzou (so linking her to the sea, and dragons, as well as Gello), defeated by a rider called Sisinnios, with the presence of the evil eye on these amulets also strongly implying the jealousy of our child-killing monsters. Even if the story the amulets were depicting wasn't exactly the same as the Melitene story, it was at least a watery, jealous, child-killing, Sisinnios-hero story: and these amulets date to around the sixth century AD – that is, about the same time as the first attestations of the legend in Mesopotamia, muddling the timeline significantly. Even earlier than these are a collection of hematite gems dating to the fourth century AD, and found around the Mediterranean. Showing a rider (who is identified as Solomon or Sisinis by the accompanying inscription) impaling a female figure with long, loose hair, these are almost certainly related to the same tradition, and further suggest that these stories were known in the West long before the first textual sources for them in Greek.

In the end, the origin of these stories is most clearly indicated by the connection of the monster to water, something that appears in all versions of the legend, whether it's found in Byzantine Greece, Mesopotamia, or Central Asia. As we've seen, this watery aspect to our demons is something that was added to the tradition in ancient Greece and Rome, where our monsters were firmly linked to the sea. Lamashtu and Lilitu, in contrast, had no oceanic interests at all. The shapeshifting of the monster is also suggestive of the Mormo, Empousa and Lamia. Lamashtu and Lilitu never took on different forms, while the demons of Greece and Rome were renowned as shapeshifters.

A Western origin for the Melitene/Gello/Sisinios story is further supported by the existence of an earlier charm story, from which it may have been derived. This story also relates to watery, female monsters being driven away by a protector who forces the demons to divulge their names, and it seems to have been Roman in origin, with the earliest attestation recorded on a tiny silver scroll, dating to around AD 300, and found in a Roman tomb in a small Austrian town.

The scroll is inscribed with a short story-charm that describes an encounter between a headache demon named 'Antaura' and the goddess Artemis. Artemis meets the demon emerging from the sea, and demands to know where the creature is going. Although the scroll breaks at this point, we can easily reconstruct what might have happened: charm stories like this appear again and again in our sources from antiquity to the medieval period.

In all these stories female monsters emerge from the ocean and are challenged by a divine force, who insists on knowing where the creature is going and what it is doing. The monster admits they're planning evil deeds, at which point the divinity will torture them until they reveal their names, thus giving mortals the tools to protect themselves against them. The protective deity was eventually Christianized, and switched to Jesus or the Archangel Michael (Michael being an obvious choice as the angel to drive away a monster, given that in the Book of Revelation he's said to defeat Satan himself).

The female demons exorcized by these charms are more complex. In most early examples, they're headache demons and, as such, their femininity makes some degree of sense: migraines are considerably more prevalent among women than men. They're also connected to the wind and the sea, emerging from the ocean and often literally called 'wind' (Aura, in the Greek). This is evident from the earliest charm: 'Antaura' literally means 'unpleasant wind'. This might also tie back to migraines – there are plenty of seaborne winds, like the Italian sirocco, which were thought to cause headaches.

These charm stories would eventually be used against our monsters as well. In one medieval version, for example, the Archangel Michael meets Gello coming out of the sea, filthy and with flowing hair. When he demands to know what she's up to, she responds: 'I go unto the creatures of God as a snake, as a dragon, as a four-legged reptile, to strike against men and women to make their hearts ache, to crush their brains and grind their teeth and to abduct their infants.'[7] Appalled, Michael grabs Gello by a lock of hair on the right side of her head and begins to torture her. She pleads with him to release her, and says that if he does she will reveal her twelve and a half names: where they are proclaimed, she will not be able to enter. Michael assents, and the names are given.*

How this collection of charms against oppressive, migraine-causing wind demons came to be linked with our monsters is up for debate. Perhaps it was the fact that the headache demonesses were female and emerged from the water that made the connection seem natural. It may also have been because migraines are connected with childbearing, pregnancy, and menstruation: even Lamashtu, in her lesser moments, was said to cause headaches (although there's no indication that this theme made it past the first millennium in Mesopotamia, let alone that

---

* 'Half' names are quite common in demonic name lists, although there rarely seems to be any particular reason why they'd be thought of as a half-name rather than a full one: they're not noticeably shorter or different from the other names in the list.

it followed the family down to the Byzantine period, so a direct link here is unlikely).

This charm (normally referred to in scholarship as a 'Michael' charm), may well have been a precursor to the longer, more complex, Melitene story. The similarities are there: female monsters connected to the sea, being caught by a protector, and tortured until they reveal the names that can be used to protect against them. If this was the case, then it provides even more evidence of a Western origin for the Melitene legends, since there is no doubt at all that the simple, Michael-type charms originated in the West, six hundred centuries before there was any sign of these kinds of stories in Mesopotamia.

There is another character in the Melitene story who we have yet to touch upon – the valiant protector* Sisinios, and his brothers. The number of brothers can change: sometimes there are two, sometimes three, and occasionally it's Sisinios alone who stands against the demon. These S and N names were crucial to the story, and although they can vary, it's very rare to see this legend told with a hero who doesn't have lots of Ss and Ns in his name. These brothers may sound like a completely new addition to the lore of our demons, but they date back almost to the beginning of our tradition. Unlikely as it may seem, Sisinios and his companions are derived from Pazuzu, the Mesopotamian demon who drove off Lilitu and Lamashtu, still dogging our demonesses right down the millennia.

The very earliest indication of Pazuzu's shift in identity is a

---

* Or, depending on which way you want to look at it, the useless brother who should have listened to his sister and nearly got his nephew killed, although the stories don't tend to portray him in this way.

Pazuzu statuette, which was found in Egypt and dates to the seventh century BC. With his snarling face, double wings and lion's tail, there can be no doubt at all that the figure is Pazuzu, but the inscription on the statuette identifies him as 'Ssm son of Pdr'.*[8] On a further Phoenician amulet, also dating to the seventh century BC and from Arslan Tash (a small city close to the Euphrates in Northern Syria) 'Ssm son of Pdr' is called to help against a flying demoness who 'strangles the lamb' and is depicted as a wolf devouring a child.[9] This monster is surely a derivation of Lamashtu, with Ssm son of Pdr playing the role of Pazuzu in driving her away. Taken together, these two objects suggest that although his name had changed, Pazuzu's appearance and purpose remained the same. It's difficult to say how this name change came about (although 'z' can turn to 's' very easily), but given that Pazuzu was frequently called 'Pazuzu, son of Hambu' in ancient Mesopotamian texts, it is nice to see that he maintained his patronymic, even if both his and his father's name had shifted.[†]

In the seventh century BC outside of Mesopotamia, Pazuzu still worked to drive away a child-stealing demoness, but his name had changed to Ssm. This is a fairly common Phoenician name, with a variant spelling of Ssmy, and both spellings can be related to the S and N names of Gello's pursuers. The reason

---

* These names are written without vowels (or 'unvocalized') because they were recorded in a script that only records consonants. Normally, the words are familiar enough to translators that the vowels can be filled in, but in the case of names we often don't quite know how they were pronounced, so the vowels can't be included.

† This, incidentally, is the simple way of looking at it, and avoids a slightly thorny issue: if Pazuzu came from Egypt (or at the very least, from outside Mesopotamia) Ssm son of Pdr might be his 'original' name, and Pazuzu a later, Mesopotamian variant.

why Pazuzu was split into two, or sometimes three, is unclear (as is the date at which this multiplication occurred) but his continued presence as a protector against members of our demonic family is beyond doubt.

The reappearance of Pazuzu only emphasizes that by late antiquity our monsters had already been around for millennia: even Michael Psellos had to acknowledge that Gello was 'an ancient and oft-repeated name'.[10] The shifts and changes in the traditions are a sign of how much they were handled, of how they were adapted to new circumstances, religions and concepts, but fundamentally, these were still monsters that Sappho, or Aristophanes, or indeed any Mesopotamia exorcist, would have recognized.

No amount of laws against Gello-belief, or calling Gello-believers 'fools', or providing religious arguments for why she couldn't exist, had any obvious impact at all. This might initially be surprising: the early Christian church was, after all, pretty good at stamping out those beliefs it disliked. Most scholars think that within a couple of centuries of Constantine's conversion, paganism had been almost entirely eradicated. Temples were turned into churches or abandoned entirely, sacrifices stopped, and belief in the old gods was consigned entirely to history within a scant few generations. And yet Gello didn't just persist, but thrived as much as our monsters ever had. How was a belief so derided by scholarly authorities able to achieve such prevalence?

The answer may well lie in the statements of John Chrysostom and Gregory of Nyssa that only 'foolish old women' believed in our monsters. Although these claims were made to dismiss those who believed in Gello, there was certainly truth to the fact that those preserving, practicing and passing on the tradition of our demons were women. When the ninth-century Abbot Theodore

praised his mother, Theoktiste, for avoiding Gello-related practices, he made it clear that these were almost exclusively female
beliefs, writing:

After giving birth, she avoided doing what other wives were
accustomed to do on behalf of their infants, when they
employ omens and amulets and certain other enchantments
to neutralize the assault of demons. They deploy these items
on couches and beds. They use necklaces and other charms
too. She, on the contrary, contented herself with the seal
of the life-giving Cross alone as her armor and shield of
protection. In sum: whereas all other women believe in the
instructive, mystical and practical power of such devices,
she alone stayed away from them ... And as a consequence,
she often drew criticism from those who were experts in
such matters.[11]

Theoktiste, according to this telling, is criticized only by
women – not men – for forgoing amulets and charms, and she is
alone among women in doing so. In all ways, our monsters are
positioned as 'old wives' tales' – superstitions that belong in the
realm of women and children and draw scorn because of it – and
sources like Theodore's show there was real truth to this: these
beliefs and traditions were, indeed, woman's lore.

Appreciating this is important to understanding how belief
in Gello survived, grew, and spread, despite the censure of the
Church. These traditions were not passed on by the elite men
who wrote that Gello was nonsense, and most Gello-believers
(emperors aside) would never have read Ignatios's sneering
account of the trial, or John Chrysostom's snippy little take on
child-snatching demons. These authorities could crack down on
beliefs in the pagan gods that relied on the public sphere and

on public acts of devotion, but changing private traditions was much harder. You can stop a religious ceremony much more easily than you can prevent a mother from telling her daughter a story – especially if that story is being told in the exclusively female environment of childbirth.

It wasn't just that the educated, scholarly men writing the majority of our surviving sources would have had very little direct influence over most women – it's that women's lore, and old wives' tales, have proven time and again to be both exceptionally durable and exceptionally long-lasting. If you want a belief to last, and you don't have access to a pulpit (or a printing press), you want it spread by women, foolish, old or otherwise.

Terms like 'old wives' tale' or 'nursemaid's story' are normally pejoratives, but the traditions they describe have a habit of surviving for centuries, and covering an enormous geographical range. We all know our fairy stories, the ultimate old wives' tales. Fables like Cinderella (which originally appears in ninth-century China) have lasted centuries and spread across continents in much the same way as our monsters: adapting to the cultures they found themselves in, shifting and changing as they were handed from one person to another, being told and retold again.

There's even a suggestion that part of the reason for the enormous spread of these kinds of traditions is that women, rather than men, tended to be the ones who made new lives away from their place of birth. While men were far more likely to stay with the land and wealth they inherited from their fathers, women were the ones who married out and left, who travelled, and integrated into the communities where their new husbands lived. Their stories travelled with them and were passed on by them to their daughters, eventually crossing continents.

And Gello, Lamia and all our monsters were not just stories to the women who told them: in many cases they were, in essence, the only medical care available to them as they faced the horrific dangers of pregnancy and childbirth, the uncertainty of infertility; the only way they had to protect their dying infants. It is hardly surprising that these beliefs continued regardless of the interventions of a group of church scholars, who could offer women only the degrees of penance they should perform if their children died (three years if the infant wasn't baptized, two years if the death was caused by neglect, one year otherwise).

Most of the time, women who pass on and practice these kinds of traditions are entirely anonymous, unknown and unknowable to us from the surviving sources. Oral traditions and private practices leave few records, and if they are eventually written down it's unlikely they'll come with much information about the person passing them on. In most cases, the traditions surrounding our demons are similar – we have no information on the individual women who believed in Gello, or who told the charm story of Melitene and Sisinios. They always appear as vague groups: 'foolish women', women who are unlike the good mother of Theodore.

But for one brief moment the sources fall in such a way that we can see some of the women who practiced magic against our demons. Their words and names are recorded on a group of objects coming from Mesopotamia in the fifth to eighth centuries AD, known as the Incantation Bowls.

4

Most Women Are Sorcerers

Stowed away in the collections storage of the Penn Museum is a ceramic bowl, unearthed in 1889 in the ruins of the Mesopotamian city of Nippur by a team of bickering Americans.* Dating to somewhere between the fourth and eighth centuries AD, it's a very plain object – small, unglazed, and identical to

* This sorry episode in archaeological history involved four adult men, lacking any understanding of the country they found themselves in, trying to steal credit for each other's work, fighting over whether travelling third class instead of first would bring 'dishonour' to their university, and involving themselves in relentless rows about who should be in charge of the expedition. The entire dismal affair led to the shooting of a young Iraqi boy, the team being driven out of Nippur, and a long-running saga of academic dishonesty and antiquities theft. It's difficult to single out an absolute low point in nineteenth-century archaeology, but the University of Pennsylvania expeditions to Nippur are definitely down there.

thousands of other mass-produced, utilitarian bowls of the period that were intended for domestic use. The interest of the bowl – the reason why nineteenth-century archaeologists bothered carting it back to America from Mesopotamia – comes in the painting on the bowl's interior: running in a spiral from the centre of the bowl until it reaches the outer rim is an Aramaic incantation. This incantation was written by a woman, named Komish, daughter of Mahlapta, who was attempting to protect herself against a demon called a 'Lilith'. This short little text reads:

> This day, from among all days, years, and generations of the world, I, Komish daughter of Mahlapta, have divorced and dismissed and banished you – you, Lilith, Lilith of the desert, ghost and kidnapper. You, the three of you, the four of you, the five of you, are sent out naked and not clad. Your hair is dishevelled, thrown over your backs ... I have decreed against you, with the curse that Joshua ben Perahia sent against you. I adjure you by the glory of your father and by the glory of your mother. Receive your gets [a type of Jewish divorce document] and your divorces, gets and divorces that were sent in the curse that Joshua ben Perahia sent against you, about which Joshua ben Perahia said to you, "a get has come to you from across the sea". In it is found written, whose mother's name is Palhan, and whose father's name is Pelahdad Lilith. Hear and go away and do not lie with her, with Komish daughter of Mahlapta, not in her house and not in her dwelling.[1]

There are around 2,000 bowls like this in museums worldwide (and plenty more that have been looted and are now in private collections). All are normal, domestic bowls with incantations written inside them, sometimes accompanied by a painted image.

They were buried upside down, usually in the corner of the house or at its threshold (and, occasionally, in graveyards), where they worked as traps, keeping the demons named in the incantations imprisoned under them and preventing them from causing harm. While the incantations cover a wide variety of topics, from curses to love spells, many acted to protect their users against Liliths, like those in Komish's bowl. These Liliths are our virgin ghosts, the Lilitu, who we last saw in the cuneiform incantations of ancient Mesopotamia mourning their untimely deaths, seducing men, and blending with the demonic, child-killing Lamashtu.

As is evident from Komish's incantation, there is a lot going on with the Liliths of these bowls that is new to the tradition of our demons, from the idea that they might 'lie with' mortal women as well as men, to the way they could have their own personal names and demonic family relations. But while plenty had changed over the few centuries that separated the last reference to Lilitu in cuneiform and the first incantation bowl, a lot stayed the same. Her name was almost identical, as were many of her behaviours – not only was she still a seductress, other bowls show us that she also attacked children and caused infertility and miscarriages.

In fact, the biggest difference between the ancient Mesopotamian Lilitu and the Liliths of the bowls is that while the cuneiform incantations that referenced Lilitu tended to be the products of elite scholarship, the bowl incantations were anything but. Bowls were found buried under the floor of numerous houses in Nippur from this period – some households even had four or five apiece. They were cheap, commonly used objects, picked from the domestic bowls of a local pottery, often poorly written, with numerous errors and corrupted spellings. Although not everyone would have been able to read them (and we even have a few that were clearly made by and for illiterate people, with the writing replaced by a collection of signs that were supposed to imitate letters), everyone would have likely known what they were.

And while most (though certainly not all) of the ancient Mesopotamian scribes were men, there is evidence that the majority of the bowl incantations were written by women. These women, like Komish daughter of Mahlapta, not only wrote bowls for themselves, but for others (whether family members or clients). These plain, low-cost objects are a window into how our demons survived despite male scholarly ridicule of the kind seen in Byzantium and ancient Greece: the knowledge of the demons was held by women, who were more than capable of passing on the information, and practising the relevant spells, themselves. As the Babylonian Talmud says: 'most women are sorcerers'[2] – practitioners of magic like the bowl rituals, and repositories of knowledge about incantations like the one Komish recited against the Lilith that was tormenting her. In these objects we are finally hearing women's voices first-hand.

When we last saw Lilitu and Lamashtu in Mesopotamia, it was in cuneiform texts dating to the time of the Persian empire in the fourth century BC. Between this and the incantation bowls, Mesopotamia had been invaded by Alexander the Great and ruled by his Seleucid heirs, who were tossed out in their turn by the Iranian Parthians, who were followed by the Romans. By the third century AD and until the Islamic conquests in the seventh century – that is, the period to which the bulk of our incantation bowls date – Mesopotamia was part of the Iran-based Sasanian empire.

From the time of Alexander's conquest of the Persian empire to the arrival of the Sasanians, our sources are largely silent on Lilitu and Lamashtu. This isn't because of a lack of interest in the demons during these centuries, but rather due to a shift in our written sources. Over time, cuneiform (and Akkadian, the language it had mostly been used to write) had slipped from use – it was being sidelined in favour of Aramaic (which was written in the Aramean alphabet) from about the sixth century BC on, with the last cuneiform document, a very badly written astrological text, dating to AD 75.

Unfortunately, Aramaic was written on parchment, which meant far fewer Aramaic texts survive in comparison with cuneiform sources, which were written on the hardy (and fireproof) clay. It's no coincidence that the vast collection of Aramaic incantations that we do have preserved from this period are those that were written on clay bowls, rather than on paper.

A change in language was not the only major shift that Mesopotamia had seen between the Lamashtu and Lilitu cuneiform incantations and the incantation bowls. Belief in the old pantheon of gods was fading, to be replaced by a whole host of new religions: Zoroastrianism was certainly around in Mesopotamia in this period, since it was a semi-state religion of the ruling Sasanians; but there were also Christians, Jews, and groups of followers of gnostic sects like Mandaeism and Manicheism.

Many of these religions were still developing at the time of the bowls – Rabbinic Judaism was in its infancy, Christianity had only been around a handful of centuries and was still working through sets of schisms, squabbles and heresies, and Mani himself – the founder of Manicheism – lived in the third century AD, and may (just) have been around when the earliest bowls were being made. And, although some of these religions (especially Manichaeism and Mandaeism) represent ethno-religious groups in the modern world, people could, and did, change their faiths (Augustine of Hippo, for example, who lived in the fourth century AD, famously converted to Manichaeism in his youth, before converting to Christianity a few years later). This was not a set of static, isolated religions but an ever-changing mess of interconnected beliefs and peoples that lived together, borrowed from each other and occasionally fought with each other.

One of the religious (or at least, quasi-religious) practices that was shared by many in this chaotic community of mingling faiths was the use of incantation bowls to drive away demons. Although the largest number of surviving bowls are written in the (Jewish-associated) Judeo-Aramaic script, and seem to reference Jewish beliefs, they appear across all faiths and languages: we have bowls written in everything including Syriac, Mandaic, Arabic and Pahlavi. The religions, too, mix in an almost dizzying fashion, so the divine names in the incantations on the bowls include not just Judeo-Christian figures like Yahweh, and the angels Gabriel and Michael, but the ancient Mesopotamian god Shamash, the Syrian Belti, and the Persian goddess Anahid.

It wasn't just the practice of bowl magic that was shared by the people of this multi-faith community – it was Lilith, who appears across the bowls, a monstrous, seductive, child-killing force, a continuation of the legacy of the ancient Lamashtu and Lilitu combined in one terrible being.

In plenty of bowls, Lilith is part of a crowd – one of multiple demons that people sought to drive away. A typical bowl incantation reads:

> You are wholly charmed and sealed and bound, that you go away and be sealed and depart from the house of Farruck son of Pusbi, Newanduch daughter of Pusbi and Abanduch daughter of Pusbi, and that they depart from them all evil Liliths, and all demons, and devils, and spells, and

idol-spirits, and the vow, and the curse, and the invocation, and evil arts, and mighty works, and everything hostile.[3]

Even in these broader spells, we can see that, much like the ancient Lilitu, Liliths were a species of demons, rather than an individual creature. In some incantations, Lilith is banished with her 'brood'; in others, as we've seen, Liliths could have individual names, and even family relations.*

Like Lilitu and Lamashtu in Mesopotamia, the monster of the incantation bowls was certainly a child-killer. She 'plagues' boys and girls, is often specifically ordered not to kill the children of the house, and is called 'the strangler', suggesting that she has maintained one of Lamashtu's principal methods of killing her young victims. She continued, too, to disrupt pregnancies: bowl incantations associate her with infertility and miscarriage, and one contains an incantation that attempts to protect a woman's 'unborn child and womb' from the monster.

Just like the ancient Lilitu, the Lilith of the bowls was also a seductive force, but the suggestion that she was a frustrated virgin ghost, attempting to enact her thwarted passions on living men, had vanished. Perhaps this is because her blending with Lamashtu rendered her wholly demonic but, whatever the reason, the idea of Lilitu as a lost young girl had slipped out of Lilith's mythology and never returned. Lilith did, however, retain her predilection for appearing to her victims in their dreams, seducing people in 'dreams of the night' and even 'visions of the day', and was still strongly associated with nocturnal emissions and wet dreams in men.

---

* Unfortunately, we can't tell much from these names – it would be interesting if they mapped onto specific actions or characteristics, but they don't appear often enough to identify any sort of pattern.

Interestingly, the targets of her seduction included women as well as men and while in some incantations it's claimed that she 'appeared to men in the form of women and women in the form of men' in many cases it isn't specified that she changed her gender (or appearance of gender) when she seduced women. There's no reason to assume that when she was accused of 'lying with' mortal women she wasn't in the form of a woman: in fact, in one unsettling bowl it's made clear that Lilith could, and did, come to women when appearing as a woman herself. The bowl is made for one 'Bardesa, granddaughter of Dade', who was attempting to protect herself from the Liliths that appeared to her 'in the form of Tata, her sister's daughter'.[4]* Oddly enough, Lili – the male equivalent of Lilitu who was said to seduce women in ancient Mesopotamia – is still around in the bowls, but he only ever appears in lists as one demon among many, fading from view as Lilith took on multi-gender seduction.

There are some images of Lilith painted in the bowls, but it's difficult to draw too much information from them – they are, to put it politely, a clear demonstration of how difficult it is to paint on a curved surface. However, even in these scrappy little drawings, we can still see the importance of Lilith's seductive qualities. The demoness is usually shown naked, with well-defined genitals and bare breasts. She wears her hair loose and wild, something reinforced by the fact that she is described as having 'dishevelled hair' which is thrown over her back (that is, worn loose) in the incantations.

Lamashtu had wild, dishevelled hair as well, but this was

---

* Bardesa does also claim that she is trying to protect her unborn child, so there is a hope that this wasn't related to any sort of incestuous seduction. Either way, the relationships in Bardesa's extended family sound awkward at best.

normally just a sign of how uncivilized she was, another aspect of her living in swamps and on the edges of society. In the bowls, though, and especially in Judaism, this loose, wild hair became a distinctly erotic feature. In Judaism, 'good' women were supposed to cover their hair and there are repeated pronouncements, even in the earlier Rabbinic writings, which make it clear that a woman's hair was considered sexual: a woman's unbound hair could, for example, be a sign of adultery, meaning a man could leave his wife without the money that was normally guaranteed to her on divorce if she went out with her head uncovered.*

If you were unlucky enough to be seduced by a Lilith, this could become a sort of perverted marriage – in one incantation, Lilith is even described as living in the house 'like a member of the family' – which meant that the best way to get rid of her was through a type of divorce. Numerous bowls order Lilith to accept her 'get' – a Jewish divorce document – as in an incantation written to protect a man and his wife (named Geyonai and Rasnoi, respectively) from their Lilith, which reads:

> And again, you [Lilith] shall not appear to them in his house nor in their dwelling nor in their bedchamber, because it is announced to you, whose father is named Palhas and whose mother Pelahdad ... that Rabbi Joshua ben Perahia has sent against you the get. I adjure you by the name of Palhas your father and by the name of Pelahdad your

---

* One rabbinic source even references a bold, Sasanian-era, hair-based chat-up line: 'Ah, you are fair my darling, your hair is like a flock of goats': truly what every woman wants to hear.

mother. A divorce-writ has come down to us from heaven and there is found written in it for your advisement … In the name of Palsa-Pelisa who renders to you your gets and your divorces, your divorces and your gets. You, Lilith, male Lili and female Lilith, hag and ghost, be in the ban … of Rabbi Joshua ben Perahia …

And thus has spoken to us Rabbi Joshua ben Perahia: A divorce writ has come for you from across the sea, and there is found written in it, whose father is named Palhas and whose mother Pelahdad … Hear and go from the house and from the dwelling of this Geyonai son of Mamai and from Rasnoi his wife daughter of Marath.[5]

The Joshua ben Perahia referenced here was a rabbinic leader in the second century AD. Although he appears frequently in the bowls, handing out divorces to demons, we have no insight as to why he was credited with performing this role.* The demonic divorce itself is often referenced as being 'from across the sea'. This was a type of (non-demonic) divorce which was used by men to separate from their (ordinary, mortal) wives when they were in foreign countries (so the divorce itself was coming across the sea). Presumably this type of get seemed appropriate because normal divorces were supposed to be handed to the wife by the husband himself, something that was impossible when the 'wife' in question was a demoness who only appeared in dreams. The get 'from across the sea' still worked to dissolve a marriage even

---

* His main other claim to fame is that, according to one passage in the Babylonian Talmud, he was supposedly a teacher of Yeshu, a figure who may or may not have been the equivalent of the Christian Jesus, leaving him with a fascinating, if slightly enigmatic, resume.

when it couldn't be given to the wife directly, making it perfect for demonic divorces.

As we'll see, Lilith's seduction of men would ultimately be portrayed by male religious authorities as her greatest evil, and it would be easy to assume that this side of her was something women had little interest in. But there are two bowls from Sasanian Nippur that tell us otherwise. The first of these bowls is a charm 'against the Liliths that haunt the house of Ephra, son of Saborduch' and his wife.[6] The bowl focuses on Liliths' propensity for seduction, and while we might be able to write this off as a fairly typical attempt to get rid of the demoness, the husband and wife wrote another bowl as well, and this one was not directed at Liliths. Instead, it contains an incantation that attempted to conjure up the love and affection of Ephra for his wife, along with the children she could not have without that love (or at least the sex that would hopefully come with it).[7] The fear of Lilith's seduction, for Ephra's wife, was her fear of losing her husband's affection (or never gaining it in the first place), and her hope that this was caused by a supernatural temptress who could be banished by a clay bowl. Her quiet desperation, preserved where she buried it 1500 years ago, is a small, heartbreaking window into a world where women were entirely dependent on their husband's affection. To lose it was a terrifying, life-destroying prospect, and something over which they might have very little control. Pushing these fears onto demons – demons that were terrifying, but that could nevertheless be dispelled – must have provided at least some semblance of comfort.

There is something else in these incantations that is strikingly familiar, but that doesn't come directly from the Mesopotamian tradition. There are a handful of bowls which tell the story of a woman, Semamit, whose children are killed by a monster called Sideros. When Semamit finds herself pregnant again she flees to a mountain, where she 'made doors for herself of bronze and bolts of iron'[8] to protect herself and her child from Sideros. Four men – Soni, Sasoni, Sanigru and Artiqu – come to her and demand that she let them in, and when Semamit reluctantly opens her door, Sideros slips through, murdering her son. The men chase Sideros to the sea intending to kill it, but the monster pleads for its life, promising them that wherever the men's names are invoked, children will be safe.

This story is also repeated almost word for word on two silver amulets from Palestine, which date to roughly the same period as the bowls. The only difference is that here the men are called 'Swny', 'Swswny' and 'Snyngly' (the last representing the least formidable name of any demon-slayer, but perhaps it was more intimidating with its vowels).

This is quite clearly the story of Gello, Sisinios and Melitene that we saw in the Greek sources, spreading into Mesopotamia. Everything is the same, from the metallic sanctuary the heroine builds and the foolish men accidentally bringing the monster inside with them, to the chase to the sea, and the extracted promise that the demon will not harm children wherever the men's names are spoken. Even the heroes' names are similar to the Sisinnios, Sisynodoros, and Sines of the Greek, with almost all of them playing with S and N sounds. Pazuzu had come back to Mesopotamia.

Only the names of the heroine and monster are different. The name of the heroine – 'Semamit' – means 'spider' (and is perhaps related to the tradition of the monster slipping into the sanctuary in the form of an insect), while 'Sideros' means iron in Greek – almost certainly another case of naming these monsters after the metal that could drive them away, as we saw with Anabardalea (an idea supported by the fact that Semamit, like Melitene, builds herself a sanctuary of metal). Sideros, in both the bowl and the amulet, is also a male demon, but given that in every other instance of this story the demon is female this seems to be a rare variation, and is perhaps just linked to the fact that the noun *sideros* in Greek is masculine.

Having found a foothold in Mesopotamia, these stories spread into Iran as well – a demon called Sesenmarg-Dew appears on Sasanian amulets from Iran, a name which means 'the demoness, death [through] Sesen'.[9] This 'Sesen' is presumably our Sisinnios, and the demon's name another (even more explicit) nickname referencing a force that could protect people from her. In the *Pahlavi Widewdad*, a fifth-century Zoroastrian text about driving away demons, a charm for a healthy birth and successful breastfeeding culminates in the statement that a demoness called the 'Aiiehia' should be driven away. Her name seems to be a feminization of *aiiah*, a word for metal (especially copper and bronze) in Avestan, one of the earliest of the Zoroastrian languages, so here we have yet another metallic demoness associated with childbirth and infant health.[10]

These metallic monsters would spread further still. In Turkmenistan, Central Asia, Armenia and even the southern parts of Russia, stories are told about a demoness called the Al, or Albasti. This creature has bronze or copper claws and iron teeth: presumably the metallic naming had transferred onto the monster itself, leaving it in the slightly awkward state of being made of the substance that could repel it. The Al also had dishevelled hair and sagging breasts, as well as tusks and a clay nose. This hideous creature was renowned for stealing the lungs, livers and hearts of women in childbirth, murdering embryos in the womb and kidnapping infants.* She is defeated by a St Sisianos, and often tries to flee to rivers with the stolen organs or children. If she is caught before she reaches the river she can be defeated, but once she has touched it she cannot be called back, and her victims are lost forever.

We can see that, as with the story of Gello and Sisinios, water plays a prominent role in the mythology of Sideros and the Al. The monsters, like Gello, flee to the sea – with the implication that if they can reach it, they will be invulnerable (an implication stated outright in the legends of the Al). The Al would even become a mermaid-like figure in Southern Russia, sitting bare-breasted with long, loose hair by rivers or lakes. In some Armenian stories, the Al is even related to the covi-mar, an ocean-dwelling sea snake that takes the form of a woman with long hair.

These watery, metallic elements were not a part of the ancient Mesopotamian tradition – Lamashtu was not associated with water, but was a monster of the steppe and wilderness, and Lilitu, likewise, was a land-dweller. Even by the time of the bowls, these stories about running to the water, or emerging from the water, or even being hunted by a man with an SN name, are still entirely lacking in Lilith's legends, and are only linked with the demon Sideros.

This tension between these mythologies – the 'original' Eastern tradition of Lamashtu and Lilitu, and the other, Western variant of it – would not remain in place for long. They collapsed back

---

* St John of Damascus, the medieval Byzantine scholar-monk, claimed that the Gello could also steal a woman's liver, so perhaps the Al's propensity for organ-stealing was another facet of the story that had slipped over from Western traditions.

into each other over the next few centuries, so that, as we'll see in the next chapter, Lilith would eventually be chased to the sea by three angels called Senoy, Sansenoy and Semangelof. This later Lilith was also associated with the water more generally – she would live in the ocean, emerge from it, and hide there from her foes. Likewise, the metal demons slowly blended back into Lilith too, so that the Al eventually took on one of the later Lilith's most famous legends, and became, in Central Asian tradition, the first wife of Adam, banished from the garden of Eden for refusing to submit to her husband.

This mess of different beliefs – of different versions of our child-snatching demons – is an insight into the continued relationship between East and West. Where we are happy to imagine the transmission of beliefs and knowledge from Mesopotamia to Greece (of, say, mathematics, or astronomy, or medicine), it's often portrayed as the Mesopotamians handing over what they had learned to the ancient Greeks and then tactfully fading away. But the relationship was dynamic and continuous – a mingling of cultures and peoples, a swapping of ideas back and forth so that a tradition of demons which started out in the East could be picked up and modified in the West, until the variant Western tradition fed back and influenced the Eastern one.

But while the bowls are fascinating for what they can tell us about this tension between the Greek and Middle Eastern versions of our demons, they are also important as a tool for understanding the type of people who were practicing these traditions, and passing them on.

There are plenty of women named on the bowls – in fact, the female/male split is about 50/50 (with a slight advantage to the men). On bowls that reference Lilith, women are more prominent, and bowls that specifically address Lilith's child-killing proclivities were almost all made for women (except for the few men who listed their children, along with their wife, house and property, as something they wanted protected).

However, the majority of the individuals named in the bowls do not seem to have written the incantations themselves. This is usually obvious from the incantations, which address the person named in the bowl in the third person, but use the first person as well – so, for example, in a bowl that was written for a woman called Newanduch, daughter of Kaphani, the incantation reads:

I have written for you [Lilith] and I have separated you from Newanduch daughter of Kahpani.[11]

Here, the 'I', the writer of the incantation, is clearly not Newanduch herself: a different, unnamed author made her bowl for her. For decades after the discovery and translation of the incantation bowls, it was assumed that this mysterious 'I' was a man. This wasn't just because writing was normally assumed to be a male skill, but also because modern scholars tended to connect the bowls with the nascent rabbinic Judaism of Sasanian Mesopotamia.

Although Judaism had been around in one form or another for centuries, rabbinic Judaism – the form of Judaism on which almost all modern forms of the religion are based – was only just coming into force in the sixth century AD. It involved the writing down of the 'Oral Torah', a set of interpretations and explanations of the Torah, which rabbinic Jews believed was handed to Moses by God at the same time as the Torah. The Oral Torah itself was then interpreted and developed, leading to even more written rabbinic scholarship, a genre normally called 'rabbinic literature'. Much of this was centred in Mesopotamia, which had been a hub of Judaism since the Babylonian exile of the sixth century BC, and was only growing in importance as the Byzantine empire's mistreatment of its Jewish population led to a large number of immigrants joining their co-religionists in Mesopotamia.

There are some obvious connections between rabbinic Judaism and the bowls: after all, there are direct references to rabbis and rabbinic traditions, especially the 'get' divorce formulae and Rabbi Joshua Ben Perahia, in the incantations. Surely – it was presumed – this was male, rabbinic learning, perhaps tied to the Mesopotamian rabbinic academies (called yeshivot), which rose to prominence in the Sasanian period. This was a sphere from which women were entirely cut off: if the bowls were part of this tradition, they could not have been written by women.

And it wasn't just the references to rabbis and Jewish divorces that led scholars to connect the bowls to rabbinic Judaism – it was Lilith.

Lilith crops up in rabbinic literature from the Sassanian period, looking very similar to the monster that appears on the bowls. The Babylonian Talmud (complied over the third to sixth centuries AD in Mesopotamia), for example, contains the instruction to men that:

> It is forbidden to sleep in a house alone, and whoever sleeps in a house alone, a Lilith seizes him.[12]

This is a fairly stern and terrifying pronouncement (although it's noticeable that the seductive danger Lilith posed to women has been quietly dropped). However, the other statements about Lilith in this early phase of rabbinic literature seem almost uninterested in the monster. Like so many of the ancient Greek sources, Lilith is occasionally mentioned as a metaphor, or a point of comparison. In one case, she's referenced in one of the curses of Eve who is said to grow 'long hair like a Lilith'.[13] In another, she's brought up in relation to a miscarried child – appropriate for Lilith, but she's only used as a comparison to the fetus, rather than being blamed for the stillbirth – the text reads: 'An abortion with the likeness of a Lilith, its mother is impure because of the birth, for it is a child, but it has wings'.[14]

Lilith also appears in Isaiah, where she is one of a number of wild beasts who haunt the divinely destroyed Edom – the translation of the Hebrew reads:

The wild beasts of the desert shall also meet with
the wild beasts of the island,
and the satyr shall cry to his fellow;
Lilith also shall rest there,
and find for herself a place of rest.*

Across all these sources, we can see that the rabbinic Lilith is, functionally, the same seductive, long-haired Lilith we see in the incantation bowls, and she was clearly well known by those reading and writing these sources – you wouldn't use something as a vehicle in a metaphor if people weren't familiar with it. But at the same time, these texts don't seem particularly excited about Lilith. She doesn't even appear in the Mishnah, one of the first major works of rabbinic literature that was ever produced. This lack of interest wouldn't remain for long – in later periods rabbinic sources would be extremely concerned about her – but it's striking how little significance she seems to have in this early period.

The indifference of these first rabbinic sources is especially clear when compared to the bowls, where Liliths appear constantly

* For more on this passage, and how it has been translated and mistranslated through the centuries, see the appendix.

► Lamashtu amulet, from around 800–500 BC, showing the demon with a lion head, clutching snakes and suckled by animals.

▼ Bronze Lamashtu amulet, from around 800–500 BC. The bottom register shows Lamashtu driven onto a boat by Pazuzu, while the entire amulet is held by Pazuzu himself.

▼ ► Bronze Pazuzu head amulet from around 800–600 BC.

▲ The courtesan Lamia is normally described as a 'hetaira', a high-level prostitute of the kind depicted in this ancient Greek kylix from around 500 BC, playing a drinking game.

◄ Fifth-century Greek vase showing Lamia tortured by satyrs. Although it has been damaged, the remains of her phallus are still visible (along with the satyr holding a flame beneath it).

▲ Byzantine amulet from the second to fourth centuries AD showing Abyzou/Anabardalea impaled by Sisinis while the Angel Araph looks on.

◄ The Phrasikleia Kore, a funerary monument dating from around 540 BC, to a girl who died before she married. The inscription on the statue base reads: 'Tomb of Phrasikleia. "Maiden" I must be called evermore; instead of marriage by the Gods this name became my fate.'

◄ Late antique wall painting from a monastery in Bawit, Egypt, showing the mounted St Sisinnios impaling a demon–woman identified as 'Alabasdria'. The fish-tailed, winged lady in the upper right-hand corner is labelled 'the daughter of Alabasdria'.

▲ Aramaic incantation bowl, from aroundxxq the sixth to eighth centuries AD made by Gushnazdukt, daughter of Ahat.

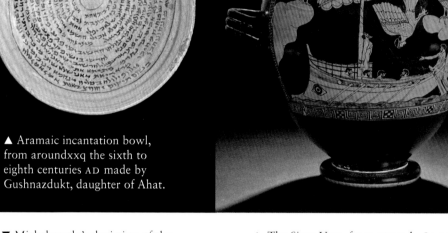

▲ The Siren Vase, from around 480 BC, showing Odysseus tied to a mast so he can hear the bird-bodied sirens that surround his ship.

▼ Michelangelo's depiction of the Fall in the Sistine Chapel, with Lilith as the blonde serpent, handing the fruit to Eve.

▲ Statuette base from the Netherlands, dating to around 1470, showing Lilith with a human head and a serpent body watching as Eve eats the fruit.

◀ A carved fifteenth-century chair from the St Senara's Church in Zennor, Cornwall, showing a mermaid holding a comb and a mirror.

Melusine's serpentine secret is discovered as her husband spies on her in the bath, depicted in a 1491 wood cut (above). Below, from a 1491 manuscript of Jean d'Arras's *Roman de Mélusine*, Melusine leaves her husband after he breaks his vow and returns to nurse her children (below).

Serge Ecker's 2013 statue of Melusine, erected in Luxembourg for the city's 1050th anniversary.

John William Waterhouse's 1896 painting *Hylas and the Nymphs*.

Dante Gabriel Rossetti's 1872 painting *Lady Lilith*.

as a primary demonic force, not just in vague references. The bowls and the rabbinic literature are undoubtedly coming from similar cultural contexts, but the former doesn't read entirely as a product of the latter.

There are other reasons, too, that the idea the bowls were written by male magic practitioners associated with rabbinic academies falls apart on closer examination. One of the main issues is that the bowls are very far from scholarly texts – the writing of most (though not all) of the incantations is rife with errors and inconsistences, rendering some bowl texts almost undecipherable, and driving their modern translators to make snide comments about 'ignorant scribes'. Even those parts that seem utterly rabbinic, like the divorce formula, are a little less official when you look closely. The 'get' divorce document, in rabbinic law, can only be given by a man to his wife. It cannot be given to multiple wives, or by a woman, or by multiple people – and yet in the bowls women give divorces to their Liliths, multiple Liliths are divorced at the same time with a single 'get', and entire families join together to give a 'get' to the demons. The bowl divorces might sound superficially similar to rabbinic 'gets', but they don't fit proper rabbinic specifications.

Even more to the point, the bowls were not a Jewish ritual practice – they were a Mesopotamian ritual practice that all the religious groups living in Mesopotamia seem to have participated in. Whether you worshipped the ancient Mesopotamian gods, or followed the teachings of Mani, or identified as a Mandaean, or were Jewish, you could use bowl magic to drive away demons. Often, the bowls were written in the language or dialect that corresponded to these religions – so we don't just have bowls written in Judeo-Aramaic (a dialect associated with

Judaism), but ones in Madaic (associated with the Mandaeans), Syriac (associated with the Manichaeans and Syriac Christians) and Pahlavi (associated with the Zoroastrians).

This cross-religious use of the bowls is illustrated beautifully by five bowls that were excavated fairly recently, and thus with decently recorded archaeological context. All five were buried in the same courtyard: three were written in Judeo-Aramaic, of which two were for members of the same family, and two were written in Mandaic for two brothers, suggesting that a Jewish family and a Mandaic family were living next to each other and practicing the same forms of magic (albeit in different languages). It's likely that the bowls they used were even taken from the same local potter, who would otherwise have been providing both families with their dinnerware.

The final nail in the coffin for the idea that bowls reference rabbinic literature, and so must have been written by educated, Jewish men, is one bowl incantation written in Manichaean Syriac (and so related to the Manichaean religion) which includes the Jewish 'get' divorce formula, right down to the reference to Rabbi Joshua ben Perahia. If this formula could be used in a bowl written using the dialect of Manichaeans (and therefore likely by someone who identified as Manichaean) its appearance is not something we have to ascribe to a rabbi, or someone from a rabbinic milieu. After all, if the author had picked up the divorce formula from a rabbinic academy, he would have picked up Judeo-Aramaic as well. The bowls might occasionally use elements of Jewish tradition to drive away demons, but that does not mean they were always written by scholarly men connected to rabbinic academies.

There is, however, another way of understanding the authors of the bowl incantations – we can look at the handful that were written for, and made by, the same person.

It stands to reason that someone who normally made bowls for other people might occasionally have reason to make one for themselves, and we do have a very small number of bowls that seem to have been written by the person named in the incantation. The incantation of Komish daughter of Mahlapta, for example, given at the start of this chapter, was certainly written by Komish herself – she is the 'I', as she clearly spells out at the beginning of the incantation, which reads:

I, Komish daughter of Mahlapta, have divorced and dismissed and banished you.[15]

The gender distribution of these first-person bowl authors overturns the idea that the bowls were written by men – in most cases the authors were women. Of the ten authors who have been identified as writing in the first person, five are women, three are a woman and man working together and one is a pair of men. In only one instance is a bowl written by a single man working by himself.* We can also identify a small number of bowls these authors wrote for other people based on their handwriting. Taken together, the number of bowls where we can identify the authors

---

* In a crowded field, this man's bowl is an absolute embarrassment – he seems to have copied the formulas he used (and very badly at that) and he had absolutely terrible handwriting. In fact, we can see that he dipped his brush into ink at the beginning of every new word, normally a sign of someone unused to writing. Not to hammer the point home further, but his paint was also far too diluted, and instead of drawing an image in the centre of the bowl he simply wrote an X. If you should ever find yourself in need of a magic bowl in Sasanian-period Mesopotamia, you'd be advised to steer clear of a man called Huniyaq, son of Ahat.

is still tiny – twenty-seven out of thousands. But of these twenty-seven, the vast majority (74 per cent) were written by women working alone. While it is always possible that this sample was skewed in some way (perhaps women were just more likely to write bowls for themselves), the available evidence suggests that some – even the majority – of bowl authors were women.[16]

We can even identify some bits and pieces about the lives and work of those five female authors who wrote the bowls themselves. Komish, daughter of Mahlapta, for example, seems to have been extremely well educated for a bowl writer (an admittedly low bar) – she has beautiful handwriting, and her divorce formula is incredibly detailed; one of the most detailed attested on an incantation bowl.

Another woman, named Giyonay daughter of Lalay, was married to a man named Hormiz, and wrote a bowl to protect them both against Lilith, using a rather pared-down version of the divorce formula. She also wrote six other bowls, all similar divorce texts, and all for her family members. In one case, she calls herself the 'maidservant of heaven',[17] a title for which we have no parallel in either the bowls or rabbinic literature.

A third woman – Gushnazdukh, daughter of Ahat – was apparently from the Mesopotamian city of Borsippa (just southwest of Babylon, on the banks of the Euphrates). She wrote a bowl to drive away witches, using elements of ancient Mesopotamian anti-witchcraft incantations: some parts of her incantation have exact parallels with cuneiform texts from hundreds of years before. It's not clear where she learned all this from, but her bowl suggests she had a strong affinity for ancient Mesopotamian beliefs.

The fourth woman was called Dukhtic, daughter of Baharoy, and her incantation bowl contains a joyous affirmation of power, reading:

I, Dukhtic, daughter of Baharoy, stand at my doorway ... I am the earth – no one can shake me; I am the high heavens – no one can reach me; I am a bright lamp – no one can fix his eyes upon me nor stand before my brilliance.[18]

Dukhtic also wrote nine other bowls for third parties, all of which contained references to the story of Semamit and Sideros – a nice example of the idea that this charm story was largely told by women.

The final woman we know of who wrote incantation bowls was called Gushnazdukh, daughter of Mushkoy. She wrote her bowl to drive malignant demons away from herself, including – almost uniquely for an incantation bowl – Satan and the Angel of Death. She even claimed that the latter figure could be dispelled by the mere mention of her name, writing:

There are names from which the Angel of Death flees, and is paralysed, and hides from them: I, Gushnazdukh, daughter of Mushkoy, and every name I have.[19]

Her bowl feels consciously rabbinic – every evil entity it protects against appears in the Babylonian Talmud, and as well as her own name she enlists the power of YHWH and His angels to her aid. She seems not just supremely confident, but highly educated as well.

There's so much information we are missing about these women: we cannot see how they learned to write incantations, whether they thought of themselves as magic users first and foremost, or whether they just occasionally made a bowl on the side. We don't know whether they practiced other rituals as well as making the bowls, or whether the bowls were the only magic they used. Did they know other practitioners and share their skills, or was this a solitary affair? What did their families think of their bowl magic? Did they make a living off their work? However, the information we have, slight though it is, has an exhilarating quality to it. It is a vision of a world we normally cannot see – one we are occasionally told did not exist at all: female magic users writing spells to keep themselves, their families, and perhaps even their customers safe. It's exciting just to know their names, to know that one of them really liked ancient Mesopotamian spells (you and me both, Gushnazdukh), to know their family relationships. It's a pleasure, as well, to see their confidence in their abilities – there is no suggestion that any of these women felt uncomfortable making bowls, or exorcising demons. On the contrary, they seem right at home.

These five women could read and write, and so don't represent the majority of women (or men) in Sassanian Mesopotamia. But there are suggestions in our sources that practising magic in order to protect one's family was widespread among women. As the famous line in the Babylonian Talmud states:

Most women are sorcerers.[20]

Yet this statement is full of negative connotations – sorcery was black magic and witchcraft. The bowl writer Gushnazdukh was making spells specifically to protect herself from sorcery. It might seem a little much to equate apotropaic magic, used against demons threatening women and children, with the 'sorcerers' of the Babylonian Talmud.

The problem is that the Talmud was written by rabbis, and their definition of sorcery seems to have included any sort of ritual and magic used by women on their own. Female practices were put into the category of dark magic – condemned as illegitimate, in contrast to the legitimate power of the rabbis. Even when men performed the same act – even when that act was specifically acknowledged as something that would otherwise be sorcery – it was not dark magic when it was a rabbi doing it. At the very worst, it was 'learning' or 'research'.* What this statement in the Talmud tells us is not that most women were evil witches, but that the rabbis felt most women practised some form of ritual or magic outside of rabbinic influence. Incantations against child-stealing, mother-killing Liliths would certainly fit into this category.

More to the point, the child-snatching, woman-seducing Lilith survived for the next few thousand years, turning up in Jewish and Islamic folklore as well as legends from across Central Asia, Turkey and Russia and surviving to the twentieth century and beyond. Since this happened despite the male-dominated religious establishment of these regions having little to no interest in the child-killing aspect of the monster, it seems likely it was women handing down these practices, working to protect themselves and their children. And this wouldn't just have included the women who wrote the bowls, but those whose names we cannot know, who couldn't write, but who could still whisper an incantation over their sickly child, or clutch an amulet during childbirth.

Men, meanwhile, either ignored these women entirely, claimed they were evil sorcerers, or ridiculed them, but as they did so they took the monsters for themselves, turning them from child-killers

---

* So when, say, Rabbi Eliezer went around filling fields with cucumbers and then harvesting them by uttering magic words, this was all perfectly fine and not sorcery at all, since he did it to gain wisdom (with the cucumbers viewed, presumably, as a by-product). In one rabbinic text, it is claimed that men who did sorcery should be members of the Sanhedrin (the Jewish high court) because they would, after all, be best at judging those cases involving sorcery.

into succubi, demons who tempted men away from their wives, slipped into the marriage bed and produced thousands of illegitimate offspring. This is the role that Lilith would fulfil in the next few centuries of Jewish lore, as she changed from a species of child-snatching monsters to become the first wife of Adam, the lover of the demon Samael, the mother of all monsters and the snake in the Garden of Eden.

5

The Other Woman

ook up at the Sistine chapel ceiling, and slightly to the right
of the Creation of Adam, where God stretches out his hand
to imbue man with the spark of life, you'll see a panel called
the Temptation, showing Adam and Eve eating the forbidden
fruit of the Tree of Knowledge. Adam is reaching up into the
tree to take the fruit himself, pulling back a branch with one
huge hand; aggressive, almost greedy. Eve, in contrast, looks
utterly at ease, lounging against a rocky outcrop. Her naked,
muscular body is facing away from the tree and she is barely
even glancing at it as she reaches up to take the fateful fruit.
It's a surprisingly casual attitude for a woman in the act of dis-
obeying God's explicit commandment, made more surprising
still given that she is not picking the fruit herself, but taking it
from the outstretched hand of a monster. This creature, with its

tail wrapped in thick, fleshy coils around the trunk of the tree, is the serpent of Eden, but in Michelangelo's painting, it has the face and bare breasts of a woman.

This is Lilith, no longer a species of demon as she is on the incantation bowls, but a single figure with a vital role to play in the creation myth. With her blonde-red hair she looks almost a twin to Michelangelo's tow-headed Adam (Eve, in contrast, is a brunette), and this isn't a coincidence: Lilith is not just the snake of Eden, but the first wife of Adam. They are made out of the same clay – hence their similar appearances – but Lilith was cast out of paradise after demanding equality with her husband. Her tempting of Eve isn't just a devil-driven strategy to bring about the Fall: it's the act of a scorned first wife, filled with jealousy at the divine couple and getting her revenge.

Michelangelo did not draw the legend of his Lilith from Christian teachings – instead, he was influenced by the Kabbalah, a form of Jewish mysticism that became increasingly popular in Europe during the Middle Ages and the Renaissance, even among Christians. Although Michelangelo was probably not a Kabbalist himself, he would have had plenty of chances of encountering Kabbalistic beliefs: one of his advisors, Egidio da Viterbo, was a student of the Kabbalah, and when Michelangelo lived at the Medici palace, he may well have come across Pico della Mirandola, one of the most important Christian Kabbalists of the time.* This Kabbalistic Lilith was not just the snake in the

---

* Just in case all of this Christian acceptance of (or at least, interest in) Jewish lore might be giving you the impression that Jewish people themselves were accepted too, the Sistine Chapel does not let you forget about their persecution: Michelangelo painted one of the Jewish ancestors of Christ, Aminadab, wearing the circular yellow Jewish *signum* that all Jews were forced to wear in Rome at the time.

garden and the first wife of Adam: she was a succubus, dangerous to all men.

Having condemned as sorcerers women who tried to protect themselves and their children against our demons, having ridiculed those who believed in them as foolish old women, a new pattern is starting here, one that we'll see repeated again and again through the Middle Ages to the modern day: men had worked out a way to turn the legends of Lilith to their own needs, to use them to reflect their own fears – principally, their fears of women.

The Lilith of Michelangelo and the Kabbalists is Lilith as the 'other woman', an interloper in Adam and Eve's marriage (albeit she was technically there first), who would go on to destroy mortal men's marriages as well. She was a destructive force, seducing innocent men, conceiving illegitimate children with them, and even demanding a demonic inheritance when her mortal lovers died. She, like the seductive Lamia before her, stood against everything a woman was supposed to be in both Jewish and Christian teachings.

Lilith had been flipped: no longer was she a way of confronting, exploring and comforting women's very real fears about the dangers of pregnancy and infant mortality; instead, she was a conduit for male fears of sexuality and sexual impurity, of women who might lead them astray, might give them illegitimate children, might tempt them away from their wife, and away from God.

The earliest, and perhaps best known, story of Lilith in Eden appears in a text known as the Alphabet of Ben Sira. Ben Sira was a respected Jewish author who lived in Jerusalem in around 200 BC, and wrote the *Sirach*, an important book of Jewish ethical teachings. The Alphabet of Ben Sira, on the other hand, dates from around AD 700–1000 (that is, the period just following the incantation bowls) and is anything but a serious text. The first, and oldest, half of the Alphabet is fairly unremarkable, and consists of some dull Aramaic proverbs,* but the second half tells the story of Ben Sira being called to the court of Nebuchadnezzar II and solving problems for the king of Babylon. These problems, their solutions, and the stories that Ben Sira tells to the king about them are odd to say the least, to the extent that the manuscript is normally described as satirical, with some people even claiming that it was an anti-Semitic text, given the way that it turns Biblical stories (and Jewish heroes) on their heads.

Ben Sira, for example (who is himself a mystically wise toddler) gets Nebuchadnezzar's overly flatulent daughter to stop farting, answers the mystery of why donkeys urinate in the urine of other donkeys, and claims to be the son and grandson of the prophet Jeremiah, conceived when his mother – who was also Jeremiah's daughter – bathed in the same fountain where Jeremiah had recently, and publicly, masturbated. To say this all sits oddly alongside so many serious religious figures is an understatement. Nebuchadnezzar's presence may well be part of the joke too – the real Nebuchadnezzar (who lived around 400 years before the real Ben Sira) was the king who conquered Judea, destroyed Jerusalem and instigated the Babylonian captivity – hardly the resume of a man a Jewish scholar should be helping out.

Among the many issues that Nebuchadnezzar asks Ben Sira to solve is the deadly illness of his young son. Ben Sira (having been threatened with death if he fails to save the boy) sits at the

---

* They are all sub-Instagram quality: 'In thy business, deal only with the upright'; 'Do not disavow an old friend'; 'Restrain not thy hand from doing good'.

child's bedside and inscribes an amulet with the names of three angels. Nebuchadnezzar asks who these angels are, and Ben Sira explains with a story. This story is so important to the lore of Lilith, it's worth reproducing it in full.

The angels who are in charge of medicine are Snvi, Snsvi, and Smnglof. When God created His world and created Adam, he saw that Adam was alone, and He immediately created a woman from earth, like him, for him. He brought her to Adam, and they immediately began to fight: Adam said, 'You shall lie below' and Lilith said 'You shall lie below, for we are equal and both of us were created from earth.' They did not listen to each other. When Lilith saw the state of things, she uttered the ineffable name and flew into the air and fled.

Adam immediately stood in prayer before God and said: 'Master of the universe, see the woman you gave me has already fled away.' God immediately sent three angels and told them: 'Go and fetch Lilith; if she agrees to come, bring her, and if she does not, bring her by force.'

The three angels went immediately and caught up with her in the sea, in the place that the Egyptians were destined to die [that is, the Red Sea]. They seized her and told her: 'If you agree to come with us, come, and if not we shall drown you in the sea'. She answered, 'Darlings, I know myself that God created me only to afflict babies with fatal disease when they are eight days old; I shall have permission to harm them from their birth to the eighth day and no longer, when it is a male baby; but when it is a female baby, I shall have permission for twelve days.'

The angels would not leave her alone until she swore by God's name that wherever she would see them or their names in an amulet, she would not possess the baby. They then left immediately.[1]

This is a charm story like those of Melitene and Gello – Lilith flees to the sea, is chased there by protectors with S and N names, and promises that she will not attack children wherever their names are written. Like all the charms, telling the story protects against the demon, since it contains both a repetition of the saints' names and the monster's promise that where they are spoken she will be powerless. It even contains within it the important information about the exact number of days that male and female children are at risk. This is a story that is focused, first and foremost, on the protection of children. It is far less concerned about how awkwardly this fits into the Eden narrative: like Gello, Lilith claims that she was created to 'inflict babies with fatal disease', a jarring statement given that we've just seen God create her as a wife for Adam, and clearly a hangover from these earlier myths. She also flies – hardly a skill a newly-made human would have possessed, and a throwback from her traditional, demonic winged form.

But while Lilith is as child-killing and sexually self-possessed here as she has been in earlier sources, and the story itself is based on one told about plenty of other monsters, the tale that appears in the Alphabet of Ben Sira still represents an astonishing promotion for her. She has been upgraded from a species of murderous demons to a single figure with a starring role in the Garden of Eden, her own motivations and knowledge of the Ineffable Name: a monster who is uncontrollable by both her husband and, to a certain extent, by God Himself. The difficulty, of course, is that while this was to become a very commonly repeated myth in the Middle Ages, this first attestation of it comes from a source so full of masturbation and dirty humour that it's hard to know what parts of it to take seriously. It's like trying to determine the plot of a film based only on its pornographic parody.

Since the Alphabet had a tendency to dirty up stories, it's quite possible that the conflict over sexual positions was part of its satire. It's also notable that Adam (and to some extent, even God) do not come across well. Adam has no control over Lilith, and his statement 'Master of the universe, see the woman you gave me has already fled away' is amusingly pathetic. God seems incredibly ineffectual as well: He cannot bring Lilith back, and even His angels are left to make terms instead of dragging her home, or drowning her as they intend. As we'll see, in later, more 'official' versions of the story, Lilith is rejected by Adam and cast into the sea by God, a much more deferential (and uninteresting) story.

However, the idea of a first wife for Adam, who pre-existed Eve, is not something invented by the Alphabet – there is even a place in Genesis for her to slot in. In the book of Genesis, there are two accounts of the creation of woman. In the first, God creates man and woman together:

And God created man to his own image: to the image of God he created him: male and female he created them. (Genesis 1:27).

However, later on, God creates Eve from Adam's rib:

But for Adam no suitable helper was found. So the Lord God caused the man to fall into a deep sleep; and while he was sleeping, he took one of the man's ribs and then closed up the place with flesh. Then the Lord God made a woman from the rib he had taken out of the man, and he brought her to the man. (Genesis ii: 20–22).

This discrepancy is almost certainly because the book of Genesis (and, in fact, all of the first five books of the Old Testament, which together make up the Torah) was written by four different authors, each telling roughly the same story. These accounts were awkwardly mashed together by later editors, leaving a whole host of odd little contradictions like this one. There isn't a missing bride in these accounts of the creation of woman, just the same story told twice in slightly different ways.

Of course, in late antiquity and the Middle Ages these sorts of explanations were off the table, and resolutions had to be found that didn't accuse the text itself of being inconsistent or imperfect. One of the explanations for these two creations of women was that there was a first wife, a predecessor to Eve, who had been removed from the scene by the time the second wife was made from Adam's rib. Lilith was tailor-made to fill this gap: in rabbinic literature that predated the Alphabet of Ben Sira, there was already a suggestion that she had slept with Adam (or, at the very least, stolen his semen).

Adam and Eve were thought to have separated for 130 years at some point after the Fall,* and during this separation, demons were said to have slept with them both, breeding a whole range

---

* It's understandable that the couple would have needed a bit of time apart – the business with the apple would have put a strain on any marriage – but this separation was originally proposed because Adam and Eve had a son (Seth) 130 years after their first sons, Cain and Abel. It was suggested that this gap in children could be explained by Adam not having sex with Eve for this period of time.

of monsters. This is discussed in the Babylonian Talmud (so, in a text written at the same time as the incantation bowls, and some time before the Alphabet), and although the female demons Adam was sleeping with are never named, on the list of demons the Talmud claims Adam fathered are the 'Lilin' – the male variants of Lilith.

In an attempt to protect Adam's reputation, it was also made clear that this demonic family was not brought into being because Adam was merrily having sex with demons left and right – instead, the demon children were created through 'semen which he emitted accidentally' and was stolen by demonesses, suggesting nocturnal emissions and again linking this unnamed female demoness to Lilith. It's likely, then, that it was this tradition that gave Lilith entry into the Garden of Eden – a lover of Adam, slipping in to become the mysterious predecessor to Eve. After all, a monster who was partnered with Adam after Eve might well have partnered with him before Eve as well.

This, too, explains another point of interest in the Alphabet: Lilith's children. In later versions of the Alphabet story, her punishment for resisting God's demand that she return to Adam is that a hundred of her children would die every day, an odd penalty given that Lilith had always been the antitheses of a mother, and had never previously shown much ability to produce her own offspring. But as the post-Fall seductress of Adam she is suddenly very prolific, giving birth to whole races of demons with her mortal lover. This demonic fertility would become an important aspect of Lilith's mythology in the Middle Ages, not to mention a vital part of her status as the archetypal 'other woman'.

Lilith's role in the Garden of Eden, and her partnership with Adam, was unlikely to have been entirely limited to the textual tradition, or even conceived for the Alphabet – the satirical notes of the story (the sexual elements, and God and Adam's slightly pathetic qualities) are unconnected to the idea of Lilith as the first wife of Adam, and our demons being Adam's first wife extended beyond Lilith as well.

To some extent, trying to pick apart what 'true' story the Alphabet was riffing off, and what elements were added by the Alphabet, is pointless – in the late Middle Ages, the story would be adopted wholesale by Jewish mystics. It may have started as a joke (or at least, a part joke), but it would eventually take on a life of its own. This would come when it blended with Kabbalism – which had already created a whole host of new Lilith traditions.

From the twelfth century on, Kabbalism – the study and practice of esoteric Jewish mysticism – grew enormously in popularity: there are plenty of Kabbalistic traditions (including Lilith-based ones) that spread widely in the later Middle Ages, both into mainstream Judaism and beyond. Although the first Kabbalistic text dates to around the third century BC, the majority are from the Middle Ages. The first one that relates to Lilith is called The Treatise on the Left Emanation, and was written in the thirteenth century by a Rabbi Isaac ben Jacob ha-Kohen in Spain – at that time a centre for Kabbalistic thought. In this text, Lilith is the wife of Samael, who was himself not only the king of the demons, but associated with both Satan and the Angel of Death. Samael even had his own connection to the Garden of Eden: it was sometimes suggested he conspired with the snake to bring about the Fall – a perfect partner for Lilith.

Rabbi Isaac had not invented this pairing himself: Samael and Lilith had been linked before, in a later manuscript of the Alphabet of Ben Sira, dating to the eleventh century. Here, instead of simply not returning to the Garden with God's angels, Lilith offers an explanation for why she cannot return. Her reasoning is:

> "I cannot return because of what is said in the Torah— 'Her former husband who sent her away, may not take her again to be his wife, after that she is defiled,' that is, when he was not the last to sleep with her. And the Great Demon has already slept with me."[2]

Here Lilith provides a scripture-based reason for not returning to Adam (it's best to ignore the fact that the Torah would not have been written by the time she fled the Garden – even Genesis would have been full of spoilers). In fact, it's a suspiciously proper reason for a woman who had recently defied God, had sex with the king of demons, and planned on spending her days murdering small children. It has been suggested that this reasoning was added to the text to try to make the story a bit more respectful to God: it wasn't that He and His angels couldn't bring her back, it was that His own commandments forbade her return. It might seem ridiculous to try and make the Alphabet story – taken from a manuscript full of public masturbation and farting – into something that was sensible and reverential, although as we'll see, this wouldn't be the only time that the Lilith story of the Alphabet of Ben Sira was taken entirely at face value.

What does seem unlikely is that this perfectly halakhic excuse would have occurred to the author of this later Alphabet variant had there not already been a tradition of Lilith and Samael sleeping together. The author of the later Ben Sira was therefore likely picking up on pre-existing legends, rather than inventing Lilith's relationship with Samael. When the Treatise on the

Left Emanation was written a couple of centuries later it was presumably still a common legend.

In the Treatise, though, the relationship with Samael doesn't just happen after the Fall as it does in the later Alphabet. Instead, it entirely replaces Lilith's relationship with Adam, both during his 130-year separation from Eve, and as his first wife. According to the text, Lilith and Samael were created together, as were Adam and Eve,* with the former representing the monstrous opposites of the latter: Lilith and Samael are evil, Adam and Eve are good; Lilith and Samael are parents to a race of demons while Adam and Eve are the father and mother of all humanity.

The Treatise also picks up on a more ancient tradition – that of Liliths as a species. There are at least two different Liliths in the text: one is the 'Grande Dame' Lilith, partnered with Samael. The other is a younger (or lesser) Lilith, who is partnered with Samael's second in command, Asmodeus. This younger Lilith was said to be more beautiful, and to have inspired the jealousy of Samael: prevented from being the 'other woman' to Adam and Eve, Lilith was here the 'other woman' to herself.

Lilith's importance to Kabbalah was compounded by her appearance in the *Zohar*. This text is one of the most important in Kabbalistic tradition, and appeared in the thirteenth century in Spain, where it was 'discovered' and published by Moses de Leon, who claimed it was written in AD 70. Given that the *Zohar* references plenty of events that occurred well after AD 70, this

---

* You might suppose that this is a text that ignores the difficulty of the two different accounts of the creation of woman in Genesis, but actually this is just another trick to try and reconcile them – Adam and Eve were created together in the Treatise, as one initial form, and Eve was only later separated from Adam as his rib.

very early composition date was questioned immediately on its publication, and it's now generally accepted that the entire thing was written by Moses de Leon himself. One man even claimed to have heard Moses' wife admit to this after Moses' death, and the original manuscript Moses said he discovered has certainly never materialized.* Given this, there were plenty of Kabbalists who never accepted the *Zohar*'s authenticity, but the *Zohar*, and some of the ideas it expressed, nonetheless became well known and popular in mainstream Judaism (and beyond).

In the *Zohar*, it's no longer Lilith and Samael who stand in contrast to Eve and Adam, but Lilith alone who opposes the divine pair. Here she is once again the first wife of Adam, but she doesn't seem like an intentional creation of God and she certainly wasn't made from clay. Instead she 'emerges' from a dark shell that God builds around the radiance of the primordial light. According to the *Zohar* she initially stayed with the cherubim, until God created Adam and brought Lilith down to be with him. When Lilith 'was no help to Adam', God created Eve, and Lilith – seeing the perfect beauty of the divine couple together – flew away in jealousy. God cast her into the bottom of the sea, allowing her to return to the world only after the Fall, to murder Adam and Eve's offspring. Here, incidentally, we can see a much more 'respectful' version of the Ben Sira story – Adam doesn't want Lilith back, Eve replaces her because she has failed at her job of being a helpmeet to Adam, and she doesn't escape to the depths of the sea: instead she is thrown there by God.

---

* The explanation for this by those who believed in the *Zohar*'s authenticity was that Moses de Leon's wife had foolishly sold the manuscript after his death, not knowing what it was. When she realized her error she was so embarrassed that she claimed it had always been a fake. No one seems to have got round to explaining where its mysterious purchaser went, and why they never produced the supposedly original manuscript themselves.

Lilith, as usual, has children by Adam, although exactly when they are conceived is a little complicated and the *Zohar* doesn't specify – maybe it was before Eve turned up, maybe it was after the Fall during that 130-year separation. There is a female demoness who does sleep with Adam during his separation from Eve in the *Zohar*, and while she is named 'Na'mah', she acts exactly like Lilith, causing wet dreams in order to steal semen to have her own demonic children.*

The irony is that despite all these complex, respectful stories – stories that had been well thought through by high-level scholars adept at Judaic lore – these are not the stories that are remembered. The legend that was told time and time again, that is repeated most (it has fifty manuscript sources) is the story from the Alphabet of Ben Sira. In the later Middle Ages it was slotted into Kabbalistic tradition as a serious legend, shorn of its context, and it has appeared in this form ever since. There are plenty of encyclopedias of Judaism, or essays on Lilith, or collections of myths, that present her story from the Alphabet with no mention of its satirical context.

There are half a dozen reasons why this might be the case – including that, as a charm story, it's likely it was passed down to protect against Lilith – but the most probable explanation is that it's simply a better story, better told, and more firmly attached to the traditions that people actually recognized. It's not just that the stories about Lilith in the Treatise on the Left Emanation or the *Zohar* are a bit dull – it's that they're told in fragments, each one trying to veil its meaning, to cram in

---

* There are already quite enough semen-stealing demon legends to keep track of here, but Na'mah was also said to have been one of the four wives of Samael, alongside Lilith, as well as Lilith's daughter or sister.

as much esoteric scholarship as possible.* The Alphabet story, on the other hand, was told to entertain. It's full of amusing characters – the pathetic Adam, the determined Lilith – and it's a tight, fun little narrative that's easily remembered. No one is trying to show off the depth of their scholarly knowledge, they're just trying to tell a good story – and succeeding. If you encounter a story about Lilith in the modern day, it's likely to be based on this one, although often the specific argument about sexual positions is removed, to be replaced by a more prosaic disagreement about equality, as if those repeating the story knew that something wasn't quite right, and were trying to subtly correct it.

That the story from the Alphabet became the most popular account was to have enormous repercussions for the perception of Lilith, especially in the twentieth century. After all, by the logic of the legend Lilith was right – she and Adam were equals, made of the same clay. There were attempts to undermine this aspect of the story – in one rabbinic version, it's stated that Lilith was made from scum and filth left over from Adam's creation, technically still clay, but definitely not equal – but these never truly took hold.

---

* Take, for example, the beginning of the Lilith myth in the Treatise, which reads: 'In answer to your question concerning Lilith, I shall explain to you that most important part. There is a tradition received from the early sages who made use of the Use of the Lesser Palaces, which is the Use of Demons, which is like a ladder by which one can transcend to various degrees of prophecy and their powers. In these sources it is explained that Samael and Lilith were born as a hermaphrodite, just like Adam and Eve, who were also born in this manner, reflecting what is above. This is the account of Lilith which was received by the sages in the Use of Palaces...' – it may be very learned (though Isaac had a habit of entirely making up what his supposed sources say), but it's hardly catchy (Joseph Dan, *The Early Kabbalah* (Paulist Press 1986), p.165).

However, whichever version of these Lilith legends was being told, all place Lilith as a malignant force in the Garden of Eden who had reasons for wishing harm on Adam, Eve and God, and it's likely because of this – as well as our demons' penchant for snakey-ness – that she's often connected with the Serpent.

The snake of Eden has always presented a bit of a problem: despite being a key player in the Fall, there is never any explanation in the Biblical account as to why a seemingly random creature suddenly decided to persuade Eve to eat the apple. The entire episode feels like an etiological, just-so story for why the serpent crawls on its belly, awkwardly inserting itself into the legend of mankind's expulsion from paradise. Because of this there are numerous versions where the serpent is given more of a personality than it has in the Bible, normally by connecting it to another Biblical figure who had an actual reason for wanting to hurt Adam and Eve.

Often this figure is Satan (or Samael, who is often himself connected with Satan) – the fallen angel returning to Eden, disguising himself as the snake (or, alternatively, persuading the snake to help him). When Lilith was partnered with Samael this drew her into the narrative even more closely, until eventually she became the snake herself: in the *Zohar* she is specifically referred to as the 'Serpent'.

This connection is further helped by the fact that when God is handing out punishments, he tells the serpent:

I will put enmity between you and the woman, and between thy seed and her seed (Genesis iii:15).

This is simply a way of saying that humanity (that is, Eve's seed) and all serpents (that is, the seed of the original, Garden serpent) will not get on. Yet with Lilith as the serpent, this suddenly takes on a new meaning: Lilith's seed refers to her demon offspring who will plague humanity, while Eve's seed refers to the children whom Lilith will kill.

It was this serpentine aspect of Lilith that made its presence most felt in the Christianity of the Middle Ages and the Renaissance. While Jews were being persecuted across Europe, interest in the Kabbalah was spreading. Some Christian commentators decried the Kabbalistic legends (Erasmus wrote crossly about his concern that people were 'backsliding' into 'unadulterated Judaism'), repeating them as they did so, and so spreading them further.* Lilith's story was one of the many that spread in this way, and it's especially well represented in art. It's not just Michelangelo who painted her – she's there in Titian's *The Fall of Man*, an oddly childish head and torso stuck on a snake tail, a pair of tiny horns protruding through her curly hair as she hands Eve the apple. She's on a Flemish statue base from the 1500s, her snake tail curling behind her, watching as a greedy Eve clutches three apples to her chest and crams another into her mouth; she's there in an image from a twelfth-century Bible, a spindly little thing with lank, loose hair, perched in her tree, and in a fresco from the 1420s in a Bologna church, a woman's head somewhat precariously balanced on a snake's body. She even appears on the carvings of Notre Dame, a busty thirteenth-century figure at the

---

* Peter Comestor, for example, a twelfth-century theologian, repeated the legend of the first wife of Adam in his widely read *Historia Scholastica*. Somewhat confusingly, he also claimed that the serpent of Eden had the face of a virgin because Eve would be more easily persuaded by an animal that looked like her. If this was an alternative Christian tradition, though, it was swiftly overridden by the idea that the serpent was Lilith.

entrance to the church, watching from her tree as Eve bites into the fruit.*

Normally Lilith is only pictured at the Fall, but we do have one medieval Christian image of her pre-Fall. In Uccello's fifteenth-century fresco of the Creation in the church of Santa Maria Novella in Florence, Lilith is crammed into the corner of the image with the animals, just underneath a very dubious-looking bull. On the other side of the panel, Adam is being made – Lilith's placement with the animals is a very clear indication that any sort of equality she might claim from the time of her creation is laughable: she is a beast rather than a true counterpart to man. Just in case there could be any mistaking this first woman, Uccello wrote her name across her forehead – but, as a reminder of just how intertwined our demons are, the careful lettering reads 'Lamia'. The two would often be equated in Europe, their connection immortalized in the Vulgate translation of Isaiah 34:13 (that passage about the ruins of Edom), which translates Lilith as 'Lamia'.†

Lilith does not just attack the divine marriage of Adam and Eve – she's also a threat to mortal marriages. Her hatred of, and attacks on, Adam and Eve are a mirror of this – just as she tries to seduce Adam away from his true wife, so she seduces men. Just as she steals Adam's semen (or has sex with him while he is asleep) to breed children of her own, so she does the same to all men.

---

* These Liliths almost never look particularly convincing – the head always seems too large, and the snake tail rarely looks like it could take the weight. Only Michelangelo comes close to making Lilith a believable animal, by giving her a thick, fleshly tail that genuinely looks like it could support a human torso, although even then you're left to wonder how Lilith got about when she wasn't in a tree.

† For more on this, see both the next chapter and appendix.

Lilith doesn't just attack men in their sleep, either. She can also appear in the day, dressed beautifully and alluringly. In one case, she is dressed 'like a harlot' and covered with 'adornments', appearing to men and seducing them before reporting their behaviour to heaven and then killing them if they try to have sex with her again.

Lilith could also cause problems when a husband and wife had sex. In one seventeenth-century text, she is 'present in the bed linen of man and wife when they copulate, in order to take hold of the sparks of the drops of semen that are lost'.[3] This is something to be concerned with especially if the copulation is taking place while the man is having sinful thoughts, as these sinful thoughts could lead to danger for the man's children. If a child is conceived when a man is 'not in a state of holiness' Lilith would be able to kill the child at any time, with even God's angels powerless to help it. The *Zohar* even includes a ritual to be performed before sex to make sure that Lilith can't get involved.

If Lilith did manage to steal a man's semen, the demonic offspring she bore could cause him enormous embarrassment further down the line, by turning up at his funeral. A sixteenth-century Kabbalist, for example, described how the illegitimate demon children would come to their human father's burial:

For all those spirits that have built their bodies from a drop of his seed regard him as their father. And so, especially on the day of his burial, he must suffer punishment; for while he is being carried to the grave, they swarm around him like bees, crying: 'You are our father,' and they complain and lament behind the bier.[4]

The best way to prevent this was for a man to forbid all his children from attending his funeral, so keeping the demonic offspring away too. There were dances that were performed at funerals to banish demon-children, and incantations were recited to ward them off, along with the passage from Genesis:

> But unto the sons of the concubines, which Abraham had, Abraham gave gifts and sent them away (Genesis xxv:6).

After death, these demonic children could continue to cause issues by claiming inheritances. An eighteenth-century text describes how a man had offspring with a demon, and allowed them to live in his cellar. When his house was sold after his death, the new owners were tormented by the demons until a rabbinic court intervened and ruled that the demonic offspring could be expelled. And Lilith's brood were feared not just because they could cause issues with lineage and property: men were anxious to dispel them because when they gathered about him at his death, God would be reminded of all the sins he had committed – all the times he had masturbated, or had sex with his wife while in an impure state. Even the prophet Elijah suffered this embarrassment – in one medieval legend, Lilith approached him and told him he could not go to heaven, since they had children together. Elijah protested that he had always been chaste, but the demon revealed that she had caused wet dreams and stolen his seed, which she used to create their shared offspring.

Misogyny, like a lot of prejudice, has a tendency to be deeply unoriginal, and in Lilith we can see a repetition of what first reared its head with the ancient Lamia – Lilith is the opposite of a good woman, a creature used to demonize those straying from the path of acceptable femininity. Eve is set up as her antithesis –

the perfect, good woman against the evil one. This might be unexpected, since a lot of traditions – especially Christian ones – paint Eve as a sinful, terrible woman who brought about the Fall. And while a lot of Jewish writing can be fairly impolite about Eve, in Kabbalah she is the perfect wife and the mother of all human-kind. Lilith is her monstrous opposite, a warning for women who might want to stray from the Eve-ideal. However, Lilith is not just a model of unacceptable womanhood – she is also a reflection of male anxieties about sex.

Judaism (especially for those of us raised in Christian cultures) can often seem astonishingly sex-positive, even in the Middle Ages. Sex between a husband and wife was always encouraged, with the commandment that mankind should 'go forth and multiply' taken seriously. There was an acknowledgement of female sexual pleasure, and even some discussion of whether or not contraception (which, at the time, took the form of a cervical sponge) was allowed while a mother was breastfeeding. Even though most felt that contraception was taking it all a bit far, the fact that the matter could be discussed at all is still surprising. As one thirteenth-century Kabbalistic work pointed out:

If we say that intercourse is repulsive, then we blaspheme God who made the genitals ... Marital intercourse, under proper circumstances, is an exalted matter.[5]

But within this quote is the important caveat – it is only sex under 'proper circumstances' that is good, and there were plenty of circumstances that were not deemed proper. Even within a marriage, sex was thought improper if a man was thinking of another woman, or drunk, or if the couple hated each other, or if a woman was menstruating. Sex purely for desire, meanwhile, was also generally looked down upon, and there was a line of

Jewish medieval thought that supported circumcision because it reduced lust.

Impurity was especially thought to stem from nocturnal emissions (one story in a popular medieval Jewish text concerned a man who, when he could not have sex with his wife because she was menstruating, slept in an uncomfortable chair or stayed awake reading the Torah so as to avoid wet dreams). Men were expected to ritually bathe before entering the temple if they had ejaculated (although the practice of this was often limited to particularly pious men). Masturbation was strictly forbidden and was known as onanism, taking its name from the biblical figure Onan who, due to complex inheritance issues surrounding his marriage to his brother's widow, did not wish to have children with her. Whenever they had sex, he pulled out, spilling his semen on the ground, an act so offensive that God Himself killed him for it. Adultery was even worse than any of this, and was often punishable by stoning. There was enormous concern surrounding the children that might result from adultery. Offspring of an adulterous relationship were called *mamzerim* (meaning estranged), a taint that could be passed down the generations: the child of a mamzer was thought a mamzer themselves.

All this improper sex is Lilith's territory – she lures men away from their wives and persuades them to commit adultery, she gives men impure thoughts even in the marriage bed, she causes nocturnal emissions and steals any semen emitted from masturbation. Worst of all, she produces hundreds of illegitimate children: symbols of her successful seductions, embarrassing men at their funerals, and threatening to destroy their legacy.

Lilith is both a symptom of these anxieties, and a consolation for them. There are ways to expel her and rituals to keep her at bay, and, more to the point, her male victims are just that: victims, all but blameless. The fault for their actions doesn't lie with them, but with the women who are seducing them and producing illegitimate children. Even holy prophets were not immune. Lilith is the other woman – and as with all other women, the true blame for a man's actions lies with her.

The extent to which the Kabbalistic Lilith catered to the fears of men, rather than women, is perhaps most obvious in the way Lilith's child-killing and mother-killing proclivities (and her sexual danger to women) are treated. In Kabbalistic sources, any threat Lilith might pose to women is dropped entirely – the risks pregnant women faced are ignored and her seduction of women is never mentioned. And while Lilith's new ability to produce children was a key focus, most Kabbalistic sources had surprisingly little interest in her propensity for killing them: the Treatise on the Left Emanation doesn't even mention it. The *Zohar*, meanwhile, contains a horrific twist on the tradition. It's not just that Lilith can kill children who were conceived when their fathers were not in a state of purity, it's that Lilith also kills 'children who deserve to be punished'. There is no comfort here, no control for women nursing ill children – just unrectifiable offenses. It's already decided if Lilith will kill an infant, whether because of an impure thought – on the part of the father – before the child was born, or because the child itself is being held accountable for vague, indefinable sins. The Kabbalistic Lilith tells desperate, terrified women that if their children are dying, there is nothing they can do but watch.

But although Lilith of the Kabbalistic texts was of little use to women, she continued in folklore as the consolation she had always been. A couple of medieval charm stories survive: one concerns the prophet Elijah meeting her and demanding to know where she is going and what she is doing. When she admits that she plans to murder children, he forces her to give him her names so they can be used to protect infants from her malice – the old Byzantine Michael charm, that had once been a defence against Roman headache demons, being used anew. One of the names that Lilith gives is even 'Abizou'. In another charm, contained within a seventeenth-century set of instructions for making an amulet to protect children against Lilith, she is once again driven away by the angels Snvi, Snsvi, and Smnglof. There were even new folk legends, including one that warns that a child laughing in its sleep was playing with Lilith, and must be tapped on the nose to be saved from the monster, and a fun little story about a canny midwife trapping Lilith in a milk jug and forcing the demon to spare the mother and child who were her targets.

The continuation of Lilith went beyond Judaism and Christianity – she crops up in Islamic folk stories as a creature called the Qarinah, a monster who appeared as a double of a husband to mortal wives, and a double of a wife to mortal husbands – an equal-opportunity seducer like the Lilith of the incantation bowls who was also said to be the first wife of Adam. And while Lilith slipped from importance in Judaism as Kabbalism fell from favour in the seventeenth and eighteenth centuries, these folk traditions continued unabated. Lilith was still warded away from infants and mothers into the twentieth (and even twenty-first) century, long after the last Kabbalistic treatise on her had been written.

But Lilith was not the only one of our demons who was used by men in the Middle Ages to reflect their concerns about sexuality: Lamia (combined with the Siren of ancient Greek legend) was to become the mermaid of the medieval church, a creature wholly stripped of her child- and mother-killing abilities and entirely focused on murderous seduction. And while Judaism in the Middle Ages might have had concerns about adultery and masturbation, this was absolutely nothing compared to the terror the medieval Christian church had of sex and women – a terror embodied by the mermaid.

6

Siren Song

Glinting golden in the storerooms of the National Gallery is one of the earliest known images of the eleventh-century cardinal and reformer Peter Damian. While the painting has a rough and ready look – the hook of Damian's crozier is just a thick black line; the edging of his cloak, although gilded, is rushed and uneven – his expression holds your attention. Glaring down at you through narrowed eyes with pursed, twisted lips, he has a judgemental, domineering appearance. He looks as if he is both uninterested in and repulsed by you at the same time.

If this was anything close to how Damian actually looked it would be entirely coincidental. The painting comes from a series of six saints, all of whom have the same mean, pinched expression, and anyway, it was painted 300 years after Peter Damian died in 1072. But the superior sneer on his face fits well with what we know about the man – he might have been a doctor of the church and placed in the highest tier of heaven by Dante in his *Inferno*, but he reads as deeply unpleasant to modern eyes.* He was obsessed with purity, especially sexual purity, and railed against masturbation (either solitary or mutual – he goes into a considerable amount of detail about it), against the 'madness' induced by excess lust, against homosexuality. He instituted flagellation as a penance (to the extent that he's often depicted clutching a flail), and suggested it be used, alongside isolation and fasting, to 'extinguish lust'. But while he believed men were struggling heroically against their desires, he writes about women as wicked corrupters; temptresses whose sole goal was to destroy male chastity. Of his many anti-woman diatribes, one is of particular interest for this book: a letter, written to Bishop Cunibert of Turin to demand the bishop no longer allow his clergymen to marry. The letter threatened monks who dared to have sex with torment and hellfire, but the true hatred is visited not on the straying men but on their female partners. Damian wrote of them as literal monsters:

> So come and listen to me, you strumpets, prostitutes ... sirens, Lamias ... who by singing their deceptive song prepare inevitable shipwreck on the devouring sea.[1]

The combination of creatures he cites – especially the Lamia and the sirens – is the key to understanding the origins of perhaps the most recognizable monster in this book, and the creature that Damian certainly had in mind when he wrote this passage: the mermaid.

* He's credited with inventing the siesta, and it's telling that even this cannot outweigh his negative qualities.

Although today she is more associated with iridescent princesses and sparkly pink and green sequins than sermons and sin, the mermaid was a creation of early Christianity, a blending of both the Lamia and the sirens of ancient Greece (with a bit of Gello and Lilith thrown in for good measure). Far from her Lamia roots as a monster of pregnancy and infant death (and even further from her siren background as a prophetic, chthonic bird-woman), the mermaid of medieval Europe was a vicious temptress who haunted monasteries and cathedrals, and stood for all that celibate churchmen feared about women and sex. Lilith had come to embody some of these ideas in Judaism, but the child- and mother-killing aspects of her remained: Jewish scholars might have had little interest in the side of Lilith that made her important to women, but the belief in her as a monster of motherhood went too deep in Judaism to be ignored. The European church had no such problem, and in the mermaid these demons lost all interest in mothers and their children, becoming monsters that were entirely fixated on seducing their male victims before killing and devouring them. In the hands of men like Peter Damian – men who had taken vows of chastity, who viewed sex as a polluting, corrupting act, who thought flagellation was a solution to sexual urges – our demons came to reflect the horror of women that ran through the medieval church, and the almost pathological level of hatred some churchmen held for any woman, real or imagined, who might make them regret their vows.

With her scaly tail and naked torso (or, if not naked, sporting only a couple of strategically placed shells), clutching a comb and a glass and singing alluringly by the sea, the mermaid depicted in the manuscripts and sculptures of the medieval church looks almost the same as she does in any children's book today. She was an immensely popular figure in the Middle Ages, and the legacy of this popularity is especially visible in medieval church buildings. In Exeter cathedral, a thirteenth-century mermaid misericord brandishes a fish in her right hand, her left hand broken. Mermaids cavort around the twelfth-century font in St Peter's in Cambridge; a bony-looking mermaid grips a snake on a corbel in Durham Cathedral's Norman chapel. In the Duomo di Modena one with flat, pancake-like breasts glares down on the crypt; there's one in Ripon Cathedral and one in Carlisle; an eleventh-century double-tailed mermaid in Saint-Dié Cathedral in France, a mermaid roundel in the twelfth-century floor mosaic of Otranto Cathedral. In fact, in most medieval church buildings you can normally find at least one, tucked under a seat or lost in the stonework. There are mermaids in manuscripts, too – they swim in marginalia, looping their tails around letters, they are referenced in the Bible, they appear in bestiaries, and are frequently discussed in the writings of church scholars.

But as popular and recognizable as she is, it is clear that the medieval mermaid was caught in an identity crisis. Even her name is not fixed: texts refer to her both as a 'mermaid' and as a 'siren', often using the two terms interchangeably within the same manuscript. Her imagery is still more confused. As many times as the mermaid appears in what we'd view as her traditional form – scaly-tailed and bare-breasted – she's pictured just as frequently with the body of a bird. These bird forms are more varied than the fish-tailed ones,* but they appear in all the same places, nestling around medieval churches and cathedrals

* There's particular confusion over where the bird form should start and finish: should only the bottom half of her body be bird-like, or should her torso be feathered as well? Should she have arms or wings?

and dotted through manuscripts, often alongside their fish-tailed sisters. Even within individual manuscripts, there's confusion over whether the mermaid should be fish-tailed or bird-bodied: the majority of illustrated texts which describe the mermaid as part bird show her with the tail of a fish in the accompanying image.

Despite the uncertainty over her appearance and her name, the behaviour of the mermaid and the lessons that were supposed to be learned from her are entirely consistent across medieval sources. The images already hint at her darker side: plenty of the mermaids (both bird-bodied and fish-tailed) clutch fish, which might initially seem like a reasonable accessory for an ocean-going creature, but in fact speaks to something more sinister. The fish stands for the human soul, and a mermaid holding a fish is brandishing a man that she has ensnared. The mermaid's bare breasts also demonstrate her evil nature – female nakedness in medieval imagery was normally used to signify lust and evil. Likewise, those two quintessential mermaid tools, the mirror and the comb, are there to demonstrate the mermaid's vanity and sexuality: vanity in primping and preening in the looking glass, and sexuality in the normally private act of combing hair, performed alluringly and shamelessly in public. The mirror was also one of the accessories of Venus, tying the mermaids to sexual seduction all the more closely, while her loose hair hinted at the same thing: respectable medieval maidens went about with their hair up, tucked away into hats and veils. Loose hair in a medieval woman was a clear sign of loose morality.

Bestiaries, or books of beasts, go into significantly more detail about the mermaid's habits. These books were widely read throughout medieval Europe and dozens of examples have survived. Beautifully illustrated, each chapter of a bestiary concerned a different animal and the lessons to be learned from its behaviour: the elephant, for example, who according to the bestiaries mates for life, teaches the reader about being a good spouse. In all bestiaries, there is a combination of real and fictional animals,* although even real animals are given completely imagined characteristics and habits (elephants, for example, don't actually mate for life, and they certainly don't begin mating rituals with the female elephant giving the bull a mandrake root and leading him to paradise). Among these creatures, in almost every surviving bestiary, is the mermaid.

Whether she has a fish tail or a bird body, the bestiaries tell us that the mermaid is fabulously beautiful, and spends her days sitting by the sea singing sweetly to passing sailors. Lured by her beauty and her song, sailors either run their ships aground on the rocks surrounding her or are lulled to sleep by her voice, at which point she will eat them alive. The lesson here, we are explicitly told, is that surrendering to lust will destroy you, that women work to tempt men, and that giving in to that temptation will mean ruin and death. Just as a mermaid will devour you if you listen to her song, so the devil will seize you if you are beguiled by lust. Occasionally, the bestiaries make the real-world significance of the mermaid even clearer by depicting her dressed in the clothing of prostitutes. Women, the mermaids teach us, are temptresses, and if you give into them you are surely doomed.

The mermaid is used to teach this lesson throughout church scholarship. For Saint Ambrose, the fourth-century theologian,

---

* The fictional beasts tend to be a mix of creatures that are very recognizable to modern eyes (like, say, the unicorn) and monsters whose myths have little purchase in the current imagination: come for the phoenix and the centaur and stay for the fire rocks – animate rocks that burst into flames when they try to mate.

she symbolized the 'figures of sexual pleasure';[2] for St Paulinus of Nola, writing in the fifth century, siren song would make a man forget his vows; in the seventh century Isidore of Seville compared mermaids to prostitutes who lured men to destitution; Damian has them leading the Bishop of Turin's monks into lust and destruction. Whether she looked like a bird or fish, whether she was called a mermaid or a siren, this was what the mermaid did, and what she symbolized to the medieval church.

It's clear from all this that the medieval mermaid drew heavily from the siren of classical Greece. These monsters are best known from their role in the *Odyssey*, where Odysseus is warned by the witch Circe about the sirens, creatures who entice sailors to their doom with irresistible song. In order to pass by safely while still hearing their music, Odysseus binds himself to the mast of his ship and has his crew stuff their ears with wax so they can row on untempted. The sirens aren't described by Homer, but we have plenty of images of them: the most iconic representation comes from an Attic red-figure vase dating to around 480 BC, which shows them clustering around Odysseus' ship. The sirens here look a lot like the bird-bodied version of the medieval mermaid – birds with the heads of women. The ancient monsters, then, share a name with the mermaid, share the deadly song that lures sailors to their deaths, and even share their bird-bodied, women-headed form. This connection is often made entirely explicit – there are plenty of medieval accounts that have mermaids tempting Odysseus.

However, look a little more closely and it's clear that the connection between the medieval mermaid and the ancient siren was not a straight line. The most obvious difference is in form – although the mermaid of the Middle Ages was fish-tailed as often as she was bird-bodied, the ancient siren is only ever depicted as a bird-woman. The classical sirens also lack the defining sexuality of the medieval mermaid: they tend not to be depicted with breasts – often the head is the only human part – and they never hold the vain, erotic accessories of the comb and the glass that medieval mermaids rarely went without (or, indeed, any other accessories that would communicate similar ideas in ancient Greece as the comb and the glass did in Europe). Even their hair tends to be neatly and properly up instead of loose – in some images they look almost asexual.

Their famous siren-song also lacks any sexual elements. It's alluring, certainly, but the temptations it offers have nothing to do with lust. When Odysseus encounters the monsters in the *Odyssey* they don't mention sex, but instead promise him knowledge, singing:

Odysseus! Come here! You are well-known
from many stories! Glory of the Greeks!
Now stop your ship and listen to our voices.
All those who pass this way hear honeyed song
poured from our mouths. The music brings them joy,
and they go on their way with greater knowledge
since we know everything the Greeks and Trojans
suffered in Troy, by the gods' will: and we know
whatever happens anywhere on earth.[3]

Even the adjective 'honeyed', the only part of this passage that sounds vaguely seductive, should probably be read as connecting the sirens to bees, animals frequently linked with poetry and prophecy, rather than its modern connotation of sweet insincerity.

This lack of sexuality remains when the sirens appear in

legends outside of the Odyssey as well. In one myth they were the companions of Persephone, and wished for wings so they could search for their lost friend after she was kidnapped by Hades – a sweet, sad little tale, that certainly doesn't show the sirens as seducers. Less sweetly, but no more sexually, in some versions their bird bodies are because Demeter cursed them for not protecting her daughter. In another myth, they lose to the Muses in a singing contest, while in *Cratylus*, Plato places them in the underworld itself, and describes them as being enraptured by Hades' song and unable to leave because they are so drawn to it. Hades here has clearly taken on the sirens' song himself, a fact that again implies it is entirely lacking in sexual elements. Plato stressed this even further in his later works by equating the singing of the sirens with the music of the spheres – the celestial harmony that was supposedly brought about by the vibration of the planets and the cosmos – which hardly speaks to lustful seduction. This lack of siren-eroticism is reflected more broadly in ancient Greece. Although 'siren' could be a synonym for prostitute in medieval Europe, in ancient Greece the term was often applied to orators, not to suggest that they were sexual tempters, but to imply that they were persuasive. This was rarely as a compliment to the orator in question, but it certainly didn't come with the medieval sexual implications: when, in the fourth century BC, the orator Demosthenes called his rival Aeschines a siren, it was to imply that his persuasiveness was something dangerous, and likely to lead people astray, not that Aeschines was a man-eating sex monster.

The ancient sirens were closely linked to the underworld (perhaps owing to their connection with Persephone, or because they caused death themselves), and they appear frequently on tombstones, but even then they had astonishingly positive attributes, functioning as psychopomps, guiding the souls of the dead on their journey to the afterlife. Sirens aren't even particularly vicious – they lure people to their deaths not out of malice, or because they want to eat their victims as the medieval mermaids do, but because they're fated to die if any man should hear their song and survive. After Odysseus listened to them and passed by unharmed, they supposedly hurled themselves into the sea to their deaths. The Greek sirens also don't live in the sea. Despite being a hazard to sailors, they sit in a flower- (and sometimes bone-) strewn meadow. Although in scenes with Odysseus they are inevitably pictured around his ship, in most other representations of sirens the ocean doesn't figure at all, and we never see them swim.

For a creature whose name was synonymous with 'mermaid' in the medieval period, there are enormous differences between the siren of ancient Greece and the siren of the Middle Ages. Where did the mermaid get her sexual side – her defining characteristic in the medieval world? Where did she get her fish-tail? When did she stop being a sad, prophetic bird-woman and morph into a scaly-tailed sex monster who wanted to eat men alive? The answer comes from the Lamia and the Gello, who for hundreds of years had been fish- (or snake-) tailed creatures, sitting bare-breasted by the sea, spending their days seducing men before eating them alive.

On the amulets and wall paintings throughout late antiquity, Gello and Lamia are shown scaly-tailed and bare-breasted, with loose, flowing hair, as mermaid-like as any creature could look. It's clear from the charms and myths that they lived in the ocean and drew power from it: the charms have Gello emerging from the sea, and her name lists include titles such as 'the one from the sea' and 'the deep'. So associated was Lamia with the sea that some commentators in late antiquity even glossed her as a fish. This association had been present in ancient Greece as well, where Aristotle called Lamia a shark, and where she was given parentage of the snakey sea-monster Scylla.

These creatures did not just look like the medieval mermaids: like the succubus sirens of the bestiaries, they were seductive and inclined to eat the men who fell for their charms, just like a mermaid devouring sailors foolish enough to follow her song. In *The Life of Apollonius of Tyana* Philostratus writes that Lamias are:

> lascivious creatures, and their passion is for making love and especially for the flesh of young men. They use the pleasures of sex as a decoy for those on whom they wish to dine.[4]

A description that any medieval churchman would have applied to a mermaid.

The Lamia of Dio Chrysostom's story of around AD 100 are as close to medieval mermaids as anything could be. His monsters live by a treacherous gulf which, once sailed into, cannot be sailed out of again. Their faces and breasts are those of beautiful women and 'all who looked into their eyes were gripped with love and desire'. However, the lower half of their bodies was that of a snake. They hunted by revealing their breasts to lost sailors, 'inflicting on men a terrible longing for sex'.[5] When their quarry approached they would seize him and eat him. In an almost exact mirror of the bestiaries, Dio Chrysostom goes on to say this story should teach us that following things we desire, things that seduce us, will often lead us to ruin.

The seductive nature of these monsters – especially the Lamia – was also talked about by church scholars, in a truly astonishing act of hypocrisy, given that all of them were mocking women for believing in the Lamia and the Gello. As we've seen, Damien was happy to reference the Lamia as a seductive force leading monks astray, and Hincmar, an archbishop of Reims in around AD 850, listed Lamias as a potential threat to marriages. Pope Gregory, writing in around 604 BC, was happy to point to Lamia as a representation of heresy.

Although the mermaid's popularity peaked in the Middle Ages, her creation seems to have come in late antiquity – when Lamia and Gello were feared by everyone from commoners to emperors, when the church was both ridiculing belief in them and engaged in rituals against them, and when the links between the siren-mermaid and the Lamia are made most explicit.

Among the earliest descriptions of the sirens as something other than bird-bodied singers come from the Biblical translations commonly known as the Septuagint (a third-century Greek translation) and the Vulgate (a fourth-century Latin translation).* These references make it clear that, in an exact mirror of Lamia's serpentine body, the supposed fish-tail of the siren-mermaid started life as the tail of a snake. In these translations, the mermaid-sirens are placed in the ruins of the divinely destroyed cities of Edom and Babylon – the Septuagint has them in both cities, and while the Vulgate kept them in Babylon, it dropped the Edom-based sirens and brought in the Lamia instead, stressing the links between the two. These translations leave no room for doubt that the mermaid-sirens (and Lamias) were snake monsters: in both the Vulgate and the Septuagint the Hebrew word *tannim*

---

* The exact way these translations mapped onto each other (and the slight wrinkle of Jerome's mistranslation of *tannim*) is described in the appendix.

(serpent) is translated as 'siren', and in the Vulgate *tannim* is also translated as 'Lamia', confirming not only the serpentine natures of both creatures, but the connection between them both. Even more interestingly, the Hebrew word 'Lilith' is also translated as 'Lamia' in the Vulgate, suggesting another snake-woman was also, tangentially, tangled into these myths. Just to make the snake-siren correlation completely explicit, the translator of the Vulgate, St Jerome, spelled out these links in a commentary to his translation, where he stated that the 'sirens' are 'great dragons'. These are no longer the bird-bodied women of ancient Greece – they are Lilith-related snake monsters.

This original serpentine nature of the siren-mermaid is still evident in later medieval sources – in some illustrations, the tail is more consciously dragon-like: covered in spikes, scales and spines and accompanied by clawed dragon-feet, while Melusine, the sister of the mermaid (discussed more in the next chapter) even takes on reptilian wings.

The addition of Lamia to the ancestry of the mermaid also explains an otherwise baffling piece of mermaid imagery: the medieval mermaid is, occasionally, shown breastfeeding an infant. In the margins of the thirteenth-century Alfonso Psalter, for example, a mermaid nurses her little scaly-tailed child; on a capital at Freiburg-im-Breisgau a mermaid with both human legs and a serpent tail is shown holding an infant to her breast. These representations are not common, but they are persistent. There's nothing in the legends of the classical sirens that connect them to children; nothing in the lore of the medieval mermaid that suggests she might have breastfed her infants (or even had children in the first place). Instead, the explanation for the image of a nursing mermaid may come from the Lamia – specifically from the Vulgate translation of Lamentations, which contains the following, astonishing, phrase:

Even the Lamia bares her breast to nurse her young ones (Lam 4:3).

Given what we know about the Lamia's child-murdering tendencies, this is certainly odd, and commentators on this passage twisted themselves into knots to explain it (perhaps the Lamia's milk is poison; perhaps this refers to Lamia before Hera forced her to devour her children), but it was a well-known phrase, and appears frequently in early Christian scholarship. Given all the links between the medieval mermaids and Lamia, it's possible that this phrase was connected with mermaids as well, that the breastfeeding sirens are the mermaid-Lamia 'bar[ing] her breast to nurse her young ones'.

The medieval mermaids, then, look and behave exactly like Lamia (and Gello), they just have the name and song of the siren – and sometimes her feathers – stuck on top. In fact, in certain cases it is impossible for modern scholars to tell the Lamia and the medieval mermaid-siren apart, and some medieval images are today identified as 'either a siren or a lamia'.[6]

Eventually, another type of mythical watery woman would be dragged into all of this – the nymph. In ancient Greece, nymphs were not generally seductive, and certainly not violently so. There is only one story where they attack a man: in the legend of Jason and the Argonauts, nymphs fall in love with and abduct Hylas, the lover of Hercules, dragging him down to his watery doom. However, this sort of behaviour is vanishingly rare for nymphs in ancient sources, and even the tale of Hylas has a variant where he doesn't drown, but lives with them happily. In most ancient myths nymphs are rape victims, rather than seducers, constantly fleeing from the men who desire them, and often being turned into trees and flowers by passing gods and goddesses to help them escape their tormentors.

In even less mermaid-like fashion, their seagoing cousins, the Nereids and Tritonesses, were credited with rescuing shipwrecked sailors, and there are no legends where they bring ships to harm. By the Middle Ages, however, the fact that they were attractive women associated with water was enough for them to be connected with both the child-killing and the seductive versions of Lamia. Although the nymphs never fully blended with the Lamia and the siren-mermaid – they are never shown with serpentine tails – Peter Damian would warn against nymphs as well as Lamias. The idea that nymphs were seducers stuck to the extent that 'nymph' was a synonym for prostitute in the seventeenth and eighteenth centuries, and they would be portrayed as sexual monsters on a par with mermaids by the Victorians. Meanwhile, by the sixteenth century in Greece, nymphs and nereids were snatching children, a role they retained until at least the 1980s.

Although the Lamia (and the Gello) were so closely related to the medieval mermaid, they eventually slipped from mermaid lore. It's not surprising that Gello, a monster so derided by the church, was never mentioned by churchmen in relation to mermaids, and it's possible that Lamia was too closely related to Gello to be entirely free of the idea that only 'foolish old women' could believe in her. However, as we've seen, Lamia was still spoken of by high-profile church scholars, and even appeared in translations of the Bible. Instead, it may be the changing nature of the Lamia that led to her separation from the mermaid: although Jerome was happy to make her dragon-like, and tied her to his serpentine sirens, by the later Middle Ages Lamia was more likely to be depicted as a quadruped than a snake monster.

Lamia had always possessed some animalistic, non-snake characteristics – even in ancient Greece she was connected to the wolf-like Mormo and the donkey-legged Empousa. However, the later medieval church's idea of the Lamia as a four-legged beast may well have come about not because of ancient memories of the Mormo, but because of a translation error. In the thirteenth century, Thomas of Cantimpré, an important Catholic theologian, wrote in his encyclopedia of nature *De Natura Rerum* that:

> The Lamia is a large and cruel animal which comes out of the woods at night, enters gardens and with its strong front legs which are more than suitable for the act, breaks trees scattering the branches all around. When men try to stop it, it fights with them and bites them. Aristotle reports a remarkable thing about its bite: a man wounded by the teeth of the Lamia will not be healed until he hears the beast roar.[7]

Aristotle, of course, said no such thing in regards to Lamia, but he did write something very like this about the beaver. Through a series of mistranslations and misunderstandings (as well as the fact that Thomas was working from the Arabic texts of Aristotle, and didn't fully understand the language), Thomas had turned Lamia into a completely different animal. Since his work was thought authoritative by the church, in later bestiaries she appears as a biting, roaring quadruped, looking and acting nothing like a mermaid.

However, although the quadruped Lamia was so prevalent in the later Middle Ages, the serpentine, water-going version of her was never fully forgotten. Not only would it return in the Victorian era, when images of Lamias and mermaids would once again be indistinguishable and their names practically synonymous, but there are plenty of versions of the seductive, ocean-going Lamia that survived through the Middle Ages as well. Up until at least the 1980s the Lamia of the Greek islands was still swimming in the sea, snake-tailed, beautiful and seductive, and likely to attack any handsome young man who came her way. Meanwhile, the mermaid of the Basque region is a creature known as a Lamiak – a beautiful woman who spends her days sitting by the water trying to lead men to their doom. Having never blended with the classical sirens, these Lamias don't sing, but in every other respect they are like the medieval mermaids.

Despite the fading of Lamia from mermaid-lore, the dual nature of the siren mermaids remained, and was never fully resolved. In the end, the sirens could never fully merge with the mermaids – there was (and still is) an uncomfortable gap between the classical and medieval monsters. Even the word 'mermaid' was a part of this awkwardness. Literally meaning 'sea woman', it doesn't seem to have referred to any creature before the medieval monster, and it was often used synonymously with 'siren': the *Liber Monstrorum* of the seventh century AD uses both 'siren' and 'mermaid' interchangeably, and Chaucer claimed it was simply an English translation of the French *sirène*. However, it was often used as a way of differentiating the fish-tailed seductress from the bird-bodied prophet-singer – a distinction that exists today, at least in English. Ask someone now to describe a mermaid and they'll come up with something fish-tailed, wearing shells and sitting by the sea combing her hair. Ask someone to describe a siren and they'll normally talk about a creature connected to water and song, something associated with the *Odyssey*, something beautiful and dangerous – but something not quite a mermaid.

Even in European languages where 'siren' is used for both mermaids and the bird-bodied singers of antiquity, the distinction is still present. In France the word *sirène* refers both to the classical sirens and the modern-day mermaid (*La Petite Sirène* is the French title of the Disney film), and *sirena* does double duty in Italian and Spanish, but the line is still firmly drawn between the seductive siren with a tail of a fish or snake and the bird-bodied siren of antiquity, with dictionaries often giving an entry for each type. Even when they share the same name, there is no doubt they are two separate, if related, monsters. The gap between them is a space that was once filled by the Lamia.

But although the mermaid shared so much of her DNA with the Lamia, the ideas about good (and bad) femininity that were embodied by the ancient child-killing demoness shifted when she became a mermaid. The mermaid is still malign womanhood – sexual, aggressive, destroying the men who came her way – just as the Lamia was. But Lamia contained within her the ideal of what a good woman should be – a loving, successful mother; a chaste, submissive wife. She, like the Gello, had tried and failed to be these things, and as such could be used to show what a good woman ought to be, despite being the antithesis of ideal woman-hood herself. The good woman who opposed Lilith, meanwhile, was external to her, but still present: Lilith might be the opposite of a good woman, but Eve was there, the good, holy wife and mother, an acceptable model for women to follow. The mermaid of the medieval church contains none of this nuance: there is no readily identifiable 'good woman' opposing the mermaid-siren.* She is femininity demonized entirely – a creature created by men who thought all women would lure men to their doom simply by existing.

---

* Except perhaps the Virgin Mary – an impossible blend of chastity and motherhood that was entirely unachievable for any actual woman.

It is no exaggeration to say that the medieval church had an absolute horror of sex. This horror had been growing throughout late antiquity, but wouldn't reach its peak until the Middle Ages – Augustine, in the fourth century, wrote about the evils of lust, but also, famously, prayed 'Oh God make me chaste: but not yet'. By the Middle Ages 'yet' had arrived, and with it, the popularity of the mermaid skyrocketed. As mermaids were being carved around church buildings, as bestiaries containing the stories of her were disseminated across the monasteries of Europe, celibacy for churchmen was becoming increasingly important, and the fears of the base, animalistic act of sex were growing ever stronger, along with an outright terror of any woman who might tempt a man to engage in it.

Horrible fates awaited clergy who did not live chaste – as Damian laid out in his letter to the Bishop of Turin, even a man who only had sex with his wife was imperilling his very soul and courting hellfire, and marriage was forbidden for priests in AD 1074 as an effort to prevent this (or at least, Pope Gregory VII absolved people of the obedience to bishops who allowed married priests, which is roughly the same thing). Even priests who simply had wet dreams were ruled unfit to perform mass the next morning, while clergymen who were not virgins were thought unworthy to touch sacred relics, and risked death if they did so. If a man had engaged in unchaste behaviour it was thought that after death his body would decay at an unnaturally fast rate, proof of the way it had been polluted in life.

By contrast, a man who had stayed a virgin would be met with the prospect of a body that remained lily-white and sweet-smelling even decades after death – Remigius of Lincoln (1067–92), Theobald of Canterbury (1139–61) and Edmund of Abingdon

(1174–1240) all had corpses that supposedly exhibited no signs of decay, evidence of their much-praised celibacy. And while his body stayed pure and unblemished, in heaven a man who had remained a virgin would display 'the sign of his virginity which was still intact' – a badge of honour even in paradise.[8] If more immediate, earthly rewards were of interest, churchmen could, and did, achieve promotions to coveted positions on the basis of their virginity. When the colleagues of Walter de Gray (1215–55), for example, expressed concern that he lacked the learning to become Archbishop of York, the Pope himself ruled that Walter's virginity alone made him worthy.

Hagiographers and chroniclers frequently stressed the virginity of their subjects, presenting it as the defining feature of men who had plenty of other achievements to their name. St Benedict (AD 480–548), for example, founded numerous monasteries and composed the Rule of St Benedict – a set of rules for his monks to follow, that became one of the most important instructions for monastic living. But in the image of him in Jean de Stavelot's *Liber de sancto Benedicto* (written in the fifteenth century) his virginity is more important than any of this. Here Benedict (who barely touched on chastity in his Rule, and certainly didn't insist on celibacy) is portrayed with the prophet Elias firmly gripping his belt so as to prevent him from removing his trousers and sinning, underscored with the caption: 'Elias guarded his [St Benedict's] virginity like a flower among thorns, he who preserves his virginity has been crowned with gold'.[9]

On the off chance that a prophet didn't have a firm grip on their trousers, some clergy took additional precautions to avoid temptations. Robert de Béthune, a onetime Bishop of Hereford (1131–48), refused to ever look at a woman, while his successor, Thomas Cantilupe, was said to draw a hood over his face if a woman passed by. He even refused to sit with his own sisters,

since any woman, even his siblings, might stir his lust.* If a clergy-
man did accidentally see a woman, he could always scourge
himself (as Peter Damian did), or lock himself in a cell until
the temptation had passed. If the medieval accounts of saints'
lives are anything to go by, churchmen flinging themselves into
bramble patches and streams to control their lust must have
been a fairly common sight – St Bernard, St Benedict, and a
Bishop Wulfstan of the eleventh century AD all decided this was
a sensible reaction to passing a woman on the street (or, in
the case of St Benedict, remembering a woman he'd seen once
some time before). Hugh of Lincoln, a twelfth-century bishop,
managed the impressive task of taking this one step further.
After being touched by a woman on the arm:

> he felt such indignation at her snakelike act that he took
> a sharp knife and cut out the small portion of his flesh
> affected.[10]

The extremes some churchmen would go to in order to remove
the temptation of sex and lust (or at least, attempt to remove it)
were symbolized by the beaver. According to medieval thought
(and as recorded in plenty of bestiaries) the beaver was supposedly hunted for its penis, which it would gnaw off to try and
make itself less alluring to hunters. So, say the bestiaries, all good

* In rare cases, men would intentionally sit with women to 'test' themselves and their resolve, an interesting take on the problem that had an
unsurprising habit of leading to scandal, as in the case of Edmund of
Abingdon, a thirteenth-century Archbishop of Canterbury, who was beset
by scurrilous rumours after he sat with holy women to prove his ability
to resist temptation – rumours that were eventually proven false by the
miraculous preservation of his body when it was exhumed a few years
after his death.

churchmen figuratively gnaw off their genitals to make themselves less obvious prey for Satan. This might seem like grotesque hyperbole, and self-castration was technically banned, but throughout the Middle Ages devout men were occasionally 'miraculously' castrated by God to help them battle their temptations.

It was in this environment that the siren thrived – a monster that symbolized the dangers these men felt they faced, a supernatural temptress that filled their books and buildings. To men who prized their virginity so highly, but who felt their grasp on it was so tenuous that they couldn't even look at a woman, a succubus with an irresistible song was a truly horrific being. But the siren was not just a fictional creature – she was the embodiment of any real-life woman who presented a danger to the celibacy and purity of men. When William of Malmsbury wrote about Wulfstan of Worcester attempting to resist the temptations of a young girl, he described her as 'designed by nature for shipwrecking chastity and luring men into pleasure' – a siren made flesh.[11]

Given that the virginal churchmen feared any woman might lead them into sin, whether she was actively trying to seduce them or was one of their sisters, calmly sitting nearby, it's unsurprising that, unlike Lamia or Lilith, the mermaid contained within her no opposing ideal of 'good' womanhood. It hardly mattered what a woman was doing, what she thought, or how chaste she was herself, if just by being in the same room as a man she could excite him to sin. Leander of Seville made this unambiguous: in his *Regula*, written in about AD 600, he claimed all women outside the monastic community were sirens. Women could either be nuns, removed entirely from society and the presence of men, or dangerous seductive menaces. There was nothing in between.*

---

* Leander was the brother of Isidore of Seville, who wrote that sirens were prostitutes who lured men to destruction and ruin. Leander wrote the

However, most men of the medieval world were not cutting out parts of their arms because a woman had touched them, or throwing themselves into streams because they remembered seeing a woman that one time – and this is reflected in the mermaid too. When the mermaid slipped the confines of her clerical beginnings and worked her way into secular stories, she took on more positive attributes and backed away from her seductive habits – a sign that for the laymen of the Middle Ages, the church's terrifying obsession with purity and virginity was far less important.

In the secular realm of medieval Europe, the siren was not just a succubus, but a figure of pathos and sympathy. This was especially linked to the idea that the siren would sing in stormy weather, and although some commentators claimed that this was because she was anticipating shipwrecks, in most cases it was said that the siren sang in the rain because she was imagining the sunny weather that was to come (and that she wept in the sunshine because she knew it had to end). As one fourteenth-century Spanish poet wrote:

In fine weather, the sirens complain and weep, fearing ill;
in bad weather they sing joyful songs and await the good
season.[12]

This is an aspect that the church never bothered with – it is only ever attested in secular sources – and it led to some beautiful poetry,

---

Regula for their sister, and while we know little else about her, given her brothers' opinions on women and their obsessions with seductive sirens we can only hope she had a happier life than her relations would suggest.

and astonishingly positive descriptions of siren-mermaids. The sweetly optimistic image of a creature singing in storms in hope of sunshine was linked to the idea that lovers would be brought comfort by singing when they were tormented by the object of their affections. In the mid thirteenth century, Jean de Dreux, a count of Brittany who had been scorned by his lover, wrote:

> Just as the Siren
> sings in stormy weather
> so I sing the more I suffer
> mindful of the relief it brings.[13]

Here, the siren-mermaid is a kindred spirit – she is not some foul temptress, but a creature that Jean can compare himself to. Her singing brings joy and relief, not dangerous lust, and the hideous, bestial seduction of the church-siren is turned into romantic (if intense and sorrowful) love.* To medieval poets, sirens could be worthy of emulation – the fifteenth-century Joan Rois de Corella praised the monsters, writing:

> What great wisdom! What brave fear! To save one's life in
> a time of misfortune for the sake of future prosperity! Thus
> the sirens sing at a time when the sea is stormy, hoping for
> calm tranquility.[14]

Beyond poetry and into folklore, secular mermaids could even have successful, if slightly unconventional, marriages. The Mermaid of Zennor is a Cornish myth first recorded in 1873, but

---

* This trope – singing in stormy weather and weeping in good – was also associated with medieval 'wild men', who, like the sirens, appear in the poetry of medieval troubadours to give hope to rejected lovers.

likely of a much earlier date. In this story, a beautiful lady comes to Sunday worship in the little parish church of Zennor every week, the only sign of her supernatural nature that she sings her hymns more sweetly than the rest of the congregation. Eventually she becomes interested in a young man, a talented singer himself, who decides to follow her home. Neither the young man nor the beautiful woman ever return to the church, but one day a ship casts anchor nearby, at which point a mermaid appears, begging them to move since the anchor is blocking the door to her home and her children are inside. The villagers conclude that this mermaid must have been the beautiful woman, that the young man had married her, and that they had started a new life together beneath the waves.

This story was likely inspired by a fifteenth-century carving of a mermaid in the church of Zennor itself – a dreaded siren of medieval Christianity inspiring the charming story of a woman who went to church, met a compatible man, married him and had children, and just happened to be a mermaid as well.

Mermaids could certainly be ominous figures outside the church. In one version of the seventeenth-century 'Ballad of Patrick Spens', a mermaid rises from the waves to warn the crew of a ship that they will never see dry land again – a prophecy that inevitably comes true. Likewise, in the mid-eighteenth century ballad 'The Mermaid' the crew of a doomed vessel spy a mermaid, and know that disaster is coming. Even in these cases, though, the mermaid doesn't seem malicious. She is warning of disaster, not the cause of it, and she isn't blamed for the ruin that comes to the men who see her.

Despite these positive mermaid portrayals, the inherent misogyny in the mermaid mythos would always be there to rear its head, even in non-religious settings. This was especially true when the archetype of the mermaid was used to attack real-life women, as was the case for Mary Queen of Scots, who, in 1567, was accused of seducing James Hepburn, Earl of Bothwell, and manipulating him into murdering her husband, Henry Darnley. Her unpopularity consequently became so great that laws were hastily pushed through in an attempt to prevent the posting and circulation of 'bills and tiquets of defamation' against the queen. Amazingly, one such bill survives, showing Mary, identified by the initials M.R., not as a human woman but as a crowned mermaid – a succubus who had led her husband to his death, and seduced her lover to commit murder. In case there was any doubt as to the meaning of this poster, beneath the mermaid is a hare identified as the earl by his initials. This animal was not only the heraldic emblem of Bothwell's house, but also, coincidentally, a symbol of lust and cowardice. This hare is surrounded by a circle of swords, implying destruction from all sides. Bothwell has been led, by the queenly seductress, into murder and ruin. This is the mermaid of the medieval church, used to accuse a real woman of being a seductive, murderous monster. Although Mary and the monarchy itself were closely linked to the church, it wasn't clergy who were making and distributing these posters – it was people who might otherwise have been telling each other the story of the mermaid of Zennor, suddenly embracing the idea that mermaids were oversexed temptresses after all. We will see the mermaid being used in the same way in the Victorian era: although mermaids could be positive creatures in poetry and folklore, when people needed a misogynistic stereotype of a femme fatale, the monster created by the sex-obsessed, woman-fearing medieval church was always there for them to use. The legacy of men who were afraid to even sit in the same room as a woman, or walk past one on the street, would remain a part of the mermaid.

There is another creature who is an almost exact reflection of the mermaid – a snake-tailed, beautiful woman with astonishingly positive characteristics who started life as a secular monster and who was only portrayed as a vicious succubus when she was spoken of by churchmen. And while the mermaid shows us that the medieval church's compulsive misogyny was not the sole way women were perceived in the Middle Ages, this new creature gives us additional perspective on the lives of women in medieval society outside of the fanaticism of the church. As we will see, this monster – Melusine – shows us clearly that medieval women were not just seductive sirens: they could be magnificent queens, cathedral-builders, and important political figures, as well as loving wives and mothers.

7

Mother of the Lords of Lusignan

Very little remains of the Chateau de Lusignan in western France, although at its height in the early Middle Ages it was one of the largest castles in Europe. A magnificent jumble of towers, walls and keeps, it went through all the normal stages of decline for a castle: it was used as a school, a prison and a source of cut stone, before finally being knocked down to make way for a pleasure garden in the 1800s. All that's left is a scatter of stone foundations on the hillside above the quiet town of Lusignan. In some ways this seems fitting: the castle was the ancestral seat of a family who had all but vanished by the late 1300s, but who in their heyday were among the most powerful families in medieval Europe, rulers of vast estates in France and Germany, as well as kings of Jerusalem, Armenia and Cyprus. Their decline came even before that of their home, with the extinction of their European line in 1314, followed by the inevitable loss of their Crusader kingdoms. By the late 1300s, their castle was inhabited not by a Lusignan but by a man called Jean de Berry.

Jean was not without impressive titles of his own. Third son of King John II of France, he was Duke of Berry and Auvergne, as well as a Count of Montpensier and Poitiers: it was through his acquisition of the latter territory that he came to inhabit the Chateau de Lusignan. Jean, bad-tempered and scruffy, with a stubby potato of a nose (if the surviving portrait of him is anything to go by), was a great patron of the arts and among the works he commissioned was a history of the family whose estates he found himself occupying, entitled *The Noble History of Lusignan*. This vast 400-page tome was written with an eye to asserting the duke's Lusignan lineage, and thus his right to rule their lands. Given the intermarriages of the medieval European nobility, this wasn't too hard for its author, John d'Arras. However, despite tying his patron to the Lusignans, and despite the fact that the history of the family was quite interesting enough in its own right, d'Arras's main focus in *The Noble History* concerns the marriage of the first duke of Lusignan to a half snake-woman called Melusine. She's so central to the narrative that the manuscript is also called the *Roman de Mélusine*.

The story is long and extremely complex, but boiled down to its utter essentials it runs as follows: Raymondin, the fictional first duke of Lusignan (the actual founder was called Hughes, along with all of his descendants, making for a very boring and confusing family tree), was hunting in the forest when he came across a beautiful woman named Melusine. He fell in love instantly, and she agreed to marry him under one condition: every Saturday she would lock herself in her room, and he would never be allowed to enter. Raymondin readily agreed, and the two were married. They had nowhere to live, but using magic Melusine built the vast Chateau de Lusignan overnight, as well as a church for them to worship in.

For years, the couple lived there happily. The fortunes of the family soared, and they became the most powerful in Europe, while Melusine birthed many sons and built many more palaces, churches and monasteries. For a while, everything was perfect. However, over the years, Raymondin grew ever more suspicious of his wife, and worried that she spent her Saturdays with another man. Eventually, overcome with jealousy, he broke his promise and spied on her through a hole in her door. There he saw Melusine bathing, but instead of legs she had the tail of a hideous serpent. Horrified, Raymondin cursed her, at which point she turned into a dragon and vanished. After she left, the prosperity and fortune which she had brought the family began to fade away, and her sons and her husband mourned her loss. Supposedly, the inhabitants of the town of Lusignan called themselves *mélusins* and *mélusines* in her memory, and there were reports that when her castle was finally destroyed in the 1800s, Melusine could be heard howling throughout the night.

This story, and all of its many variants, is the secular version of the mermaid in Europe – a Lamia-related monster who moved westward independently of the serpentine siren, and who, untethered from her child-killing and seductive qualities (at least to some extent) gives a view on women in the Middle Ages from outside the confines of the sex-obsessed church. It is the story of a woman who (snake-tailed or not) was a powerful matriarch in her own right, a good mother, and a joyous lover.

Jean d'Arras didn't invent the story of Melusine, nor her connections to the Lusignans,* both of which are attested in a slightly less complex form from the early 1200s, but it does seem odd that he would draw so much attention to such an ancestor when he was trying to incorporate his patron into the family. Even odder is that Jean de Berry wasn't the only noble of the late medieval period who proudly claimed to be descended from Melusine. After Berry's attempt to secure his rights to Lusignan lands through Melusine, Guillaume l'Archevêque, Lord of Parthenay, commissioned a retelling of the story in verse. Although the main narrative was left fundamentally unchanged, this version stressed the descent of both L'Archevêque and his English Plantagenet allies from Melusine, and therefore their rights to the contested Lusignan estate.

There were also noble claims of Melusine-ancestry unconnected with the Lusignans: the Counts of Luxembourg maintained that she had married their founder, Count Siegfried, in the tenth century and the Dukes of Anjou had their own story in which Count Fulk III of Anjou (970–1040), sometimes called Black Fulk, found Melusine in the Holy Land while he was crusading and married her. Even Richard the Lionheart claimed descent from the snake-woman, and was apparently fond of saying that he and his family came 'from the Devil, and to the Devil we shall return' because of their unusual matriarch.

---

* Although he did go some way towards ruining it. A story full of Crusaders and magical snake-women should be fun, but d'Arras's text is an inconsistent mess. A lot of people claim it's a masterpiece, but they always follow this by talking about its 'ambiguities' and 'ambivalence'. One scholar points out that it's not 'unproblematic, "readerly" fiction destined for mass consumption' but a 'writerly text' with an 'obstinate resistance to interpretation'. All 400 pages of the epic are available for free online, if you think that sounds like a good time (Donald Maddox, Sara Sturm-Maddox, *Melusine of Lusignan* (University of Georgia Press, 1996) p.3).

Non-noble versions of this story cropped up, normally with an unnamed knight as the hero (or at least, a knight with a name that isn't recorded). In all cases, the story follows a similar arc: the couple meet in woods, or among some ruins, after the hero has become lost while hunting. They fall in love, and marry under the condition that Melusine cannot be seen on a particular day of the week (or, occasionally, that her husband cannot see her naked, or when bathing). The condition is met for a while, and a happy, prosperous marriage follows. Melusine will often build castles, churches and monasteries and will always produce children. Then, inevitably, the taboo will be broken, and Melusine's husband will see her at the forbidden time, or in the forbidden manner, revealing that his wife has the tail of a snake instead of legs. Often suspicious friends or relatives goad him into the betrayal. Melusine will then vanish, to be mourned by her husband, occasionally appearing at family births and deaths, or to nurse her infant children, or, in some cases, at seven-year intervals. It's often suggested that she is in torment, possibly even in hell, and will only be saved on Judgement Day.

These stories were solidly popular. Numerous copies of Jean d'Arras's text, as well as L'Archevêque's poetic version, circulated in the late Middle Ages. By the mid 1500s, it had been translated from the Latin original into French, Middle English, Dutch, Spanish, Czech and German. It passed into Denmark and Sweden and by the early 1600s had even been translated into Russian. Families and cities took their associations seriously, and Melusine appears on various crests, including those of the Lusignan and Limburg-Luxembourg families.

Interest in Melusine continued to bubble along through the eighteenth and nineteenth century. Goethe wrote a tale about her in *Wilhelm Meister's Travels*, which was later turned into a play. Six separate operas about Melusine were performed in

Hungary, Germany and Barcelona, a ballet about her was staged in Vienna, and Mendelssohn composed music inspired by her. Today, her impact is still clear in those towns which regard her as a patron: in 1997 Luxembourg issued a stamp commemorating Melusine (in a very sparkly, Disneyfied version), and a bright purple ceramic Melusine statue was installed near Neumünster Abbey in the city centre in 2013, to commemorate the city's 1050th anniversary. In the rest of Europe, however, the story has largely faded, with one odd exception: one of the most common modern symbols, the Starbucks logo, is Melusine.*

Melusine's origins are far from clear. She first appears in the *Otia Imperialia* ('Recreation for an Emperor'), an encyclopedia written in the very early 1200s for the entertainment of the Holy Roman Emperor, Otto IV, by a scholar called Gervase of Tilbury. Jean d'Arras certainly drew on Gervase's text (and even cites him in his introduction), and it's likely to be where he found the name 'Raymondin' to insert into the exclusively Hughes-based Lusignan family tree. But while the two stories follow an almost identical arc, Gervase's Melusine has a couple of differences.† Firstly, Gervase

---

* Probably. The company founders claim that the image (which has changed significantly since it was first used by Starbucks in 1971), was taken from a sixteenth-century book of Norse woodcuts. It's unclear what they meant by this, given that there aren't any books that fit this description, but the image they used looks identical to one in a 1962 book called *A Dictionary of Symbols*. This image was taken from an illustration of d'Arras's *Noble History of the House of Lusignan*, and is of Melusine (she also wears a crown, something few mermaids did in the Middle Ages, but was a natural fit for the noble Melusine).

† Incidentally, the Melusine story in the *Otia Imperialia* is far more enjoyable to read than Jean d'Arras's version. In fact, the entire book is a wonderful example of medieval speculum literature (books of marvels).

tells a far simpler and shorter story (two pages to d'Arras's 400), and sticks to the barest facts – Melusine's marriage, Raymond's promise, and his betrayal. Furthermore, Gervase's hero, Raymond, is Lord of Aix, the medieval capital of Provence, not a Duke of Lusignan. This may be an attempt by Gervase to make his hero an Anjou (the family ruled Provence in the twelfth century) but this is never explicitly stated. Either way, the association doesn't seem to have had a lasting impact on the city, where the legend has been entirely forgotten: there are no stamps of Melusine issued here, and no plastic mermaid statuettes available in the gift shops. Despite Gervase's scholastic tendencies, there's little information on where the story might have come from: he presents it as truth, for which he was 'once given a reliable account'.

With so little to go on, how do we parse Melusine? The association with mermaids is fairly clear: she's occasionally called one in the texts, she sometimes lures her husbands to her by singing, and when she's seen in the bath she's often brushing her hair and staring into a mirror. However, this is apparently a later connection: the sources which call her a mermaid and give her a comb are more recent versions. Instead, it seems likely that Melusine wasn't a child of the mermaids, but a cousin who came into the Western tradition independently (if perhaps concurrently).

Her derivation from the earlier Eastern monsters is undeniable: Melusine looks every inch the Lamia or Gello. This isn't just because of her snake tail – unlike the mermaid, she often keeps

---

When Gervase is discussing women who turn into snakes, for example, he admits that the prospect is 'remarkable', but thinks that it is 'not to be repudiated'. His reason for believing in snake-women? '[I]n England we have often seen men change into wolves according to phases of the moon.' Then he's off into an examination of the origins of the term 'werewolf'. It's a medieval *Brewer's Dictionary of Phrase and Fable* and there's something charming on every page.

the wings of her Byzantine forebears as well, which is presumably why she's sometimes called a dragon. Her seductive element, and her links to the wilderness, also suggest this connection. When Paracelsus (a sixteenth-century physician and theologian) wrote about 'Melusines', turning them into a species as opposed to a character, her name could be substituted for that of any of her Eastern relatives:

> Melusines are the daughters of kings who are tormented because of their sins. Satan seized them and transformed them into phantoms, evil spirits, ghosts and frightful monsters. They live without a rational mind in a fantastic body ... it is believed that these phantoms inhabit deserts, forest, ruins and tombs, empty vaults and the edge of the sea.[1]

Melusine may well have slipped into Western mythology via the Crusades. This is evident first and foremost in the timing of Melusine's myths: they are set just as the Crusades were heating up, and by the time they were being written down, as the Crusades were finishing, they were clearly already popular and well known. But the biggest indication that she followed the Crusaders home comes from the stories themselves, and the families they were associated with. The Lusignans and the Anjous were all heavily involved in the Crusades, and possessed large Crusader kingdoms. The Melusine of the Dukes of Anjou is even found and married in the Holy Lands.* It's also fitting

---

* The Duke of Anjou named Black Fulk, who is normally Melusine's bridegroom in the legends, did actually marry a fierce and impressive woman in the Holy Lands: Melisende (1105–1161). Eldest daughter of Baldwin II of Jerusalem, she was raised as heir presumptive to the crown, ruled jointly with her husband, defeated him in various palace intrigues and crusaded with Eleanor of Aquitaine. It seems likely that this marriage is one of the

that it was England's Crusader king, Richard the Lionheart, who supposedly claimed Melusine as an ancestor.*

This is all nice and neat, but the more you look at Melusine, the more it becomes clear that she isn't a typical demon. There is an odd strand running through these myths: Melusine is demon*ic*, certainly, but she has bizarrely positive traits as well. She brings genuine wealth and power to her husbands, all while building churches and monasteries. When her serpentine nature is exposed her husbands are never angry at her, or horrified by her monstrous form, but are instead filled with guilt for betraying their vows. In Jean d'Arras's version, for example, Raymond cries out on losing his wife (and this is only part of a lament that goes on for three pages):

Ah, Melusine, lady of whom all the world spoke well ...

reasons why Black Fulk, as opposed to any other Duke of Anjou, is typically associated with Melusine, and may also account for the unique detail in the Anjou versions wherein the bride is found in the Holy Land. It has been suggested that Melusine's name was based on Melisende, and while this might sound plausible, there are half a dozen alternative etymologies as well. One has it that 'Melusine' comes from 'Mere d'Lusignan' ('mother of the Lusignans'), although there's no reason why the 'd' would have dropped, and anyway, when her name is first attested, in Gervase, she's more closely connected to the Anjous. There's also an idea that Melusine comes from the Breton words 'me' (half) and 'llysoewn' (snake) and means half-snake.
* The case of the Counts of Luxembourg is more awkward: this family were one of the few who never involved themselves in the Crusades. It's possible, of course, that the legend was loose enough that it didn't have to fit with crusading families. The stories rarely actually mention the Holy Lands, and knights errant were clearly quite capable of bumping into Melusine without any suggestion that they'd also travelled to the East.

Now I have lost beauty, goodness, sweetness, affection, wisdom, charity, humility ... all the modest honor God has lent me was by way of you, my sweet love ... I have betrayed you with my deceitful poison. Alas, you had healed me of my early cruel venom. But I bitterly fulfilled my oath to you when I betrayed you and broke my promise to you.[2]

Melusine is also an exceptional mother. In d'Arras's text, he describes how:

Melusine had excellent nurses and herself took such good care of her children that they flourished and became so strong that all who saw them marveled.[3]

When her sons ask to go crusading she acts like a good medieval mother should: she weeps, and then allows them to leave, sending them off with loving advice. After her husband's betrayal, she frequently comes back to care for her children, especially to breastfeed her youngest infants. Melusine was often depicted nursing in her snakey form, sometimes with surprising tenderness. One typical example, from the mid fifteenth century, shows Melusine feeding her infant when he has woken in the night. She is in her serpent form, and no attempt has been made to hide it, but the focus of the image is on the bond between mother and son: the one lying, comforted, in her arms, the other with her eyes half closed, gazing at her child while smiling tenderly, every inch the perfect mother. Surrounded by other sleepers – two adults (presumably nursemaids) in a bed behind, and the second child still asleep in his crib – the scene is one of quiet gentleness. Some of the images even deliberately invoke the Virgin Mary nursing the baby Jesus, the most widespread – not to mention sacred – scene of a mother and child in the

Middle Ages and an astonishing connection for a half-serpent woman. Many of the woodcuts that accompanied stories about Melusine show her in a sympathetic light, often underplaying or lessening her monstrous body. She also has a far more modest look than her demonic sisters: even in her snakey form she tends to keep her hair neatly and properly tucked away in a bonnet. When she's shown bathing she can sometimes appear more dishevelled, for obvious reasons, but even on these occasions she is frequently depicted with her hair up instead of in the seductively loose style of mermaids. Noble families proudly claiming descent from a demon is distinctly odd, but Melusine is an almost respectable ancestor.

These positive elements of Melusine's story were interwoven with other strands and traditions, influenced by them, and likely influencing them in turn – especially in the case of those stories relating to the Queen of Sheba and the Sibyl.

In 1391, at almost exactly the same time as Jean d'Arras was publishing his story of Melusine, Andrea de Barberino wrote an Italian chivalric romance called *Il Guerrin Meschino* ('Guerrino the Wretch'). It's a fun, bouncy read, which follows the adventures of the tricksterish, wily orphan, Guerrino, as he attempts to find his father. At one point in his travels, Guerrino comes to a mountain pass in the Apennines, near Norcia, when the devil suddenly appears and tells him that a great enchantress, the Sibilla, lives nearby. The enchantress, the devil explains, rules over a vast subterranean kingdom, an earthly paradise that will be Guerrino's to enjoy. The hero finds the entrance to this kingdom, overcomes its anticlimactic guardian (a supposedly terrifying snake called Malco who is defeated instantly when Guerrino steps on him) and discovers a realm of wondrous enchantment. Trees flower and bear fruit at the same time, there is no pain and no age, and all the inhabitants are young and beautiful. The most beautiful of them all is the Queen, Sibilla, who tells Guerrino that she is the Cumaean Sibyl, the great Roman prophetess who was visited by Aeneas and burned her books of prophecies in front of the emperor Tarquin when he tried to haggle over their price. For a year, Guerrino is perfectly happy in this fairy kingdom, but eventually he notices that every Saturday the Sibyl and all her ladies lock themselves in their rooms. Overcome by curiosity, he peers through the door, and sees that all of them have transformed, and have monstrous snake tails instead of legs. Horrified, Guerrino escapes, and goes to Rome to be absolved of his year of sinful living.*

This story was retold in 1420 by Antoine de La Sale, tutor to the son of Louis III, in a book of entertainments La Sale wrote for his pupil. La Sale even claims to have explored the Apennine mountains near Norcia, where the entrance to the Sibyl's kingdom supposedly stood. The locals were able to show him the way but he disappointingly decided not to enter. The story he tells is slightly different from the story of Guerrino: his hero is a German knight, the Sibyl's legs turn to a snake tail on Friday, not on Saturday, and when the knight eventually leaves, the Pope refuses to grant him absolution. On hearing this, the knight returns, shrugging happily, to live forever in earthly paradise with the beautiful Sibyl as his lover.

The legend of the Apennine Sibyl had a long-lasting, if localized, impact. Huge numbers of pilgrims tried to access her cave in the mountains of Norcia, to the extent that Rome threatened

---

* In proper fairy-tale fashion, Guerrino then heads off to his next adventure with Prester John in India, before eventually discovering that he is the son, and therefore heir, of the Duke of Burgundy.

to excommunicate anyone who went there. When this failed to discourage would-be paradise-dwellers, the entrances to the caverns were filled in (in the seventeenth century) and dynamited (in the nineteenth century).

The links between the Apennine Sibyl and Melusine are undeniable: the beautiful woman who locks herself away for one day of the week to become half snake, and who is eventually found out by her spying lover. It's unfortunately unclear exactly how the story of Melusine relates to the story of the Sibyl and whether one was inspired by the other or if they both grew from the same root. Melusine is attested before the snakey Sibyl, but given that these are likely to be oral traditions, the first one written down is not necessarily the first one created, especially since the gap between them only amounts to about ten years. Making the connection to our demonic tradition even clearer, the Hebrew 'Lilith' in Isaiah 34, sometimes translated as Lamia, was, in some cases, translated as Sibyl as well.[4]

The parallels between the Apennine Sibyl and Melusine are also evident in their more positive attributes – for a monstrous seductress, the Sibyl comes across as very pleasant. It's true that both her lovers feel they've sinned enough to seek absolution from the Pope, but they also both enjoy themselves fully while they're in her kingdom. La Sale's knight even comes back, happily, and lives contentedly for the rest of eternity. Admittedly, La Sale was clearly writing with his tongue slightly in his cheek (the book which includes this story is called 'la Salade', a pun on his name 'because in a salad one puts many good herbs'), but the detail of the happily returning knight figures in other, more melodramatic versions as well.

The story of Tannhäuser, best known in modern times from Wagner's opera, tells the same story as La Sale, except the German knight Tannhäuser spends his year in an underground paradise in the Venusberg mountains with the goddess Venus. After he grows tired of her (she has no monstrous transformations), he returns to Rome and begs the Pope for a pardon. The Pope tells him that forgiveness for such behaviour is as likely as the papal staff blossoming. Days later, the staff miraculously erupts into bloom, but it is too late: Tannhäuser has already returned to Venus's kingdom. It's unclear if this inspired or was inspired by La Sale but the appearance of the returning knight in the Tannhäuser myth is a clear sign that it wasn't just an amusing finale added by La Sale to keep the jovial tone of his book. It suggests that in both cases, the fairy kingdom is not terrifying and dark but a place of happiness and enjoyment, albeit one that doesn't have the full approval of the Catholic Church.

This leaves us with the same question presented by the myths of Melusine: how did snake-tailed seductresses with demonic ancestry come to possess such oddly positive qualities? One part of the puzzle may lie in the Islamic tradition of the Queen of Sheba.

The Queen of Sheba has always been a shifting figure: sometime wise woman, sometime seductress and often redeemable, she makes her appearances in all three of the Abrahamic faiths, travelling from a far-off land to meet King Solomon and test his famous wisdom. In the Christian tradition she is exotically and supremely beautiful, but in both the Jewish and Islamic mythology something is off. On the surface she seems lovely, but Solomon is not fooled. He orders a polished sheet of glass to be laid on the floor of his throne room, and then invites the queen in. Thinking that the glass is water, she draws up her skirts, revealing horror and shame beneath. In the slightly anticlimactic Jewish version, this shame is her hairy legs. Solomon rebukes her on her grooming habits, she ignores him, and they get on with her riddles. The Islamic mythology is more developed. Beneath her skirts she has not human legs, but the legs of a donkey. Solomon realizes that this deformity is because she has still not accepted the true faith, and goes about convincing her of it. He eventually succeeds, she converts, her legs become normal legs and (in some versions at least) she marries him.

In Melusine and the Apennine Sibyl's stories we can, perhaps, see echoes of this myth, in the poorly hidden, misshapen legs and the husband or lover who eventually reveals the truth. We know that, as with so many stories, the legend of the Queen of Sheba's deformed nether regions jumped westward with the Crusades and became fairly popular in Europe. One twelfth-century German manuscript tells the tale, and in the portal of Saint-Bénigne cathedral, in Dijon, the Queen of Sheba was shown with webbed flippers under her dress. She appears with a griffin's foot in an image in a chapel near Prague, painted in the 1400s, and a 1492 print from Ulm, Germany, shows her with the webbed foot of a goose. A Western connection with the Melusine/Sibyl/mermaid myths is also evident.

In a roundel in the 1165 mosaic floor of Otranto Cathedral is a snake-tailed woman. With her split tail, one end held in each hand, this creature could just as easily be Melusine as a mermaid, and the mosaic does not allow us to distinguish between the two. However, this snake-woman is associated with the Queen of Sheba, and her Islamic tradition specifically: the roundel appears at the top of a panel in the mosaic showing the queen. In this image, she holds her shoe in her right hand, and her bare foot is wedge-shaped, without the carefully delineated toes of the other barefooted humans shown in the Otranto mosaics. Even more tellingly, in one German poem, composed between 1347 and 1348 and describing Solomon's revelation of the Queen of

Sheba's monstrous feet, she is described as 'Sibilla' or Sibyl. Even if this was primarily a way of referencing her wisdom, it still suggests that the similarities between the myths of Melusine, the Queen of Sheba and the Sibyl had been noticed by their tellers.

As well as lending to the myths of Melusine and the Apennine Sibyl the story of her hidden deformities, the Queen of Sheba may also have given these two figures some of her respectability. As a woman so revered for her wisdom that she became a suitable bride for Solomon, an association with her can only have improved the image of the snake-women. However, both the Sibyl, and Melusine especially, were also soaked in European lore and stories, and it is these tales which give us the greatest insights into the better sides of our demons.

Many early legends from Europe (especially France and Germany) concern beautiful fairies who agree to marry mortals under particular conditions. The marriage results in luck, prosperity and numerous offspring until the mortal partner inevitably breaks the conditions and the fairy leaves forever. Often the fairy is female, but with refreshing frequency the story is told about male supernatural creatures as well. Both male and female variants of the stories appear extremely early in the written record.

The tale of Lohengrin, for example, tells the story of a sleeping knight who was pulled across a lake in a boat by a beautiful white swan. When the boat came ashore in the Low Countries, the knight awoke and saved a local princess who was lost in the forest. Utterly besotted, the princess proposed marriage. The knight accepted with great happiness, and prophesied a joyous union, under one condition: the princess could never ask where he came from, or know anything about his origins. The princess accepted gladly, and the two lived many long years together, and had many children. But this couldn't last forever. One day their children came to the princess and begged to know more about their father's ancestry. The princess, moved by their pleas, asked her husband the fateful question. Without saying a word he sadly shook his head, walked away, and got back into his boat. The last the princess saw of him was the swan pulling the boat into the mists, as he lay down to sleep. Although this story might be best known from Wagner's composition of the same name, it is referenced as common knowledge as early as 1190.

The inevitably broken taboo is a familiar storytelling device. In the tale of Bluebeard, the new wife must always open the forbidden door, in the *1001 Nights* a man left alone in a castle by forty beautiful women must go into the room they have told him not to enter. It gives the story an instant framework, an instant tension, and makes us curious: what is behind the door? Why can't Raymondin see Melusine on Saturdays? In the case of Lohengrin we don't even have to learn the answer to the mystery for the story to be satisfying.* Certainly the existence of this trope in both Melusine and the old, European fairy myths is not enough to suggest that they were part of a shared tradition.

However, it is not just this element that makes the tales so similar. In both the early fairy myths and the Melusine story, the marriage is genuinely happy and successful, and blame for its dissolution lies entirely with the mortal party who could not keep their promise. Perhaps even more to the point, the early fairy stories are notable for a lack of dire consequences. No one is damned to eternal torments until Judgement Day, nor condemned

---

* The mystery is resolved in the *1001 Nights* tale, incidentally: the forbidden room contains a flying mechanical horse, which kicks out the protagonist's eye and flies him to an island full of similarly one-eyed men who also broke their promise to the forty beautiful women.

by the Pope for their actions – in fact, the Church stays entirely out of the narrative. The worst that happens is the break-up of a happy marriage and the loss of the prosperity that the fairy lover brought. These are not monstrous succubi, who will destroy all those foolish enough to fall for their charms: there is no underlying sense of menace to the mystery, and no suggestion that anyone is doing anything wrong. The mortal half of the partnership isn't putting themselves, or their soul, in any grave jeopardy by marrying a fairy: the only danger is that they will eventually lose their supernatural lover. Moreover, the fairy is a delighted and willing participant.*

These stories were popular in the Middle Ages, especially in Germany and France, that is, at just the right time, and in just the right areas, to be feeding into the tradition of Melusine. This combining of legends helps to explain some of the odd tensions in Melusine's legend. Just as with the fairy marriages, Melusine's partnership is genuinely happy and non-threatening, and her husband is sincerely sorry to lose her, always taking the responsibility for his betrayal as opposed to accusing her of lying to him about being a mystical half-snake woman (something that most people might take rather badly, broken vows or not). These early European traditions can also be seen feeding into stories about the Apennine Sibyl, although the exact relationship between

* The happiness of the fairy sets these legends apart from the stories of selkies, often suggested as inspirations for Melusine. In these tales, the beautiful seal women shed their skin to come on land once a year (or once every ten years, or on some sort of schedule). Prospective husbands must steal the skins, after which the selkie will be forced to remain human, and marry the possessor of their skin. However, these supernatural creatures are miserable in their forced marriages, and the moment they find the skin they return to the sea as seals again. These tales were current in Scotland in the late Middle Ages, with little overlap in England, and certainly no presence in the German and French Melusine hotbeds.

them is harder to parse. The Tannhäuser tradition, outlined above, does suggest a concurrent set of myths which don't involve the snakey transition, but there's no way to tell if these predated the Sibyl or were inspired by it. However, the more general early European ideas of a happy marriage to a fairy creature and a happy time spent in a fairy kingdom almost certainly played a part in shaping the character and tone of the Sibylline legends.

Being a child or a descendent of these fairy marriages was viewed as something to be proud of: a sign of greatness much like being a child or descendent of a god in ancient Greece or Rome.* Perhaps here is the reason why so many medieval nobles claimed Melusine as their ancestor.

Neither Melusine nor the Sibyl quite escape either their demonic connections or the later Christian beliefs which over-laid these pre-Christian fairy stories. In the case of the Sibyl, her lovers have to travel to Rome to seek absolution. Melusine fares even worse: her children are often cursed, and sometimes she is left tormented in hell until Judgement Day. But the European, pre-Christian tradition gives our demons, if only for a short time, a genuinely happy marriage to the highest nobility in medieval Europe and, often, a loving family.

We have seen that the mermaid and Lilith were both very different in secular myth when compared with how they were presented by religious authorities. The succubus Lilith, the stereotype of the other woman who threatened men in Kabbalah was, in Jewish

---

* Take Lancelot, for example, who was said to be the son of the Lady of the Lake (who is herself occasionally connected with Melusine). This is not an embarrassment for Lancelot: instead it is a source of pride and sign that he is destined for greatness.

folklore, a tool for protecting women and children. Likewise the mermaid, the literal man-eater of the medieval church, was a sweetly hopeful singer or a great and noble matriarch in secular literature. But this was to change in the Victorian period where all the positive qualities of our monsters would be dropped, even outside of religious contexts, and Lilith, Lamia and the mermaid were to become the ultimate femmes fatales, luring men (and even the British empire itself) to lust and ruin. The clearest sign of this focus on the negative aspects of these creatures is that the legends about Melusine would almost entirely fade away. Despite being popular enough to form the subject of a Mendelssohn overture and a Goethe short story in the eighteenth and early nineteenth centuries, a serpentine, self-possessed woman who had happy relationships with her lovers had no place in the Victorian imagination.

8

The Monster Outside

I n January 2018 the Manchester Art Gallery removed John William Waterhouse's 1896 painting *Hylas and the Nymphs* from display. Part of an artistic 'takeover' of the nineteenth-century galleries that included masquerade, drag artists and a performer handing out selfies, the removal prompted cries of censorship from critics who wrongly believed that the painting would not be returned. In fact, as planned, it was put back a week later, alongside a small case of comments that visitors had been encouraged to write during the painting's absence. Many of the comments were from visitors riled up about perceived censorship, but there were plenty who, while stressing that censorship is rarely the answer, nonetheless expressed discomfort with the image. It's easy to see why.

The painting depicts the scene described in the third century BC by both Theocritus and Apollonius of Rhodes: Hylas, the lover of Heracles, goes to a lake to fetch water. The lake is inhabited by nymphs who fall in love with him and drag him underwater, killing him in the process. Waterhouse shows Hylas kneeling by the pool, bending over dangerously and surrounded by seven nymphs. The central nymph holds his arm, pulling on it gently and staring hypnotically into his eyes. Another plucks at his tunic, a third offers pearls in her outstretched hand. It's clear that soon the central nymph will tighten her grasp and drag him under, but the painting keeps him in the moment before his death – unbalanced and enchanted.

Many of the issues raised about the image centre on the youth of the nymphs, and how Waterhouse is clearly inviting the viewer to enjoy the naked bodies of extremely young teenage girls. But the problems go deeper than this. Waterhouse is telling us that these girls, despite their youth and apparent innocence, are actually dangerous little Lolitas; that any girl, no matter how sweet and naïve she might seem, could still be setting out to seduce a man, and that – in a blatant contradiction to Victorian reality – this will spell ruin for her lover, and not for her.

It is the painted illustration of Waterhouse's fellow Pre-Raphaelite Burne-Jones' claim that:

A woman at her best, self-denying and devoted, is pathetic and lovely beyond words ... but as soon as you've taken pity on her, you're the one to be pitied, so beware.[1]

In portraying women this way, Waterhouse and Burne-Jones were hardly unique. The treacherously sexual woman obsessed the Victorians, who portrayed her in literature and art again and again. This woman was created almost entirely from the tradition described in this book, combining the forms and myths of Lamia, Lilith, mermaids and sirens. Though she sometimes appears more mature than Waterhouse's nymphs – less a deceptively innocent waif and more a strong, self-possessed woman – she is always the doom of any man foolish enough to fall under her seductive spell, strangling her lovers in her snake-like hair, pulling them down to their watery graves or even sucking their blood. In extreme circumstances she will be the downfall of the country if she goes unchecked. She is the Victorian femme fatale, the 'Monster Outside',* a counterpart to the 'Angel in the House' who represented the chaste, submissive spirit of ideal Victorian womanhood.

Unlike the succubi Lilith and mermaids, the Monster Outside was not limited to religious contexts, and while she was still the embodiment of male anxieties, these were no longer solely related to sex. Instead, they covered everything from concerns about the expansion of women's rights to the perceived degeneration and feminization of masculinity, and even the end of empire.

Although she appears in the form of numerous different demons, the Monster Outside is best understood as a single archetype. People had always been aware of the blurred lines between sirens, mermaids, Lamias and Liliths, but this is the point where they became completely interchangeable, where they collapsed together into a single figure, and a woman sitting by the water with a snakeskin and a hapless male victim could be any one of them. Waterhouse's paintings are a prime example of this – he depicted serpentine, watery women constantly, from mermaids and nymphs to Lamias and witches, and in every image they are

* A term coined by Gilbert and Gubar in *The Madwoman in the Attic* (Yale University Press, 1979).

almost identical. His 1909 *Lamia*, for example, is indistinguishable from the nymphs in his *Hylas*, sitting by a lily-filled pool, lifting her hair on either side of her head in an exact mirror of the pose of one of the *Hylas* nymphs. The snakeskin lying across her legs hints at the Lamia's transformation, but also makes her appear, at first glance, like a snake-tailed mermaid. Snakes that twine around Lilith become the tails of sirens which become singing mermaids, which become pearl-wreathed, watery Lamias.

This serpentine, watery, beauty appears repeatedly – she was such a favourite of the Pre-Raphaelites that in 1897, when Waterhouse exhibited his *Hylas* at the Royal Academy, a critic referred to Burlington House as the 'cavern of the mermaids'[2] because of the sheer volume of paintings of seductive, snake- and fish-tailed women on display. She crops up constantly in literature as well as art, whether 'mermaid' is used to refer to the supernatural creature herself, or as a metaphor for a dangerously alluring woman.

The new interchangeability of these monsters brought in more than just the core group – it extended out, dragging in a whole host of previously unrelated creatures who would henceforth be represented as succubi. In 1905 Herbert James Draper painted a kelpie, a mythical water-horse from Scottish legend who occasionally took the shape of an angry old man. However, Draper's *Kelpie* has no hint of any equine or masculine attributes – instead, she is a beautiful naked woman sitting by a stream, indistinguishable from Waterhouse's Lamias or nymphs.

The easiest way to understand the Monster Outside – who she was, what she did, and why she so beguiled the Victorians – is through her two principal attributes: her snakes and her hair.

Snakes crop up constantly in depictions of the monster. Lamia is almost always painted with at least the suggestion of her previous snake-form, either in the process of transformation, or with a snakeskin wrapped around her. The beaver-based quadruped Lamia who appears in the Middle Ages and the Renaissance was all but extinguished, despite being such a popular motif in previous centuries: the Victorian Lamia is a snake above all else. The mermaid's tail, too, is more consciously serpentine than fish-like – a reversion to its original roots after the period of being firmly fish-based during the eighteenth century. Although Lilith is rarely depicted as the actual snake of Eden itself, she twines it about her naked body (as in John Collier's 1887 painting *Lilith*) or lays it over her legs, often in an overtly sexual manner. This is made explicit in Rossetti's poem 'Eden Bower' where Lilith claims that the snake of Eden was once her lover. In George MacDonald's hallucinatory fantasy novel *Lilith*, serpents flood from her shoulders, and their poison leaks into the wound in her side.

The snake also appears with women who had never before been connected to our demons, a sign that they, like the kelpie, were being made a part of the Monster Outside. In Pre-Raphaelite paintings of Circe, the witch who turned Odysseus' men into pigs in the *Odyssey* and tried to seduce Odysseus himself, the sorceress often wears the necklace of a snake and in Waterhouse's 1892 *Circe Invidiosa*, she stands on a hideous snake-like beast while wearing a dress of serpentine green. Ayesha, the monstrously beautiful femme fatale of Rider Haggard's 1886 adventure novel *She*, appears wearing a clinging, low-cut dress and a belt in the shape of a 'double-headed snake'.[3] Sometimes, snakes are hinted at rather than present, as in Rossetti's seductive 1874 *Proserpine*, where the coiling, climbing, vine framing the image, and the subject's twisting, twining fingers, sinuous neck and wavy hair all gesture to the serpentine.

Snakes have always been important to our demons, from Lamashtu 'creeping in by the door socket like a snake' to Lilith appearing as the snake in the Garden of Eden in both Jewish and Christian lore. It's no surprise, then, to see the snake cropping up in reference to these monsters, but there is a deliberateness to its use in the Victorian era that was never present in any previous incarnations of the demons (or at least not to the same extent). The men who painted and wrote about these creatures no longer believed in them, but were instead using them to make their own myth-based allegories. As such the serpentine nature of these creatures in Victorian England was weighted with a whole wealth of metaphor and meaning that would never have occurred to the Mesopotamians.

Perhaps the most jarring new addition to the mythology is the recasting of the serpent as a distinctly female and erotic creature, an animal made up entirely of seductive and sexual coiling. In *The Ethics of Dust*,* Ruskin populates his Valley of Sinbad with beautiful singing snakes, and in his *Queen of the Air* he describes a snake's motion as being full of feminine curves. Seductive women themselves become snakes, as in Rossetti's twisting, serpentine *Proserpine*, or in Arthur Hacker's faintly ridiculous 1894 *The Temptation of Sir Percival*, which shows the knight perching primly on the edge of a rock while the tempting devil, appearing as a pleasantly chubby woman in a flouncy floral dress, slithers and curves across the ground towards him.†

* A bizarre little book that is part geology, part moral philosophy and part mythology, with the deeply misleading subtitle *Ten Lectures to Little Housewives on the Elements of Crystallisation.*
† The RA did not find the painting remotely ridiculous – it was one of only two by Hacker that they ever exhibited.

But snakes didn't just coil around seductively – in their constantly shedding skins, they were also transformative and changeable, qualities that the Victorians frequently identified as particularly feminine. Occasionally, this is presented as a good thing: Ruskin wrote that 'the true changefulness' of women is that they must be 'infinitely variable' in their service to others.[4] More frequently, though, the transformative power of women was associated with the idea that they were capricious, fickle and untrustworthy, something further stressed by the association between snakes and lying; the notorious untruthfulness of snakes' tongues.

Lamia seemed to be tailor-made for this – the snake who could transform into a beautiful woman, and, as per Keats and Theocritus, could only be revealed by someone who knew her true form. Paintings frequently reference her previous serpent state: in Herbert James Draper's *Lamia* and both of Waterhouse's paintings by this name the monster is shown as a beautiful woman with a snakeskin draped over her legs. In Isobel Gloag's 1890 *The Kiss of the Enchantress*, her transformation is still incomplete – she appears like a land-bound (and gravity-defying) mermaid with a snake tail that ensnares the feet of her knight while she distracts him with kisses. This idea of mutability was transferred onto sirens and mermaids as well. Although these creatures didn't technically transform, their serpentine half could be hidden beneath the water and they could at least appear like beautiful women to the unobservant viewer.

The mermaid-like girl hiding her bestial nature beneath an attractive, charming exterior was used often in literature to refer to non-supernatural monsters. Prominent among these un-magical mermaids is Becky Sharp, the protagonist of Thackeray's *Vanity Fair*. Beautiful, alluring and completely amoral, Becky works her way upwards in society through advantageous marriages and the favours of wealthy men, seducing left and right.

She doesn't care who she hurts on the way, putting down the meek, unassuming Amelia Sedley (who is the ideal of Victorian womanhood, and utterly dull in consequence), and, it is hinted, even murdering her eventual husband Ros.

Thackeray was glad to point out the comparisons between Becky and mermaids – he drew her as a mermaid, smiling and half naked with her tail tucked behind her, and he references her as such frequently in the novel. Finally, he makes the analogy almost entirely explicit:

> In describing this siren, singing and smiling, coaxing and cajoling, the author, with modest pride, asking his readers all around, has he once forgotten the laws of politeness, and showed the monster's hideous tail above water? No! Those who like may peep down under waves that are pretty transparent and see it writhing and twirling, diabolically hideous and slimy, flapping among bones or curling around corpses; but above the water line, I ask, has not everything been proper, agreeable and decorous...[5]

Just as Lamia is able to shift her shape to hide her monstrous form, so Becky is able to appear a beautiful woman by hiding a hideous, murderous snake beneath the waves. But although she can disguise her serpentine nature with her pretty face and charming manners, the snake will always be her true self.

This trope reoccurs constantly in Victorian literature: pretty women who are concealing something – their true feelings, their pasts, their unpleasant tendencies – are described as mermaids or Lamias. Gwendolen in George Eliot's *Daniel Deronda* – a beautiful woman who seduces the wealthy Grandcourt and marries him despite promising his mistress that she won't – is described as having a 'lamia beauty'.[6] Her husband eventually drowns, with Gwendolen herself partially to blame, further driving the connection between her and the murderous sirens. *Middlemarch*'s externally lovely Rosamond, determined to maintain her social standing by concealing her husband's financial embarrassment, is called both a 'siren' and a 'mermaid'. In *Lady Audley's Secret*, the titular heroine seems beautiful and kind, but is also murderous and hiding a dark past, and is unsurprisingly referred to as a 'mermaid' throughout.*

This downgrading of the supernatural in the Monster Outside meant that a serpentine nature could be hidden in almost any woman – you no longer had to be a literal man-hungry, murdering mermaid to be swallowed by the Victorian serpent woman archetype. All you needed to be was beautiful and hiding something, anything, whether it's a murder or an unappealing character trait. Even the Angel of the House herself – the woman described in Patmore's eponymous poem – is a serpent underneath it all. The titular subject, the defining model of the perfect, self-denying woman:

To the sweet folly of the dove,
She joins the cunning of the snake,
To rivet and exalt his love;
Her mode of candour is deceit[7]

---

* *Lady Audley's Secret* suffers from one of the modern issues with a lot of Victorian fiction: we feel sympathy in places we're clearly not meant to. The heroine's dark, unforgiveable secret is that when she was a teenager she was abandoned in penury with an infant by her husband, who popped off to Australia without even telling her. She leaves the child in suitable care and ends up marrying a kindly lord (without telling him about her past), presuming, after many years, that her husband is dead. It's difficult to feel anything but sympathy with Lady Audley, and when her first husband shows up bursting with self-righteousness we might feel he deserves to be pushed down a well.

The Angel may be using her serpentine cunning to praise a man, but it is present nonetheless. No matter how kind, meek and submissive a woman might be, if she is beautiful then she is always a mermaid, hiding the snake beneath the waves.

There is another facet to the monster outside, linked to the transformative power of snakes and women: the vampire. The vampire-as-seducer had been a staple of literature since Polidori's 1819 *The Vampyre*, but in most of the mid-nineteenth-century follow-ups, the vampire is a man, luring unwary women to their doom. It was only in Sheridan Le Fanu's 1872 story, *Carmilla*, that the seductive vampire was a woman (in this case, one who preyed on other women), and this trope was only fully realized by Bram Stoker in his 1897 *Dracula*, which saw the vampire fully incorporated into the lore of the Monster Outside. Most modern adaptations of *Dracula* centre on the eponymous vampire and his own seductive power, the precursor to all the glittery, boyfriend-ready vampires that populated YA shelves in bookshops ten years ago. However in Stoker's original novel the majority of the vampiric characters are female, and the plot revolves around them. From the wives of Dracula who try to seduce Harker in Dracula's castle (and who, Harker is at pains to note, are more terrifying and horrible to him than Dracula himself), to Mina, halting her transformation halfway and using it to lead the band of men to the vampire's lair, vampire women are front and centre. Most prominent of all is Lucy Westenra, the beautiful, sweet girl who, once she is bitten, becomes a violent, seductive monster.

In most adaptations of the novel, Lucy tends to be portrayed as a succubus from the beginning, with her vampire-hood and subsequent destruction used to punish her for her earlier wanton behaviour. In Francis Ford Coppola's 1992 *Dracula* she is at best a confirmed flirt. The much-panned 2020 Mark Gatiss and Stephen Moffat adaptation takes this even further – Lucy is a vain prostitute who begs Dracula to turn her into a vampire so she can be young, beautiful and seductive forever. In these films, Lucy's behaviour as a vampire is not much different to Lucy's behaviour as a mortal.

However, in Stoker's original, the transformation is key. The Lucy of the novel is nothing but kind and meek before Dracula appears – her oft-quoted wish that she could marry all three men who have proposed to her coming from a genuine concern for her suitors' feelings and a guilt that she will have to hurt at least two of them, rather than any voracious sexual appetite. After she is bitten, Lucy is constantly described as having undergone a 'terrible change' as she shifts – like a mermaid or a Lamia – from perfect woman to vicious seductress. When her lover, Arthur, looks on her new form he sees that, like a snake-tailed siren revealing her true self:

[Lucy's] sweetness was turned to adamantine, heartless cruelty, and the purity to voluptuous wantonness.[8]

In this state, she is 'hungry' for her lover and murderously seductive, the Monster Outside incarnate. Like Waterhouse with his nymphs, Stoker is showing us that no matter how lovely a woman might seem she can always turn into a snake – the Angel of the House's serpentine cunning can always be brought to the surface. In his later horror novels Stoker removed the male vampire character entirely, leaving us only with shifting temptresses. In his 1911 *The Lair of the White Worm*, for example, the plot centres entirely on Lady Arabella March, who changes from a beautiful society lady to a hideous, coiling white worm, a clear relative of the Lamia-snake or mermaid tail.

Pre-Raphaelites were delighted to have yet another type of seductive woman to add to their canon, and the painting *The Vampire* by Philip Burne-Jones was exhibited at the RA in 1898. It shows a woman in a white nightdress straddling a sleeping man in his bed, his shirt falling open to expose his neck. The woman, with her dark hair curling around her, shows her teeth as she smiles down at him, preparing to strike. As catalogue copy for this image, Rudyard Kipling wrote his poem 'The Vampire'. As with Becky Sharp's mermaid-hood, here the monstrous nature of the vampire is entirely metaphorical. The woman Kipling describes does not literally drink the blood of her lover, but instead takes his material possessions and his attention, bleeding him dry financially and emotionally before eventually abandoning him to his misery. As in the final verse of the poem:

> The fool was stripped to his foolish hide
> (Even as you and I!)
> Which she might have seen when she threw him aside—
> (But it isn't on record the lady tried)
> So some of him lived but the most of him died—
> (Even as you and I!)[9]

Lamia, Gello and Lilith had always had faintly vampiric tendencies but here in the late nineteenth century they were drawn closer still, as the transformative, seductive vampire became another face of the Victorian femme fatale.

Alongside snakes and snakelike transformations, the Monster Outside had another telltale characteristic – her hair. Weighted with symbolism, a woman's hair could have positive connotations in Victorian England: golden hair could form the angelic halo of a righteous woman, while the 'hair bower' (described with pleasing informality by William Tindal as when 'your girl, lying on top of you, lets her long hair down around your head'[10]) was viewed as an almost sacred space. Browning, in *Pauline*, describes his lover's hair as 'a screen; to shut me in with thee and from all fear'.[11] In Rossetti's *The Stream's Secret*, the hair bower created by his beloved is 'sheltering' him in a 'nest' of 'warm silence'.[12] But even in these cases, the erotic charge of a woman's hair is clear – an eroticism that inevitably came with negative associations when it was connected to the Monster Outside.

Mermaids had been combing their hair since the early Middle Ages, an action used to symbolize female vanity and carrying with it the allure of a normally private action performed publicly. Pre-Raphaelites were happy to paint their mermaids in the act as well. Waterhouse's *The Mermaid* shows the siren coiled up on a distinctly chilly-looking beach dragging a comb through her beautiful locks. This combing-as-seduction transferred easily from the mermaid to other facets of the Monster Outside, so that in Rossetti's painting *Lady Lilith*, Lilith herself looks every inch the mermaid, her glistening, golden hair taking up at least a third of the image as she pulls a comb through it.

But hair was not just alluring – it could also be used to literally ensnare and kill unwary men. On his watercolour replica of *Lady Lilith*, Rossetti attached to the frame the description of Lilith from Goethe's *Faust* (as translated by Shelley):

Beware of her fair hair, for she excels
All women in the magic of her locks,
And when she twines them round a young man's neck
She will not ever set him free again.[13]

Here hair is a noose, an idea repeated by Rossetti in his own poem *Lilith*, where he describes Lilith seducing a man and leaving 'round his heart one strangling golden hair'. The hair-as-snare was also depicted by Waterhouse in his *La Belle Dame Sans Merci*. This painting is based on Keats' poem of the same name, which tells of a beautiful 'faery's child' who seduces a knight and then abandons him, leaving him wandering desolate and forever in her thrall. In Waterhouse's depiction, the Belle Dame leans forward, looping her long hair around the knight's neck, a literal noose of which the knight seems perilously unaware. As with Waterhouse's nymphs, her wide eyes, extreme youth and half-open mouth give her the look of an ingénue being seduced herself, but the way she twines her lover in her trap shows differently. She may appear a naïve young woman, but she is a dangerous seductress, and the knight is surely being led to his doom.

The twining nature of hair allowed it to connect back to snakes, as in *Eden's Bower*, when Lilith commands the snake to:

Wreathe thy neck with my hair's bright tether,
And wear my gold and thy gold together![14]

Even without an actual snake present, hair could be serpentine.* In Christina Rossetti's 'The Prince's Progress', the titular Prince is seduced by a milkmaid who shows her monstrous tendencies by trapping him in snake-like hair:

---

* The ultimate snake-haired woman, Medusa, was, oddly enough, rarely depicted as a seductress herself in Victorian England. Instead she tended to be treated more as that other favoured archetype of Victorian womanhood: the fallen woman. William Morris in his *The Doom of the King Acrisius* depicts her in an especially sympathetic light, with his Perseus eventually killing her out of pity and love to save her from continued torment. Clearly a literal head of snakes was a bit too prominent to be disguised by charming manners, and the rape of Medusa too violent to be considered seduction.

[She] twisted her hair in a cunning braid,
And writhed it in shining serpent-coils,
And held him a day and night fast laid
In her subtle toils.[15]

This snakey, alluring, strangling hair is both what attracts
men to these women and the tool they use to entrap them. It
works as bait as well as a snare because the golden hair that
gives an angel her halo is indistinguishable from the golden
hair of a monster; the hair-bower of a good woman can quickly
become the hair-noose of a femme fatale. Just as with a Lamia
or mermaid disguising her serpentine nature beneath apparent
innocence, failure to discern the monster beneath can have deadly
consequences for unwary men.

The Victorian femme fatale is still instantly recognizable as
our demons – long-haired, seductive and serpentine – but it's
telling that all the positive characteristics of these monsters had
dropped away, along with any danger they might pose to women
and children. Even in 1837, Hans Christian Andersen could
write his Little Mermaid as a broadly good woman, earning
her soul through her silent, painful and unrewarded devotion
to her prince, rescuing men from shipwrecks, never seducing
anyone, and doing good works for a hundred years. By the time
the Pre-Raphaelites were painting a few decades later, this had
been downgraded to the idea that mermaids longed for land
and human lovers, but still, certainly, murdered sailors while
doing so.

In creating the Monster Outside the Victorians had focused
solely on the negative, seductive, dangerous elements of these
myths. By the end of the nineteenth century there could be no
equivocation – these creatures were evil and seductive, and
nothing else. A kindly, sympathetic, non-erotic mermaid was all

but unthinkable in the Victorian era. Why was this? And why were the Victorians so obsessed with their serpentine femme fatale?

1897, the year when Waterhouse exhibited his *Hylas and the Nymphs* at the Royal Academy and a critic described Burlington House as being a 'cavern of mermaids', was also the year that Millicent Fawcett founded the National Union of Women's Suffrage Societies, the largest women's rights association in Britain. A bill for women's suffrage had come perilously close to passing in the Commons, and the perception of a woman's place in society was changing rapidly. Education and employment prospects were improving, with the first four women to ever take degrees in the UK graduating in 1880. Sexual freedom for women was also dawning both socially and legally – by the late 1800s divorce laws allowed women to retain at least some of their property upon leaving their husbands, and procuring a divorce itself was getting easier. Although there was still marked discomfort about women having and acting on sexual desires, there were plenty of role models for it in literature and the real world. The writer George Egerton happily divorced and had a string of well-publicized affairs even while her marriage lasted; Ellen Terry, the actress, divorced her tedious Pre-Raphaelite husband (who had married her when she was only fourteen), had two illegitimate children with the architect Edward William Godwin, married Charles Kelly (another actor) separated from him and went on to have an out-of-wedlock relationship with Henry Irving. In fiction, Nora, in Ibsen's *The Doll's House*, leaves her husband to follow her own wants; in *The Heavenly Twins* by Sarah Grand the protagonist does not allow her husband to consummate their marriage, refusing to give her husband's desires precedence over her own. These women who sought an education, sexual freedom and voting rights were called New Women (a term coined in 1894), and are often connected to the Monster Outside.

Certainly the monster included powerful, politically engaged women – queens and would-be-rulers like Ayesha, Circe and Lilith – and the stories told about them spoke to the dangers of ever allowing these women power. In the uncontainable and dangerous sexuality of the monster there are also elements of the sexual freedom demanded, and taken, by the New Woman, and in the unproductivity of this sexuality (the monster never produces children) there are hints at the New Woman's rejection of motherhood. Bram Stoker came close to making this connection explicit: the New Woman is referenced dismissively in *Dracula*, and while Lucy, the seductive monster who murders children, is brutally killed, Mina, the devoted wife and mother, saves the day.

But there is something missing in this analysis. If it is as simple as Lucy's vampire-bite transforming her from Angel of the House to a New Woman, you might expect her to put on some comfortable clothes and get an education, or involve herself in politics, or ride a bicycle and enjoy light exercise. Millicent Fawcett was not campaigning for the right to chase men around crypts in a skimpy nightdress. *Punch*, always a good barometer of the stereotypes of the day, supports the idea that the New Woman alone was not responsible for the Monster Outside – Punch's cartoonists tended to portray the New Woman not as a seductress but as a sexless spinster or a statuesque Amazon on a bicycle – she is never a simpering flirt. There are certainly elements of concern about the growing women's movements in these monsters, but it is not the entire picture. This is because the Monster Outside was not focused on women – it was focused on men, and male anxieties. And while men were worried about the movement for women's rights, they had plenty of other fears besides.

1897 was also the year of Queen Victoria's Diamond Jubilee. There were parades, imperial and commonwealth conferences, and beacons lit on the hills of England in displays of celebration and power. Superficially, the British empire looked to be at the height of its strength – ruling over a vast portion of the globe and continuing to expand. Internally, there were growing worries about imperial overstretch and imminent collapse. Between the mid and late 1800s the mood of the empire had shifted. Expansion had once been a sign of strength and connected to growing prosperity and power: now it was viewed as necessary for survival. Uprisings of native populations seemed to be continuous, and the fiasco of the Boer War was just on the horizon. Other European nations were also starting to compete, developing and expanding their own empires and challenging Britain in industry and manufacturing – once arenas where Britain had held undisputed power. Even the pre-eminence of the British Navy – the tool with which Britannia 'ruled the waves' – was uncertain. No longer did British supremacy seem unquestioned and unchallenged.

This led to a growing siege mentality in Britain, not helped by its increasing isolation from Europe. So unpopular was British foreign policy that by 1900 it was deemed inadvisable for Victoria to travel to France, and there was an ever-present fear of invasion and a coming European war (notably missing at the Diamond Jubilee celebrations was Victoria's grandson, Kaiser Wilhelm II, out of concerns that he might cause trouble at the event). This was the era of the famous 'invasion narratives': popular novels like *The Riddle of the Sands* (1903) and *The War of the Worlds* (1898) that imagined the invasion of Britain by a foreign enemy.

This declining strength of the empire was tied to what was seen as an increasing permissiveness in British society, and the New Women were only a part of this perceived moral backsliding. The scandals of Oscar Wilde, the dandy movement and a collection of high-profile divorces, as well as the involvement of the Prince of Wales in a gay brothel, were all taken as evidence for a loss of virility and moral fibre. Numerous purity organizations were founded to combat this, many with a terrifyingly nationalistic and militaristic bent. Societies like the Boy Scouts and the Catholic Boys' Brigades were also part of the pushback, aimed at teaching boys how to be one very narrowly defined type of men.

We can see these fears – of foreign invasion, of slipping morality, of 'feminized' men – all coming together in *Dracula*. The book is, fundamentally, an invasion narrative about a foreigner attempting to conquer England: Dracula is clear in his intention to take over the country and the empire. Aiding him are hideous inversions of women, who are irresistible to weak men. Standing against him is Van Helsing, the 'ideal' man, who does not shirk from killing the transformed Lucy, who does not tremble after close encounters with vampires, and who shows Arthur, Lucy's lover, how to behave when he is in danger of giving in to her. It is Van Helsing who persuades the vacillating Arthur to brutally stake and decapitate Lucy when he initially shies away from the task, Van Helsing who jumps between Arthur and Lucy when she advances on him with outstretched arms, and Van Helsing who bodily throws Arthur across the room when it looks like he might go to her himself. Here, Arthur's lack of proper masculinity, his inability to resist or kill the beautiful monster, threatens the downfall of the empire and of social order. Van Helsing, the paragon of manhood, has to show him (and the reader) the right way to behave to avert these disasters.

The hero who can resist the seductive woman appears frequently in relation to the Monster Outside, often as a counterpart to more easily corrupted men. In Waterhouse's *Circe Offering the Cup to Ulysses*, we see the enchantress with her breasts slipping loose from her transparent gown, long hair coiling around her shoulders and the pig men who succumbed to her charms at her feet. She holds aloft the potion-filled cup to tempt Ulysses, whom we see reflected in her mirror behind her, and we know that here is a man who will not be seduced by her (and who will later have sex with her in a 'proper' way – with him in a position of power, rather than her). This is not a painting about the power of women, but about the dangers of losing your masculinity, of giving in to degeneration and becoming a pig at a woman's feet. At the same time it shows the correct way to be a man, in the strong, un-seducible Ulysses.

Sometimes the focus shifts to look solely on the degraded, degenerate men who cannot resist, and their punishment for this failure – whether it is Waterhouse's *Hylas and the Nymphs*, Philip Burne-Jones' *Vampire*, or Edward Burne-Jones' *Depths of the Sea* (where a beautiful, childlike mermaid drags down the lifeless body of a man). The message is clear: Kipling's 'fools', the men who aren't masculine enough to save themselves, their gender and their country, will die horribly. The Monster Outside was not only about New Women and women's rights, but about men terrified of themselves, terrified of losing control, terrified that they might become pigs or fools or just drowned victims if they couldn't push back against the loss of virility, masculinity and empire.

This is the complete usurpation of women's lore – the demons that had originated as a way of consoling women through the very real dangers of childbirth had become, in the late Victorian era, about the fears of men over the imagined degeneration of masculinity.

Although the Monster Outside was particularly tied to the political and social fears of late Victorian Britain, she did not remain attached to this one place and time. By the end of the nineteenth century she had hopped the Channel and appeared in mainland Europe, becoming a favourite of the Symbolist movement and appearing in the works of artists from Gustav Klimt to Edvard Munch. Even more famously, the monster found a new home in twentieth-century cinema in the form of the femme fatale.

The links between the noir femme fatale and the Monster of the Victorians are strikingly direct. Kipling's poem *The Vampire* inspired the 1913 film of the same name, which focused on a beautiful woman, played by Alice Hollister, who seduces a man away from his fiancé before taking everything he owns and leaving him. The title cards even contained verses from the poem, which was often read before showings. Alice Hollister was labelled the original femme fatale of cinema alongside Theda Bara, who appeared in the 1915 *A Fool There Was*, another silent film that riffed on Kipling's *Vampire*. In *A Fool*, as in the 1913 *Vampire*, a man is seduced away from his family and career by a beautiful woman, ending the film a raving drunk. Although the main character is called 'The Vampire' in the credits, she, like the vampire in the poem and Alice Hollister's character in the 1913 film, is not a supernatural being – just a seductive woman who will lead a man to ruin. Films of *She* were also made right through the early 1900s (Georges Méliès even made a version in 1899), always focusing on the ruinously sexual Ayesha.

Throughout the era of the silent film and in early Hollywood, the femme fatale (or 'vamp', a term directly derived from the 1913 and 1915 'vampire' films) continued to be a stock character. Although the symbols of the Monster Outside – the snakes and the coiling hair – were largely abandoned, the fundamental archetype of a dangerous seductress who would destroy any man who fell for her charms remained. Despite never appearing as actual mermaids, the term 'sirens of the silver screen' suggested that their origins were still, to some extent, remembered.

These early 'vamps' were the direct precursors to the femme fatale of film noir and detective fiction. In a genre of twists and turns where nothing is quite as it seems, the femme fatale was perfect as the guilty woman who appears innocent – the mermaid hiding her coiling tail beneath the waves. The great noir writers Dashiell Hammett, Raymond Chandler and James Cain, much like Burne-Jones, all felt that women were at their most treacherous if you pitied them. Carmen Sternwood – baby-ish, and petulantly sucking her thumb when Marlowe first meets her in *The Big Sleep* – is in fact more dangerous than any of the hardened criminals the detective encounters. Brigid O'Shaughnessey in *The Maltese Falcon*, with her wide-open eyes and nervous manner, is a cold-blooded murderer – although Hammett's hero, Sam Spade, is clearly well versed in his siren lore, and identifies her as truly dangerous when she reveals that she is in serious trouble and pleads for his help, throwing herself (apparently) entirely on his mercy. Some film noir dames are more overtly sexual and threatening: in *Double Indemnity*, Phyllis Dietrichson meets Walter Neff dressed only in a towel and almost immediately proposes he help murder her husband. However, even Phyllis is not above playing the victim, telling Neff that her husband hits her, a statement the truth of which we are left to guess at. Mae West, who played many of cinema's foremost femmes fatales, famously claimed: 'There are no good girls gone wrong, only bad girls found out' – the perfect distillation of the Monster Outside and her transformative powers.

Like the Victorians, noir was obsessed with condemning the types of men who fall for the femme fatale, and praising those who resist her. Neff, like Hylas or the vampire's victims, is ensnared by the charms of his monster and ends up committing murder for her, shot by her, and ultimately hanging for her, his only redemption being that at least he brings her down with him. Meanwhile Sam Spade and Marlowe, like Ulysses and Van Helsing, remain un-seduced. Marlowe throws out Carmen Sternwood when he returns home to find her naked in his bed and Spade even specifically states, before he turns Brigid over to the police for murder, that he will not be another in the legion of men who've already succumbed, telling her:

> I'm not going to play the sap for you. I won't walk in Thursby's and Christ knows who else's footsteps.[16]*

This is a man who has peeped down beneath the waves, seen the writhing mermaid tail coiling around her victims and decided he will not be one himself. It is clear that we are meant to feel the actions of men like Walter Neff are understandable – he has been viciously manipulated with the suggestion of sex, after all – but the ideal hero is the one who can turn a woman down flat.

Even in the late twentieth century, there were still plenty of femmes fatales who maintain the classic persona – sexual, transformative and ready to lead men astray through their seduction. Sharon Stone in *Basic Instinct* manages to capture all of this – aggressively

---

* Spade does try to have his cake and eat it in an Ulysses-like way: he still wants to sleep with the femme fatale, but only after she has been stripped of her powers against him. His Circe, on the other hand, seems less enamoured by the prospect: when Spade hands Brigid over to the police and tells her that he'll wait for her if she gets twenty years and 'if they hang you, I'll always remember you', she seems profoundly unimpressed by the idea (as well she might be).

sexual and the ruin of any man foolish enough to fall for her, but nonetheless swinging dizzyingly from monster to victim and back again over the course of the film.

Glenn Close's Alex Forrest in the 1987 *Fatal Attraction* embodies the Monster Outside to an even greater extent. Seductive, self-possessed and rejecting gender roles (in one painfully on-the-nose scene she opts to have sex in the sink on top of some washing up – the 'good' woman of the film, Beth, would presumably just have cleaned the dishes),* this is Lilith once again taking on the role of the ultimate other woman, but in this case her demonic side is also evident in her feminism, her career, her refusal to take a man's lead. Michael Douglas's hapless Dan is the Walter Neff of the piece: presented as all but blameless for falling for her charms, while Alex tempts the otherwise good husband and father away from his home and family and into her arms. In a throwback to earlier iterations of Lilith, she even threatens him with illegitimate children, and is connected to water: emerging from the bath when we first meet her (her arms crossed across her chest as if she is a vampire rising from a coffin, as well as a mermaid coming out of the waves). Alex cannot even be drowned, despite Dan submerging her head underwater in the climax of the film.

The men who wrote, starred in, and directed *Fatal Attraction* were not shy about the fact that, for them, Alex's character represented a takedown of feminism, an attempt to show that women who broke free of gender roles were both miserable and dangerous. The director, Adrian Lyne, claimed that feminism is 'kind of unattractive ... it fights the whole wife role', the scriptwriter James Dearden was clear that 'in reality you don't want to

---

* One can only hope there's a middle ground of womanhood, where you don't have to clean anything but can also have sex somewhere comfortable.

spend your life with a woman like that' ('that' being Alex Forrest), and Michael Douglas stated that he was 'sick of feminists', since 'some women now, juggling with career, lover, children, wifehood, have spread themselves too thin and are very unhappy' (so sweet of him to worry).[17]

The 1982 show *Cheers* (and its spin-off, *Frasier*) features a character called Lilith, a woman who is presented as over-educated, mannish and lacking all the softness and sweetness a woman 'ought' to have. This Lilith is a 'comical' (and viciously misogynistic) depiction of a feminist as a monster – 'weird', constantly called a man as a 'joke', so frigid that her ex-husband claims she could have been used as an ice sculpture at their wedding (although Bebe Neuwirth's acting gives her a vulnerability and depth that the script doesn't suggest). Here, yet again, is our monster as the opposite of what a supposed good woman ought to be. After a few millennia, the entire stereotype feels a little tired.

However, media like *Fatal Attraction* and *Cheers* were some of the last that used these figures to mock (and demonize) women. While monstrous succubi do occasionally still appear in modern media (especially in horror films and video games, where a beautiful woman emerging mysteriously from the woods or the water is absolutely never to be trusted, in a manner any medieval monk would have agreed with), in the twenty-first century, if you do encounter a Lilith in popular fiction, she'll probably be portrayed as an icon, instead of a warning. And that's because, from the twentieth century on, there was a slow-building, and largely successful, movement to reclaim these figures as feminist heroes. After all, what could be more inspiring than a woman who spurned God, her husband, and paradise because she had been denied her equality?

9

Lilith Rewritten

n early 2020, just before the pandemic struck, Calida Rawles' exhibition A Dream for My Lilith was displayed at the VSF Gallery in Los Angeles. The exhibition primarily focused on a series of acrylic paintings showing Black women and girls submerged or part submerged in water. They look entirely self-possessed, eyes closed in private peace as they move their limbs slowly through the swirling water. The images are almost photo-real, but the more you look at them the more you can detect an enhanced, supernatural quality. The water is somehow bluer than it should be, the smooth swirls of the waves deeper and darker than you would expect, and the girls themselves glow, the brown paint of their skin having been mixed with gold and bronze. Combined with their serene expressions, the effect is one of divinity and latent power.

There is a superficial similarity between Rawles' work and Waterhouse's painting *Hylas and the Nymphs* – both, after all, depict beautiful young girls floating in water, and both equate them with iterations of our demons – but they are separated by a vast gulf in understanding and approach. Rawles based her version of Lilith on the story of Ben Sira, interpreted not as a ribald folk tale, or an esoteric legend, or a child-protecting charm, but as the story of a woman who was inherently equal. Made from the same clay as man, this is a Lilith who would rather leave paradise and rebel against God than accept a life of oppression. There is no implication of seduction or danger in Rawles' invocation of Lilith – instead Rawles referenced the demon because she wanted to 'expand on the legacy of Lilith … towards the notion of liberation and strength held in the bodies of black women and girls'. Rawles' Liliths are not something to be feared, but are a source of 'inspired rebellion'.[1]

As with the Lilith of Ben Sira, Rawles' Liliths have faced, and still face, oppression. Despite their peaceful appearance the girls are surrounded by symbols of Black trauma – Rawles links the water in which they float to the water of the Middle Passage, as well as the segregated swimming pools and beaches of the Jim Crow South. In one case, the seemingly random patterns of water and light on a girl's ankle form a map of Coral Springs, where a Black girl was brutally beaten by a police officer. And yet, as with Lilith, even in the midst of their traumas, Rawles' women are powerful, in control and at peace.

Rawles was certainly not the first women to look at the myth of Lilith from a feminist perspective, to identify with it, and draw inspiration from it. As women struggled for equality throughout the twentieth century, the story was re-examined, and has become a tale of female empowerment, drawn on by all types of women – from middle-class housewives to Black women struggling against the dual forces of racism and misogyny, and women in the LGBTQ community. Indeed, more of our demons have evolved to be the symbols of feminist and LGBTQ movements, so that the mermaid, as well as Lilith, once a misogynistic stereotype of a seductive woman, became the last word in joyous femininity, as well as a source of inspiration for trans women.

Even in the nineteenth century there were depictions of our demons that did not cast them as wholly evil beings, especially in the case of Lilith. In Emma Southworth's novel *Lilith: a Sequel to 'The Unloved Wife'*, written in 1891, the (fully human) Lilith is a kind, meek paragon of Victorian womanhood. In a fit of causeless jealousy, her husband, Tudor Hereward, accuses the innocent Lilith of having committed 'unspeakable ... incomprehensible evil' and throws her out of the house. Lilith is blameless – the assumption of evil is there because of her beauty and her gender. Hereward believes the tropes about Lilith and womanhood and by the end of the novel is forced to see the truth, at which point he apologetically takes back his wife.*

The outward symbols of the mythological Lilith are all there – Southworth's creation is beautiful, long-haired, and associated with mirrors – but the novel shows that none of these things can be taken as evidence of Lilith's inner character, and that all the blame for the horrors of her life can be laid firmly at her husband's feet. Tudor might feel himself seduced, or manipulated, by her

---

* Interesting as it is for the purposes of this chapter, the book is almost unreadably bad – Lilith's blamelessness quickly becomes boring, and the plot is full of half-baked contrivances (like a Florentine prince who shows up at the end to marry the kindly ex-lover of Hereward). It was, however, middlingly popular at the time, and ran to five editions over the ten years from its initial publication.

beauty, but that is on him and not on her. Despite Southworth's rather regressive gender attitudes, Lilith is even allowed a righteously furious conversation with Hereward's previous lover, where they both rail at the unfairness of Tudor's behaviour, and men in general.

It is not necessarily surprising that a woman wrote this – this is Lilith from a female perspective, written by someone who could at least imagine what it was like to be accused of seduction simply because they were attractive. Other women were also gently subverting these tropes – George Eliot's 'lamia-like' Gwendolen, for example, is abused and tormented (not to mention horrified that her husband dies), and Eliot certainly wants us to sympathize with her.*

There were men, as well, who were less focused on Victorian concerns about the loss of masculinity and empire and wrote with interest and empathy about Lilith. In Browning's short poem 'Adam, Lilith and Eve' the three titular characters (or, at least, mortal stand-ins for them) are sitting together as friends. Jolted into confessions by a terrifying storm, Lilith admits that she always loved Adam, and Eve admits she never did. This is far from a feminist retelling of the story – Lilith claims that if Adam had only kissed her after she rebelled, she would have been his 'slave – soul, body and all' – but it at least shows an interest in her internal life and emotions (and while Lilith acknowledges she spoke 'venomous' words, she is certainly not evil, or seductive).

C. L. Moore's 1940s story, 'Fruit of Knowledge', although written significantly later, is about another of these tentatively

---

* This does not mean that every woman took this view – there were plenty who clearly agreed with men that Lilith, Lamia and the rest were dangerous rather than inspiring (the author of *Lady Audley's Secret* certainly held no sympathy for her 'mermaid' antagonist).

sympathetic Liliths. It is a story told from the perspective of Lilith, who, as in the *Zohar*, emerged from 'Darkness and Air', long before Adam was made out of clay. She visits Adam in the Garden to persuade him to join her as her partner, planning that they should combine their power to overthrow God. However, over the course of their interactions Lilith finds herself falling for Adam. When she leaves his side one morning she returns to discover that God has replaced her with Eve. Adam, despite claiming that he misses Lilith and wants her back, seems quite taken with the meek, almost childish nature of his new wife and in her fury, Lilith teams up with a serpentine Lucifer to trick Eve into eating the apple. All four of them – Adam, Eve, Lucifer and Lilith – are cast out of the Garden by God as a result, but not before Lilith promises that she will murder Eve's children whenever she can.

Lilith here is still defined as 'evil' and still acts with malice, but there is a distinct feeling that God Himself is not necessarily good, and Lilith's behaviour, while not ideal, is understandable. C. L. Moore is determined to make us empathize with Lilith's hurt and anger at being replaced by Eve, and Adam's preference for a more submissive partner. As with Browning's poem, Lilith seems to be the one who truly loves Adam, extracting a promise that no harm will come to him when she schemes with Lucifer. Eve, meanwhile, has very little loyalty to her husband and is more than happy to have her head turned by Lucifer. Lilith is not an inspirational figure in Moore's retelling, but her frustration over Adam's preference for the docile, almost childlike Eve is comprehensible for any intelligent, powerful woman who has felt that the man she loves might prefer someone a little less smart and a little less empowered.

Lilith also had a positive role in occultism in the late nineteenth and early twentieth centuries, where she was often seen as a powerful, impressive figure rather than a manipulative, evil one. In the religion Thelema, founded in the early 1900s by the famous (and infamous) mystic Aleister Crowley, Lilith was connected to the goddess Babalon (a figure based on the Whore of Babylon), who is identified with female sexuality and liberation.

The works of the late-nineteenth-century folklorist Charles Leland featured Lilith prominently. Leland was not, technically, a pagan or a witch himself, but he made a lot of claims that inspired the movement: he is perhaps best known for proposing that the women murdered as witches in the Middle Ages were, in fact, following a pre-Christian pagan faith that looked a lot like witchcraft. Leland also claimed he had found an actual handbook that was still being used by witches in Tuscany, a claim instantly disputed by almost everyone given how little evidence he provided for his statements (and his inability to produce any of these Tuscan witches) but he nonetheless managed to publicize it widely. In this alleged handbook there are plenty of powerful, witchy goddesses, the most important of whom is Aradia, or Herodias. Leland claimed (with his customary vague shrug in the direction of evidence)* that this goddess was in fact an early form of Lilith.

* He says that 'In Slavonian spells and charms, which are generally very ancient, and of Oriental origin, Lilith appears the same as Herodias' (Leland, *Etruscan Roman Remains in Popular Tradition* (Beyond Books Hub, 1892) p.180). He is presumably referring to a Russian charm, first published in the nineteenth century, that describes a Saint Sisynie driving away twelve daughters of Herod who have emerged from the sea (Herodias being the daughter, or wife of Herod). This sounds a bit Lilith-y, and is undoubtedly based on the Lilith/Gello charm stories, but these 'daughters of Herod' specifically state that they are fever demons, who are there to 'torture all mankind, those who do not rise up early and say their prayers,

In Wicca, a religion developed in the early twentieth century by Gerald Gardener (and which drew heavily on the work of Charles Leland), Lilith is likewise prominent, with Gardener claiming that there had been continuous worship of Lilith from ancient times to the present day. This, of course, is tenuously true – this entire book has, after all, been about the continuity of Lilith – but in Gardener's telling she was a powerful goddess for all this time, which as we've seen is certainly not the case. Lilith was also picked up on by Doreen Valiente, a high priestess of one of Gardener's covens in the mid twentieth century, who claimed that Lilith was one of the most important Wiccan goddesses.*

It's notable that, at least in the beginning, occultism and Wicca were heavily male-dominated religions, the leaders and founders of which all tended to be men. It's tempting to see this as the reason that Lilith was treated so cavalierly by them, run together with a lot of other 'strong' women and female legends, with little effort made to distinguish between them. Crowley's daughter, for example, was named 'Nuit Ma Ahathoor Hecate Sappho Jezebel Lilith Crowley' – a random blend of historical and mythological women he thought were connected – and Lilith was often viewed as another name for various goddesses in a way that completely ignored their very evident differences. Gardener claimed, for

---

who do not keep the festivals, and who indulge in eating and drinking in the early mornings'. These are not child snatchers, or seducers, and this seems like a case of the charm story and protection of Sisinios being repurposed for a different use. It's interesting, but it certainly isn't enough to say that Lilith and Herodias 'appear the same'.

* Doreen Valiente was also famous for joining far-right, white supremacist movements in the 1970s, and then leaving when she found out that they opposed women's and gay rights: a surprising oversight that has led to the suggestion she joined these groups to report on them to intelligence agencies. Those in a less charitable mood might be tempted to point out that she doesn't seem to have raised any issues with these groups' racism.

example, that she was identical to the Mesopotamian goddess Ishtar and the Egyptian Isis, primarily because Ishtar and Isis were also female, powerful and sexual, and despite the fact that these were clearly distinct figures, despite some similarities. Not only was this a fairly intellectually lazy approach to a fascinating creature (biases of the current author aside), it also feels tokenistic – it seems to be saying that sexual, powerful women were so surprising and unique that every single one throughout history must be the same figure, deep down.

However, all this had a relatively minor cultural impact – Wicca, occultism and Crowley all had a degree of prominence in elite circles, and often attracted the attention of the press, but their followers were limited to a handful of individuals. After Lilith's period in the sun during the Victorian era, she faded, to some extent, from popular culture. She was at best an ambiguous figure: powerful, threateningly sexual and associated with a lot of very loose historical interpretations. She might have remained such, had it not been for Judith Plaskow and second-wave feminism.

In 1972, Judith Plaskow, a feminist Jewish theologian, published a Midrash based on the Alphabet of Ben Sira story of Lilith. Lilith, in Plaskow's retelling, leaves the garden because Adam resents their equality and orders her about, trying to make her do all the 'daily tasks of life'. As in Ben Sira, Lilith pronounces the ineffable name and flies away, leaving Adam to complain to God, who dispatches angels to bring her back. When they fail at their task, God makes Eve from Adam's rib, and for a while, everything is peaceful.

However, over time, God becomes increasingly uncomfortable with how closely Adam identifies himself with Him, and worries that banishing Lilith and so enhancing Adam's power was the wrong thing to do. Lilith, meanwhile, is lonely, and tries to breach the walls of the Garden, leading Adam to build them up stronger than ever before. To enlist Eve's help in this, he tells her that Lilith is a vicious demon who kills women in childbirth, but when Eve finally catches a glimpse of her she realizes that Lilith is just 'a woman, like herself' and not a demon at all. Eventually, overcome with curiosity, Eve climbs over the garden wall by way of an apple tree, and meets Lilith. She and Lilith

> sat and spoke together of the past and then of the future. They talked for many hours, not once, but many times. They taught each other many things, and told each other stories, and laughed together, and cried, over and over, till the bond of sisterhood grew between them.[2]

Eventually, the two of them return to the Garden, 'ready to rebuild it together': at their approach, God and Adam both are 'expectant and afraid'.

This is a consciously religious, Jewish text. Over the course of her career, Plaskow spoke time and again on the importance of readmitting Jewish women's experiences to the history of Judaism, pointing out that when only the male side was told, half of the Jewish story was lost. In her famous book *Standing Against Sinai*, she wrote:

> We must render visible the presence, experience, and deeds of women erased in traditional sources. We must tell the stories of women's encounters with God and capture the texture of their religious experience ... To expand Torah, we must reconstruct Jewish history to include the history of women, and in doing so alter the shape of Jewish memory.[3]

This is what is portrayed in 'The Coming of Lilith': God's discomfort at the power of Adam is a reflection of the overvaluing of the male side of Jewish history, and the return of Lilith and Eve is understood as a restoration not just of women's voices, but of a divine order, of the perfection that was unbalanced by Adam's original misogyny. Lilith's return stands for the return of all Jewish women's stories to Judaism and Judaic history. However, despite this explicit religiosity, the story struck a far broader chord, chiming perfectly with the larger discussions of second-wave feminism that were going on when Plaskow was writing.

Second-wave feminism is normally understood to have begun with the publication of Betty Friedan's *The Feminine Mystique*, in 1963. Friedan's book centred on the domestic roles that women were still expected to play: she was concerned by the assumption that women should give up any fledgling careers for husbands and children as soon as they married; that women were generally told their ambitions should be limited to their family. Although second-wave feminism had a lot of (mainly achieved) goals, concerning everything from women's reproductive health to the legalization of no-fault divorce, the overriding message was that women needed a place in the world beyond the home.

In this context, the legend of Lilith told in the Alphabet and then retold by Judith Plaskow feels extraordinarily relevant. Plaskow may have intended her Midrash to be about the rebalancing of Jewish history, the Alphabet may have been trying to tell a fun little charm, but within a movement that was discussing how women should be free of domestic shackles, it reads as a story of a woman who flees from her life of servitude with her husband to find freedom in the world beyond her home.

This new version of Lilith spread immediately as a point of inspiration to other feminists; a spread almost certainly helped by the fact that the majority of the second-wave feminist leaders were Jewish themselves: Betty Friedan, Andrea Dworkin, Germaine Greer, Lily Rivlin, Susan Gubar – all were Jewish or had Jewish backgrounds. In the December of 1972, Lily Rivlin wrote her article 'Lilith' for *Ms. Magazine*, where she meditated on the inspiration provided by the demoness, pointing out that, as every good second-wave feminist should:

> Lilith prefers life without a mate – or at least, a mate like Adam – to giving up her integrity and independence.[4]

More famously, in 1976, *Lilith* magazine was launched, with the tagline 'Independent, Jewish & Frankly Feminist'. The very first issue of this contained an op-ed called 'The Lilith Question', written by Aviva Cantor. This looked at Lilith within an explicitly Jewish context, exploring her relevance to Judaism, and asking whether she could be a 'model for Jewish women', but also clearly tied Lilith into broader ideas. Looking at the Alphabet of Ben Sira, Cantor points out that it is a story of a woman 'immediately recognizing tyranny for what it is' and resisting it – she is 'courageous and decisive, willing to accept the consequences of her actions'.[5] Cantor also further compares Lilith's rebellion to that of a modern woman leaving her home and husband, claiming that Lilith forsakes the 'economic security of the Garden of Eden': the Garden, to Cantor, is the economic safety of the family, of being supported by a husband, happily abandoned when it might stand in the way of equality.

And it wasn't just her leaving home that allowed Lilith to slot perfectly into second-wave feminism. *The Female Eunuch*, Germaine Greer's 1970 book about how women had been separated from their sexuality and libido, was crying out for someone like Lilith as its figurehead. Lilith does, in fact, appear briefly in *The Female Eunuch*, where Greer calls her 'the harlot beckoning from outside the prison of domesticity',[6] sexual in a way Eve is never allowed to be. And Lilith wasn't just sexual: the most famous legend told about her concerns the time she refused sex she did not want with Adam before heading off to sleep with demons: her sexuality is not in the service of men, is not for the pleasure of others, but for her pleasure and hers alone. Again and again, when talking about the myth of Lilith, women stressed her sexual self-possession and her determination to follow her own desires as inspirational, as something that drew them to her legend, and allowed them to rethink their own sexuality.

This sexuality was not just heterosexual, either. On the incantation bowls, Lilith happily seduces women and, given that there had always been a suggestion that Eve had sex with the Serpent of Eden, there's certainly a frisson when Lilith appears as the snake herself. When Lilith and Eve side with each other in Plaskow's Midrash, their relationship could be read as romantic as well – Eve is fascinated by Lilith's beauty and strength – and this probably isn't a coincidence: Plaskow herself came out as lesbian in the 1980s.

Lilith still chimes with the LGBTQ experience today – in a 2018 article for the blog Autostraddle, Aliza Cohen discussed how it wasn't just Lilith's relationship with Eve that drew her to Lilith's legends, but the fact that she was forced to leave her home to find freedom. In a world where those in the LGBTQ community may not be safe with their own families, where LGBTQ youth are often made homeless by parents who reject them for simply being who they are, this is an important aspect of Lilith's legends. As Aliza puts it:

I suspect this shared experience is what draws so many of us to Lilith, and to each other. She knows what it is to choose liberty over home, family, and God. She knows what it is to choose exile. After all, there are plenty of lady-monsters, but only one who knew, and fled, Paradise.[7]

Lilith's significance was not just limited to feminist and LGBTQ spaces – she was appearing once again throughout popular culture, restored to a significance she had not known since the Victorian period, albeit often with a new feminist-y twist. Lilith joined the Marvel comic cannon in the later 1970s (in this case, she was the daughter of Dracula), and while she was still clearly intended for the assumed male readers – painted in skin-tight suits thrusting out her chest – the authors of her first outing (Marv Wolfman and Gene Colan) did link her to feminism (if with painful clumsiness) by having her going around violently avenging abused women. The icy, highly educated, self-possessed Lilith on *Cheers*, meanwhile, was likely given her name to make it clear that she was a parody of feminists and feminism. Since Plaskow's Midrash, Lilith has starred in countless films and TV shows (Michelle Gomez as Lilith in *The Chilling Adventures of Sabrina* is a personal favourite), there have been operas written about her, heavy metal albums named after her, and she appears repeatedly in video games. The feminists had brought Lilith back into the popular consciousness.

One of the casualties of this new, feminist Lilith was Eve. Although in Judith Plaskow's Midrash Eve joins forces with Lilith, in most interpretations Eve is portrayed as a traitor to her gender, a colluder, a woman who accepts her inferiority, who doesn't have the strength to leave the Garden. Where Lilith decides that she will have her equality, where she leaves paradise to find it, where she refuses to accept her lot, Eve remains, the helpmeet of Adam, made not out of the equality-giving clay but from her husband's rib. C. L. Moore casts her as a simpering child, Lily Rivlin calls her 'a submissive, blonde creature', and in her op-ed 'The Lilith Question', Aviva Cantor specifically calls out Eve as an enabler-in-chief, and claims that in contrast to Eve:

> Lilith is the embodiment of the woman who refuses to be an enabler.*[8]

There are certainly women who spend their lives reinforcing misogyny, and are viciously sexist themselves – and others who just quietly support the systems into which they were born. Women trying to achieve equality have often faced an astonishing degree of hatred from other women, and it's no surprise that plenty of the interpretations of Lilith come with this anger for those who seem content to accept their lot, or who try to hurt, and not help, those who want something more.

However, this doesn't mean that every woman who stays in her metaphorical Garden is meekly accepting her fate. Cantor lauds Lilith for abandoning her 'economic security' and 'accepting the consequences' of her actions, but there are plenty of women for whom outwardly standing up to misogyny, fleeing

---

* Also accused of being part of the patriarchy were those women throughout history who had used amulets against Lilith, who, according to Lily Rivlin, were also Eves, encouraged by men to 'weave charms and carry amulets for protection against their own repressed instincts'. The closest Rivlin gets to acknowledging that perhaps women were using these amulets for their own healthcare is to suggest that there might have been a caring, maternal version of Lilith who women used to pray to, an idea without any basis in historical fact.

their oppressors, and building a new life is impossible, who are trapped by systems that they cannot escape.

This was one of the major criticisms of second-wave feminism – that it was focused on middle-class women for whom embracing freedom came at a cost, certainly, but a cost that was affordable. Lilith is brave and rebellious, but at the same time there is no real suggestion that staying in the garden would have been a good idea – the choice she has to make is clear. But what about women who cannot leave? This is something addressed in one of the most interesting and nuanced treatments of the Lilith legend: Octavia Butler's 1979 sci-fi novel *Dawn*.

In *Dawn*, Lilith is a Black American woman who, along with the rest of humanity, has been abducted by aliens and kept in suspended animation on their ship. These aliens can only reproduce with another species and want to use humanity to breed, reviving Lilith so she can bear their offspring and reconcile the surviving humans to their fate. Despite the sci-fi setting, the comparisons with Lilith's myths go beyond the heroine's name – the alien ship is a living organism, and the interior of it seems like a garden. The aliens themselves are covered in serpentine appendages and place Lilith in an Adam-like situation with a human man who assumes it is his right to have sex with her and attempts to rape her when she refuses his advances. Given that Lilith eventually bears a human/alien hybrid child, she ends up producing a species of creatures that are viewed by most humans as 'demonic': Butler's Lilith becomes the mother of all monsters. However, the story is not just a surface-level mirroring of Lilith's myth. Instead, Butler uses the story of Lilith to meditate on the nature of consent and freedom in a situation where people have little to no control or power.

Butler's examination of this hinges on one striking difference between the legendary Lilith and her own heroine: Butler's Lilith cannot flee the garden. She is imprisoned on the alien ship, and although she desperately wants to leave there is no way out. There is no suggestion that she desires freedom any less than her mythical counterpart, or that she is any less mentally free – she is simply in a situation that she cannot escape.

This makes all of her choices infinitely more complex (something reflected in her surname – Iyapo – a Nigerian word that translates as 'hard choices'). She must do what the aliens ask: it is quite clear that if she refuses, she will be put back into suspended animation with no suggestion that she would even be woken again. This means that she has to find her freedom where she can – by refusing certain low-stakes requests or by trying to get the aliens to see her point of view. She does this partly for self-preservation, and partly with an eye to the future: she knows that she might be able to use the extremely limited power she has to advocate for humanity and try to win them extra freedoms. She becomes, to some extent, the mother of humans as well as demons, and, along with her continued presence in the garden, this gives her an Eve-like role. Through Lilith's struggles, Butler helps us see that perhaps Eve was as desperate for freedom as Lilith was, just trapped in a position where she couldn't flee her oppressors.

Butler's Lilith even has echoes of the Virgin Mary, and allows for a re-examination of her myth as well. The alien/human child is conceived when Lilith and her human lover Joseph have sex while 'supervised' and 'aided' by the all-powerful alien, who impregnates her. Lilith, like the Virgin Mary being impregnated by God, has very little control in the situation. Technically, the alien has asked for her permission, but, as with everything else, it's clear that Lilith has no real power to refuse. Butler's telling suggests that even the Virgin Mary, the supposed ideal of submissive womanhood, is as mentally free as Lilith (and Eve): her inability to turn down the all-powerful being who has decided that she must bear its child has no connection with her desire to escape. Even Mary, the mother of God, is not an enabler, but a trapped woman trying to do the best she can in horrible circumstances.

Butler also shows us that all of this coercion, all of this unwanted childbearing and sexual assault, is almost harder because the aliens are outwardly non-violent, and always ask Lilith's permission, even though all of their asking is backed by the fact that, if she refuses, she can be put back into suspended animation again. This forces Lilith to collude in her own imprisonments and assaults, actively doing the bidding of her captors with the appearance of it being of her own free will. She is even accused of collaborating with the oppressor aliens by other human women, just as Eve was in Butler's time.

Butler talked and wrote extensively about this tendency to blame those without the freedom to resist for 'accepting' their own oppression. In one interview she spoke of how, as a child, she had tagged along to some of her mother's cleaning jobs. Hearing the vile things that her mother's (white) employers said about her, while her mother went 'selectively deaf'; watching her mother submissively enter through back doors, Butler admitted that she had initially blamed her for refusing to stand up for herself – for her apparent obedient acceptance, like Eve, of her situation. It was only later that Butler realized her mother's behaviour was what kept her fed and housed; that as defiant as her mother may have wished to be – may well have been internally – there was no other course available to her if she wanted to care for herself and her child. When writing about her grandmother, Butler talked of how she spent her life washing clothes, cutting sugar cane, and having children. This, Butler said, was the 'kind of life that she had no choice but to live'.[9] It was exactly the sort of grim domesticity that second-wave feminists thought women should shrug off, but Butler was clear that her grandmother (and women like her) should not be criticized for not having a moment of glorious rebellion and leaving it all behind. Undoubtedly she would have done so if she could. Butler wants us to understand that no one is an enabler for living this way: that the oppressed must not be blamed for their oppression, and that living with oppression when there is no other way to survive is not the same as accepting it.

This was an argument of particular importance to Black women in the 1970s: within the Civil Rights movement at the time, there was also dismissal and blame for those who were seen as having colluded with their oppressors – but who were, themselves, slaves. Malcolm X, in his famous speech 'Message to the Grassroots', talked about the slaves who worked in the house of the slave-owner, claiming they 'loved the master more than the master loved himself'. These slaves were often women (and being a house slave often involved sexual slavery as well as domestic chores) – and were frequently portrayed using the cheerful 'mammy' stereotype, or even as willing, if dependent, lovers.

Octavia Butler addressed these issues in the specific context of slavery in her novel *Kindred*, where a modern Black woman, Dana, time-travels back to a plantation. Through Dana's eyes we see the lives of women like Alice, a slave repeatedly raped by her owner, who has her will broken over time, and Sarah, someone who Dana initially views contemptuously as a 'mammy' figure, before eventually understanding that her apparent submission is brought about by fear that her last remaining child might be sold, and thus separated from her permanently. These women are not colluders or enablers, as Malcolm X would have it – they are trying to survive, trying to protect their loved ones where they can, in a situation where there are no good options. In many ways, *Kindred* is Butler's response to the Civil Rights movement's arguments about Black women as collaborators, and *Dawn* is her response to the white feminists. Although both novels are fantastic, it must have been incredibly frustrating to have to spell out the same lessons to both of the progressive movements Butler was involved with.

Despite this, Butler's writing is too nuanced to categorize *Dawn* solely as a rebuke to the wealthy, white feminists who had the freedom to flee their home and husbands if they wanted to, and who claimed anyone who didn't was an enabling Eve. Butler might have taken the problems with this view as a jumping-off point, but she uses them to explore something much more interesting and wider-reaching, refusing to allow for any sort of simplification.* Nonetheless Butler makes us see that Eve was even more trapped, though just as desperate for freedom as Lilith was – that the people who cannot fly free are just as valuable, and may be striving as much as they can for their emancipation: that simple survival can be a means of resistance, and one that we, the children of those who survived, should be grateful for.

This is a treatment of Lilith that far surpasses the limits put on her legend by second-wave feminists, and considers issues that apply to a far wider range of women. And our monsters would also surpass their original setting of second-wave feminism in the inspiration and understanding they have provided to trans women.

* She never did – when asked why she had given the Black, female protagonist of *Kindred* a white boyfriend, she replied that it was to complicate things, as if being a 1960s Black woman time-travelling uncontrollably back and forth from modernity to the antebellum south was not already complicated enough.

Lilith is an important figure in the trans movement. Her name is taken by numerous trans women – one, an incredible woman who moved from Pakistan to Germany and now works with transgender refugees, stated that to her, 'Lilith was the woman who was always there',[10] a neat blending of her own internal womanhood and the idea that Lilith, as the first woman, has always been around. Again, the issue that trans women (and the LGBTQ community in general) all too frequently face – that they are often forced to leave their families, their communities and the lives they have known in order to be true to their selves – makes Lilith a sympathetic figure. As Shana Carroll, a trans woman who was obliged to leave her career as a pastor when she came out, wrote:

> Like Lilith I have had to flee what was a career, and a community.[11]

However, as significant as Lilith is for some trans women, another one of our creatures has more significance still: the mermaid.

Over the twentieth century mermaids saw perhaps more change than any of our demons. Especially after the Disney film of 1989, mermaids became associated less with seductive femmes fatales, hiding their grotesque, serpentine tails, and more with the ultimate expression of femininity. If someone was accused of being a mermaid today, or was portrayed, as Mary Queen of Scots was, as a mermaid themselves, it certainly wouldn't communicate that they were leading men astray with their sexuality. Instead, mermaids are associated with princesses, with girliness, sequins and prettiness (not to mention fabulous hair and make-up). Mermaid tails are no longer the grim, slimy things of Thackeray, writhing just under the water level, but incredible, iridescent silicone fins worn by 'mermaid' swimmers. This in itself is a reclamation – a trope that was used to attack women for being overly sexual, turned into a glorious celebration of glitter, rainbows and femininity.

Moreover, mermaids have been entangled with queer narratives since the publication of Hans Christian Andersen's *The Little Mermaid*. Andersen was himself bisexual, and his tale of the mermaid yearning unrequitedly for a prince who only ever cares for her platonically (while he marries the princess he truly loves) was written after Andersen was rejected by Edvard Collin, who found himself 'unable to respond' to Andersen's affections.

This queerness comes through even more strongly in the Disney film. The music was written by Howard Ashman, himself a gay man, and included 'Part of Your World', a song about a desperate longing to be somewhere different, to be accepted in a different community.* The hatred Ariel's father has for land, and his destruction of Ariel's hoard of human objects, mirrors the bigotry and lack of acceptance that many queer people face from their own parents. Even drag queens make their way in, with the joyously camp sea witch Ursula modelled heavily on the drag legend Divine.

Along with all this femininity and queerness, the appeal of the mermaid myth to trans women also comes from the fact that the story of the Little Mermaid itself focuses on the trading of

* Tragically, Howard Ashman died of heart failure caused by HIV/AIDs in 1991 when he was only forty-one, having written for musicals including *Little Shop of Horrors*, *Beauty and the Beast* and *Aladdin* as well as *The Little Mermaid*. The dedication of *Beauty and the Beast*, which was released only a few months after his death, is: 'to Howard Ashman, who gave a mermaid her voice and a beast his soul, we will be forever grateful'.

Ariel's tail for legs. As Janet Mock wrote in a 2017 article for *Allure* magazine:

> Like Ariel, I was told I wasn't a real girl because of my body, and this common struggle to be seen as normal, to just belong, tethered my trans girl self to Ariel's mermaid girl self. Plus, it didn't hurt that my childhood heroine was gorgeous – the epitome of femininity – despite struggling to exist in an untraditional form.[12]

Even without the transition narrative of the Little Mermaid story, the mermaid tail renders genitalia irrelevant and invisible – unimportant to the identity of any mermaids we encounter. It is no surprise that mermaids are used as the logo of charities like the Trans Kids Purple Rainbow Foundation, or as the name of the UK trans charity Mermaids.

In one other way trans women can also end up feeling a grim kinship with the mermaid. As Janet Mock wrote, again in her article for *Allure*:

> Like mermaids, trans women are wrongly accused of seducing men, which is one of the driving factors as to why the killings of trans women of colour are largely left unsolved and under-investigated.[13]

The idea that trans women are a seductive danger to men – to such an extent that the so-called 'trans panic defense'* is still

---

* This legal strategy allows a defendant to claim their violence was precipitated by learning that a sexual partner (or even a potential sexual partner) was trans, and has led to reduced sentences for murderers as recently as 2013.

a legitimate legal strategy for murderers – bears with it all the hallmarks of our monsters, not least the idea that the responsibility for male sexual behaviour and violence lies with anyone but men themselves.

Although some of our demons have faded into insignificance (Lamia and Gello have very little name recognition in the modern world), figures like Lilith and the mermaid are progressive cultural touchstones. They appear again and again in our stories, often with feminist and LGBTQ positive spins (no matter how clumsily executed). Their names are attached to numerous organizations and charities – from the feminist, Jewish magazine *Lilith*, numerous trans charities, to the Lilith Fair (an all-woman music festival held in the 1990s) and the Lilith Fund (a charity that helps women fund abortions in Texas).

They have proven enormously adaptable to women's causes – symbolizing everything from the need to leave home and husband to find equality to sexual freedom and LGBTQ rights. Some of this significance is undoubtedly because Lilith's story in the Alphabet of Ben Sira is just an astonishingly inspirational one, if you want to read it that way – the legend of a woman who refuses to live a life of oppression and defies every possible authority, from her husband to God Himself, to make her own path.

From ancient Greece through to the modern day, our monsters have been used as embodiments of every type of unacceptable womanhood – and unacceptable womanhood, it turns out, has existed in almost every form. Our monsters hate children, want to be mothers more than anything but are unable to be, and are the mothers of multitudes. They are incredibly beautiful, hideously ugly, ugly but able to appear beauties; they are vulnerable young girls and women who are 'past their prime'; they have hunted men down for sex, turned men down flat, been too sexual and too frigid, too feminine and too manly. They are self-possessed queens, and innocent ingénues. They have been both too vain, and scorned for the fact they don't take enough time over their appearance. They have had penises, vulvas, and no genitalia at all. It is no wonder that so many women identify with our monsters: at one point or another, they have embodied almost every aspect of womanhood.

There are women who are more likely to be demonized: women of colour especially are exoticized, sexualized, and accused of being too masculine, too loud, too angry, to a vastly higher degree than white women, and men have used (and are, appallingly, still using) the idea that trans women are nefarious seducers to get away with hideous crimes. But the catalogue of our demons' qualities is a clear demonstration of what every woman knows on some level: there is no way of being a woman that can keep you safe from demonization, that frees you from criticism. And while this is a depressing realization, it's also a freeing one – if you'll be painted as a monster no matter what, you might as well make your own choices, and take control of your own destiny, rather than attempting to mould yourself to a contradictory ideal of womanhood that can be taken away from you no matter what you do. As symbols of 'unacceptable' women, Lilith and our demons are symbols of us all.

Epilogue: Survival

Among the ancient ruins and fertile fields of the Greek island of Naxos, you can find Apiranthos, a village of around a thousand inhabitants built across the gently undulating foothills of Mount Fanari. Founded in the 1400s, the village is all tiny cobbled lanes and Venetian architecture,* dominated by a jarringly huge fortress tower and boasting a glorious five museums. It feels like a place that preserves and values its history, and it must have looked very similar to how it does now when an anthropologist named Charles Stewart visited it in the 1980s.

While he was researching the folklore of the community, Stewart was told by some of the older women that they used to recite what they called 'the Yalou prayer' over their children, to prevent a demoness from strangling them in the night.[1] The prayer, as they described it, was an exorcism wrapped in a legend, which told the story of a woman named Melitini, whose six children were murdered by the Yalou. When the seventh child was born, she hid with it in a tower, but her brothers, Saint Sisinios and Saint Isidoros, begged her to let them in. When she

---

* The Venetians ruled Naxos for about 200 years, built some lovely houses, failed to defend the island against Ottoman raids, and eventually ceded the taxes from it to the Ottomans while largely continuing to run the island themselves. The whole lot of them, Venetians and Ottomans alike, were driven from power in the Greek war of independence in the nineteenth century.

finally relented and opened the door, the Yalou crept in with them, strangling Melitini's child. The brothers chased the Yalou to the sea, and forced her to reveal her names, which can be used to defend any infant against her.

Although Stewart was told that this charm was rarely used anymore, there were other precautions that women still observed: to prevent a Yalou trailing a person to their house and murdering any unbaptized children inside, mothers placed a cross made from cane and a piece of bread beneath their child's pillow, and hung reed crosses on the doors and windows of the house. Women also refused to leave a child's clothing hanging outside to dry at night, lest a Yalou should cling to it. One woman told a story of the time the devil attacked her when she was unchurched (that is, during a period of supposed impurity occurring in the forty days postpartum), and Stewart noted that in other towns on the island the same story was told with the Yalou taking the place of the devil.

Sometimes, the Yalou shades into another creature, the Lamia, which was known to attack children, and also swam in the seas around the island. Sometimes, recalling the ancient Empousa, this Lamia was said to have goat legs. If any handsome young man should take a dip at midday, it was said she would drown him. In some tellings, the Yalou also had a habit of drowning people in the sea, blurring these monsters further until, in some contexts, Stewart deemed it impossible and largely pointless to try and separate them.

In some ways, the story of the demons that has been described in this book is a deeply disheartening one. Their tradition was initially something that gave women a degree of comfort and control in the horrifyingly dangerous situation of childbirth and pregnancy, and helped them through times when their children were sick or dying. Over time, however, it was appropriated by men, who co-opted these demons into appallingly misogynist stereotypes that focused entirely on men's own imagined fears (no matter what Peter Damian seems to have thought, it doesn't seem likely women were queueing up round the block to seduce him). At the same time they mocked women for believing in these figures and using them to try and keep themselves and their children safe.

But this is not a history of men overpowering women and women's stories. We have already seen how the figure of the succubus has been repurposed as a symbol of women's rights, and here, in the folklore of Apiranthos, we can see the survival of the monsters that helped women through pregnancy and the illness of their children, almost unchanged across the centuries. Here are Gello and Lamia, alive and well, snatching children, dwelling in the sea, part of the legend of Melitene and Sisinios, just as they had been for thousands of years. These stories were passed from woman to woman across millennia (barring the occasional seductive Lamia story, it was only women who told Stewart about the Lamia and the Yalou, only women who remembered the Yalou prayer). These child-snatching demons have crossed continents, facing ridicule and censure from those in power, and yet here they are, in the 1980s, just as they always were. They survived far beyond Apiranthos as well: stories about the Albasty demon, child-stealing, metal-clawed and inhabiting riverways, are still widely attested in the Caucasus. In Jerusalem, charms are still sold (if rarely) to ward off Lilith from children and the childbed.

Over the last century, belief in these demons has certainly ebbed. In Stewart's study of Apiranthos, the Yalou charm was only remembered and not in current use, and while mothers tended to take in their children's washing before night fell, and still used cane crosses to ward away the Yalou lest it followed them home, most claimed that these monsters no longer attacked children as much as they used to. There were, overall, what Stewart called 'present day reservations about the existence of these monsters'.[2]

Stewart himself suggested that this was because of the introduction of street lights to the village: with the darkness easily driven away, the demons that lived in it vanished too. This is a suspiciously pat explanation (and one that certainly doesn't explain why a midday-murdering Lamia would have vanished as well), and it seems unlikely that it's the entire story. The reasons for the fading of these sorts of folk traditions are numerous and complex – encroaching modernity, increasing access to education (and Stewart's street lights) all undoubtedly had some impact.

However, it seems especially likely that advances in modern medicine, especially in maternal and infant care, had a significant impact on beliefs in our demons. Over the course of the nineteenth century, C-sections went from being a method of extracting a baby from a dying woman to a way of saving both mother and child; with the development of antibiotics into the twentieth century, there was finally a way of treating puerperal fever, one of the worst killers of new mothers; doctors (at last) listened to the research that said they should wash their hands before assisting in a birth;* blood transfusions (first developed in the nineteenth century) were able to save women who would otherwise have died from haemorrhages. Abortions were made available to end dangerous pregnancies, and contraception meant that women

---

* It was discovered that the unwashed hands of doctors were a leading cause in maternal deaths in the early 1800s, but it took until the 1900s before any real changes were implemented on the basis of this.

could limit the number of births they went through in their lives, thus limiting their overall danger of dying in childbirth. Meanwhile, improvements in hygiene, including proper sewage disposal and access to clean drinking water, reduced infant mortality dramatically. Formula milk was available, allowing infants to be fed even in cases where the mother could not breast-feed. Vaccinations prevented children from dying of illnesses from diphtheria to measles, and non-viable pregnancies could be terminated – still an agonizing decision for any woman, but something that at least prevents the trauma of giving birth to a child only to watch them die (and potentially harm the mother as well). Although infertility still affects many couples (around one in seven in the UK), there are now treatments for it, covering everything from sperm and egg donations to IVF, and the expansion of women's rights means that children are no longer seen as the be-all and end-all of a woman's life.

In the UK today, around 1 in 10,000 women die in childbirth, instead of the 8 in 100 women prior to the modern period. The infant mortality rates have also improved dramatically – it's estimated that around 4.3 per cent of children die in the UK before their fifth birthday, as opposed to the 33 per cent that never made it to adulthood for most of history. Each one of these deaths is an appalling tragedy, but they are no longer the norm.* And it's not just that mothers and children are safer: if a

---

* Not that we should get too smug about maternal healthcare – there are still a shocking number of issues with it, from the systematic racism of the healthcare system that leads to higher maternal mortality rates for Black mothers to the arguments that still rage around contraception and abortion, from the exclusion of trans men to the inequality of maternal healthcare provision around the world. As the far right seek to make parts of reproductive healthcare illegal, maternal mortality rates will only rise. We have come a long way, but there is still much further to go.

mother today is worried about her child's health, or her own, the (relatively) easy access to healthcare and the trust in its efficacy means she is more likely to call a hospital or doctor than turn to an amulet.

For millennia, the men who mocked our demons as old wives' tales had little to offer in their place. When Plato suggested that in his ideal republic women would no longer tell stories about our monsters, he wasn't proposing a robust maternal and infant healthcare programme to replace them. He just wanted the women and children who were dying in droves to do it more quietly.* Some ancient men explicitly stated that women should not be emotional about the loss of their children (whether they should be emotional about the risks to their own lives was apparently not even worth discussing). The Christian church, meanwhile, could only suggest that women do penance for their sins if their children died, and often refused to baptise children until they were a few days old, dooming those that died earlier to hell (or at least limbo), despite the pleas of mothers (life certainly did not begin at conception for most of the history of Christianity). The new, male-orientated versions of the demons were similarly unhelpful: mermaids had no connection to mothers or children, while the Kabbalistic version of Lilith had absolutely nothing to say about maternal mortality and largely ignored her

---

* He did want all children to be reared as a group, bred only from the eugenically desirable men and women, and without a specific mother (or father) figure to care for them (Plato did, occasionally, have good ideas, but he had an absolutely uncountable number of terrible ones as well). This might mean that mothers would be less attached to their children if they did get ill (although the idea of being separated from your child, and then having to watch it suffer from a distance, is perhaps even more horrific), but Plato didn't have the imagination to propose anything that might limit infant mortality, or help mothers through childbirth.

child-killing. Even where Lilith was responsible for children's deaths, it was suggested that she killed them because of their own sins, or the impure thoughts of their fathers – the Lilith of the Kabbalah offered women no comfort, no help, no sense of control.

With these as the alternatives, it's no wonder women went on with their demons as they had before. But with the advent of modern medicine, for the first time, Liliths, Lamias and Gellos were up against something that could save the lives of women and their children. It's difficult not to draw the conclusion that the child- and mother-killing iterations of our monsters have faded from view in the last few decades only because they are, at last, no longer needed.

There is too much in the history of our demons that strikes a chord with anyone familiar with women's healthcare – the neglect of women's needs and the idea that women should suffer in silence are all still issues in the modern day. As women's reproductive healthcare and rights come under increased assault, we must remember these horrors, and how prevalent they were – must remember what happens when women are denied life-saving abortions and treatments. Where women's voices were often silenced or unrecorded through history, or overwritten by male sources (the fact that a few male ancient authors stated that women *shouldn't* get upset if their infants died led to a now debunked hypothesis that women actually *weren't* upset), our demons are a testament to what women and their children have faced for millennia, to the heartache, pain, and terror of bearing a child in the pre-modern world.

But our demons are also a testament to the resilience of women's traditions and beliefs: surviving for millennia, for the most part either ignored, mocked or appropriated by men, but passed nonetheless from woman to woman down through the centuries, vanishing only when women had found a new way of protecting themselves and their children. Spanning over 4,000 years and crossing continents, the tradition described in this book is one of the oldest and furthest-reaching continuous traditions of humanity. Against seemingly insurmountable obstacles, the story of our demons is the story of the triumph of woman's lore.

Appendix

I n some translations of the Bible, both the sirens and the Lamia
haunt the ruins of the divinely destroyed cities Edom and
Babylon, but the links between the two go further than this
surface similarity and are evidenced most clearly by comparing
different early translations of the Bible. Biblical translations are
a complicated, incestuous mess, but the versions that have most
to do with mermaids, sirens and Lamias are the Septuagint and
the Vulgate (and the original Hebrew text).

The Septuagint was a Greek translation made in the third
century BC in Alexandria. With no offence to the seventy-two
scholars Ptolemy II supposedly assembled to make it, it is a
very free translation of the Hebrew, often veering wildly away
from the original text, sometimes for reasons that are entirely
unexplained, and inexplicable. Despite these shortcomings, as
the first translation of the Hebrew Bible into Greek it became
the accepted text of the Old Testament in the Christian Church.
There were Latin translations circulating, known as the *Vetus
Latina*, but these were made from the Septuagint (or an alternative Greek translation), and were not particularly reliable.

In around AD 390, St Jerome went back to the Hebrew texts
and made a Latin translation directly from these. At first this
translation was used alongside the Septuagint (and the *Vetus
Latina*), but increasingly Jerome's version grew in popularity,
eventually earning the name 'Vulgate' (or, 'commonly used'). In
the sixteenth century, this was affirmed as the official Latin Bible

of the Catholic Church. But just because Jerome was setting himself apart from the Septuagint and going back to the original Hebrew didn't mean that his work was completely free of its influence. He kept in things that the Hebrew never mentions but that appear in the Septuagint, and in his commentaries he refers to it repeatedly.

Comparing Jerome's Vulgate with the Septuagint and the Hebrew text gives us considerable information about the siren-mermaids, and their connections to the Lamia. The first set of passages to look at is Isaiah 13:21–22, where the desolation of Babylon is described:

Septuagint:

Now beasts make their home there
and an empty echo is heard in the houses.
Sirens have their habitation there
and demons dance.
Onocentaurs dwell there,
and hedgehogs breed in the halls

Vulgate:

But wild beasts shall rest there,
and their houses shall be filled with dragons
and ostriches shall dwell there,
and the hairy ones shall dance there
and owls shall answer one another there,
in the houses thereof and **sirens** in the temples of pleasure

Hebrew:

But wild beasts of the desert shall lie there;
And their houses shall be full of owls;
and **owls** shall dwell there,
and satyrs shall dance there.
And the wild beasts of the islands shall cry in their
desolate houses,
And **jackals** in [their] pleasant palaces.

Jerome's inclusion of sirens in this passage is presumably down to the influence of the Septuagint, since there's nothing in the Hebrew that suggests them. He has, however, moved them. In the Septuagint, they are the translation for the Hebrew 'owls' (Jerome's 'ostriches'). In the Vulgate, 'sirens' are now the translation for jackals. This move allowed Jerome to render 'pleasant palaces' as 'temples of pleasure' and so to hint at the siren's seductive qualities, but it also let him draw a comparison between the jackals and the sirens. This might seem like a strange link to make, but Jerome expands on the connection in his commentaries and it's clear from these that he confused '*tannim*' (jackals) with '*tannin*' (dragons):* he describes the *tannim*, and the sirens, as 'great dragons, who are crested and fly'.[1] In fact, this translation error occurs throughout the Vulgate (it's even in the passage given below). Just in case there could be any doubt that this was a link between the sirens and the reptilian Lamia, Jerome also translated 'tannin' as 'lamia' in the Lamentations passage about the breastfeeding Lamia. In the Vulgate, then, the same word (or at least, what Jerome thought was the same word)

---

* He made plenty of other mistakes too – in Hebrew, 'horns' and 'glory' are the same word, and when Moses comes down with the 'glory of God on his countenance', Jerome decided to translate this as 'the horns of God', leading to a lot of confused medieval images of a horned Moses.

can be translated as either 'Lamia' or 'siren' – an undeniable sign of a connection between the two in early Christian thought.

The second set of passages (Isaiah 34:11–14) are more complex but tie the Lamia to the sirens even more explicitly. They describe the ruins not of Babylon, but of Edom.

Septuagint:

And nettles shall sprout up in their cities and in the
securest places of the land
and the hamlet shall be full of **sirens** and the house shall
be full of sparrows
And spirits shall meet with onocentaurs
And they shall call to each other;
There shall the onocentaurs halt, for they shall have
found rest for themselves.

Vulgate:

And thorns and nettles shall grow up in its houses,
and the thistle in the fortresses thereof:
and it shall be the habitation of **dragons,**
and the pasture of ostriches.
And demons and onocentaurs shall meet,
and the hairy ones shall cry out to one another,
There hath the **lamia** lain down,
and found rest for herself.*

Hebrew

* M. R. James, incidentally, based a ghost story on the phrase *ibi cubavit lamia* ('there hath the lamia lain down'), and a very good one it is too.

And thorns shall come up in her palaces,
nettles and brambles in the fortresses thereof:
and it shall be an habitation of **jackals**,
[and] a court for owls.
The wild beasts of the desert shall also meet with
the wild beasts of the island,
and the satyr shall cry to his fellow;
Lilith also shall rest there,
and find for herself a place of rest.

The first thing to note is that Jerome has again made his *tannin/
tannim*, dragon/jackal error, further stressing that he really did
mean to draw a comparison between siren-mermaids and dragon-
lamia in the first passage.*

Jerome has also removed the sirens of the Septuagint, and put
in a Lamia where there wasn't one before, in either the Septuagint
or the original Hebrew. Although the Lamia isn't swapped in
directly for the siren, it nonetheless gives the sense that one works
as a replacement for the other: in the ruins of Edom, Jerome kept
the sirens despite their absence in the Hebrew. He would surely
have done the same here – there's even the word *tannim* for him
to use, which this time he simply translates as 'dragon' – unless
he felt that the sense had been captured elsewhere. Lamia, here,
seems to be standing in for the sirens. Even more interestingly, we
can see that the word rendered by Jerome as 'Lamia' was, in the
original Hebrew, 'Lilith'. It's not surprising that another snake-
tailed, bare-breasted temptress who figures in churches across

---

* Was the Septuagint making the same comparison and mistake that
Jerome was making when it translates *tannim* as 'siren' in the third line?
Maybe, but given how bad the Septuagint's translation of the Hebrew is,
any conclusions drawn like this are on shaky ground – and we don't have
an equivalent to Jerome's commentary to point us in the right direction.

Europe would be mixed up with the mermaids, and it's nice to see it suggested, even if only tentatively, by the texts.

Acknowledgements

With enormous thanks to all the colleagues and friends who have helped this book become a reality. To The London Library and especially the Emerging Writers Programme, Claire Berliner and my wonderful peer group for giving me so much in the way of advice, encouragement and resources; to Dr Moudhy Al-Rashid and Dr Selena Wisnom for their reading of, and advice on, the Mesopotamia chapter (any mistakes are all mine); to my editor Georgina Blackwell; my agent Hayley Steed; Catherine Cho, who signed me in the first place; Elinor Davies who has been unwaveringly helpful; Nina Elstad for the fantastic cover design; Elodie for all her copyedits; to Tabby and Katie for being such wonderful colleagues while I was writing. To my friends, especially Afy, Danni and Georgia, who are better friends and people than anyone could hope to have in their lives; to my father for my love of history and my mother for her help.

And, of course, to Max – this book would not exist without the happiness and support you have given me for fifteen years. I love you more than anything.

Select Bibliography

CHAPTER 1: THE CRADLE OF CIVILIZATION

Walter Farber, *Lamaštu: An Edition of the Canonical Series of Lamaštu Incantations and Rituals and Related Texts from the Second and First Millennia B.C.* (Eisenbrauns, 2014).

Walter Farber, "Lilu, Lilitu, Ardat-lili", *Realexikon der Assyriologie und Vorderasiatischen Archäologie* Vol.7 (de Gruyter, 1987–1990).

Markham Geller, *Forerunners to Udug-Hul. Sumerian exorcistic incantations* (Franz Steiner Verlag, 1985).

Markham Geller, "New Duplicates to SBTU II", *Archiv für Orientforschung* Vol.35 (1988).

Nils Heebel, *Pazuzu* (Brill, 2002).

M. Stol, *Birth in Babylonia and the Bible* (STYX Publications, 2000).

J. A. Scurlock, "Baby-snatching Demons, Restless Souls and the Dangers of Childbirth: Medico-Magical Means of Dealing with Some of the Perils of Motherhood in Ancient Mesopotamia", *Incognita* Vol.2 (Brill, 1991).

CHAPTER 2: VIRGIN GHOSTS AND FAILED MOTHERS

Sarah Iles Johnston, *The Restless Dead* (University of California Press, 1999).

Daniel Ogden, *Dragons, Serpents, and Slayers in the Classical and Early Christian Worlds: A Sourcebook* (Oxford University Press, 2013).

Mary Lefkowitz, *Women's Life in Greece and Rome: a source book in translation* (Bloomsbury, 2016).

Konstantinos Kapparis, *Prostitution in the Ancient Greek World* (de Gruyter, 2018).

Richmond Alexander Lattimore, *Themes in Greek and Latin Epitaphs* (University of Illinois Press, 1962).

CHAPTER 3: FOOLISH OLD WOMEN

A. A. Barb, "The Mermaid and the Devil's Grandmother", *Journal of the Warburg and Courtauld Institutes* Vol. 29 (Warburg Institute, 1969).

Jeffrey Spier, "Medieval Byzantine Magical Amulets and Their Tradition", *Journal of the Warburg and Courtauld Institutes* Vol. 56 (Warburg Institute, 1993).

Richard Greenfield, "St Sisinnios, the Archangel Michael and the Female Demon Gylou: the Typology of the Greek Literary Sources", *Byzantina* Vol. 15 (Centre for Byzantine Research of the Aristotle University of Thessaloniki, 1989).

Richard Greenfield, *Traditions of Belief in Late Byzantine Demonology* (Adolf M. Hakkert, 1988).

Karen Hartnup, *On the Beliefs of the Greeks* (Brill, 2004).

CHAPTER 4: MOST WOMEN ARE SORCERERS

Edine Dallos, "Albasty: A Female Demon of the Turkic Peoples", *Acta Ethnographica Hungarica* Vol. 64 (Hungarian Academy of Sciences, 2019).

Rebecca Lesses, "Exe(o)rcising Power: Women as Sorceresses, Exorcists and Demonesses in Babylonian Jewish Society of Late Antiquity", *Journal of the American Academy of Religion* Vol. 69 (Oxford University Press, 2001).

James Montgomery, *Aramaic Incantation Texts from Nippur* (Museum of the University of Philadelphia, 1913).

James Nathan Ford and Matthew Morgenstern, *Aramaic Incantation Bowls in Museum Collections* (Brill, 2019).

Martin Schwartz, "*Sasm, Sesen, St. Sisinnios, Sesengen Barpharanges and 'Semanglof'", *Bulletin of the Asia Institute* Vol. 10 (Bulletin of the Asia Institute, 1996).

Martin Schwartz, "On Aiiehiia, Afflictress of Childbirth, and Pairika: Two Avestan Demonesses (with an Appendix on the Indo-Iranian Shipwrecked Seaman)", *Bulletin of the Asia Institute* Vol. 22 (Bulletin of the Asia Institute, 2008).

Dorit Kedar, *Who Wrote the Incantation Bowls* (unpublished PhD thesis, Berlin, 2018).

Shaul Shaked, James Nathan Ford, Siam Bhayro, *Aramaic Bowl Spells: Jewish Babylonian Aramaic Bowls Volume One* (Brill 2013).

Joseph Naveh, Shaul Shaked, *Amulets and Magic Bowls: Aramaic Incan-*

tations of Late Antiquity (Magnes Press, 1997).

CHAPTER 5: THE OTHER WOMAN

David Biale, *Eros and the Jews: From Biblical Israel to Contemporary America* (University of California Press, 1997).

Joseph Dan, "Samael, Lilith, and the Concept of Evil in Early Kabbalah", *AJS Review* Vol. 5 (Cambridge University Press, 1980).

Jeffrey Hoffeld, "Adam's Two Wives", *The Metropolitan Museum of Art Bulletin* Vol.26 (The Metropolitan Museum of Art, 1968).

Raphael Patai, *The Hebrew Goddess* (Wayne State University Press, 1990).

Gershom Scholem, *On the Kabbalah and its Symbolism* (Schocken Books, 1965).

Howard Schwartz, *Tree of Souls: The Mythology of Judaism* (Oxford University Press, 2004).

Virginia Tuttle, "Lilith in Bosch's 'Garden of Earthly Delights'", *Netherlands Quarterly History of Art* Vol. 15 (Stichting Nederlandse Kunsthistorische Publicaties, 1985).

Eli Yassif, *The Tales of Ben Sira in the Middle-Ages: A Critical Text and Literary Studies* (The Magnes Press, 1984).

Siegmund Hurwitz, *Lilith: The First Eve* (Daimon Verlag, 1992) (This is the English-language edition of the original German work *Lilith – die erste Eva*, published Daimon Verlag, 1980).

CHAPTER 6: SIREN SONG

Katherine Harvey, "Episcopal Virginity in Medieval England", *Journal of the History of Sexuality* Vol. 26 (University of Texas, 2017).

Roger Boase, "The 'Penitents of Love' and the Wild Man in the Storm: A Passage by the Knight of La Tour-Landry", *The Modern Language Review* Vol. 84 (Modern Humanities Research Association, 1989).

Roger Boase, "The Siren in the Storm and the Wild Man's Solace", *EHumanista* Vol.32 (Department of Spanish and Portuguese, University of California Santa Barbara, 2016).

Michael Bath and Malcolm Jones, "'Placardes and Billis and Ticquettis of Defamatioun': Queen Mary, the Mermaid and the Hare", *Journal of the Warburg and Courtauld Institutes* Vol. 78 (The Warburg Institute, 2015).

Hana Šedinová, "The 'Lamia' and Aristotle's Beaver: The Consequences of a Mistranscription', *Journal of the Warburg and Courtauld Institutes* Vol. 79 (The Warburg Institute, 2016).

Debra Hassig, *Medieval Bestiaries: Text, Image, Ideology* (Cambridge University Press, 1995).

William J. Travis, "Of Sirens and Onocentaurs: A Romanesque Apocalypse at Montceaux-l'Etoile", *Artibus et Historiae* Vol. 23 (IRSA s.c., 2002).

CHAPTER 7: MOTHER OF THE LORDS OF LUSIGNAN

Gervase of Tilbury, *Otia Imperialia*, edited and translated by S. E. Banks and James Wallace Binns (Clarendon Press, 2002).

Donald Maddox, Sara Sturm-Maddox, *Melusine of Lusignan* (University of Georgia Press, 1996).

Jean d'Arras, *Melusine; or, The Noble History of Lusignan* translated by Donald Maddox and Sara Sturm-Maddox (The Pennsylvania State University Press, 2012).

Marina Warner, *From the Beast to the Blonde: On Fairy Tales and Their Tellers* (Chatto & Windus, 1994).

Misty Urban, Deva Kemmis, Melissa Ridley Elmes (eds), *Melusine's Footprint: Tracing the Legacy of a Medieval Myth* (Brill, 2017).

CHAPTER 8: THE MONSTER OUTSIDE

Rebecca Stott, *The Fabrication of the Late-Victorian Femme Fatale* (Macmillan, 1992).

Sandra M. Gilbert and Susan Gubar, *The Madwoman in the Attic* (Yale University Press, 1979).

Mashey Bernstein, "The Fatal Attraction of Lilith", *Christianity and Literature* Vol. 42 (The Johns Hopkins University Press, 1993).

Elisabeth Gitter, "The Power of Women's Hair in the Victorian Imagination", *PMLA* Vol.99 (Modern Languages Association, 1984).

Virginia M. Allen, "'One Strangling Golden Hair': Dante Gabriel Rossetti's Lady Lilith", *The Art Bulletin* Vol.66 (CAA, 1984).

Peter Trippi, *J. W. Waterhouse* (Phaidon Press, 2002).

Cathy L. Baker and James K Baker, "The 'Lamia' in the Art of J W Waterhouse", *The British Art Journal* Vol. 5 (British Art Journal, 2004).

CHAPTER 9: LILITH REWRITTEN

Judith Plaskow, *The Coming of Lilith* (Beacon Press, 2005).

Lily Rivlin, "Lilith", *Ms Magazine* (1972).

Aviva Cantor Zuckoff, "The Lilith Question", *Lilith Magazine* (1972).

Aliza Cohen, "Escaping Eden: Finding Lilith in Queerness", *Autostraddle* (2018).

Shana Carroll, "Becoming Lilith" on the blog *The Transition Transmission* (2018).

Janet Mock, "Beauty Beyond Binaries: The Mermaid Trend Has an Extra-Special Meaning for Many Trans Women", *Allure* (2017).

C. L. Moore, "Fruit of Knowledge", *The Best of C. L. Moore* (Del Ray/Ballantine Books, 1980).

Octavia Butler, *Dawn* (Grand Central Publishing, 2021).

Charles Leland, *Etruscan Roman Remains in Popular Tradition* (Beyond Books Hub, 1892).

Ann R. Shapiro, "The Flight of Lilith: Modern Jewish American Feminist Literature", *Studies in American Jewish Literature (1981–)* Vol. 29 (Penn State University Press, 2010).

EPILOGUE: SURVIVAL

Randi Hutter Epstein, *Get Me Out: A History of Childbirth from the Garden of Eden to the Sperm Bank* (W. W. Norton, 2011).

Charles Stewart, *Demons and the Devil: Moral Imagination in Modern Greek Culture* (Princeton University Press, 1991).

Notes

CHAPTER 1: THE CRADLE OF CIVILIZATION

1 Walter Farber, *Lamaštu: An Edition* (Eisenbrauns, 2014), p.281.
2 Ibid., p.309.
3 Markham Geller, *Forerunners to Udug-Hul: Sumerian exorcistic incantations* (Franz Steiner Verlag, 1985), p.31.
4 Markham Geller, 'New Duplicates to SBTU II', *Archiv für Orientforschung* 35 (1988), p.14.
5 Benjamin Foster, *Before the Muses* (CDL Press, 2005), p.848.

CHAPTER 2: VIRGIN GHOSTS AND FAILED MOTHERS

1 Plutarch, *Plutarch's Lives with an English Translation by Bernadotte Perrin*, vol. 9 (Harvard University Press, 1926).
2 Daniel Ogden, *Dragons, Serpents, and Slayers in the Classical and Early Christian Worlds: A Sourcebook* (Oxford University Press, 2013), p.98.
3 Ibid., p.100.
4 Ibid., p.106.
5 *Women Writers of Ancient Greece and Rome: An Anthology* ed. Ian Michael Plant (University of Oklahoma Press, 2004), p.50.
6 Daniel Ogden, *The Strix-Witch* (Cambridge University Press, 2021), p.86.
7 Ibid., p.51.
8 *Cut These Words into My Stone: Ancient Greek Epitaphs* trans. Michael Wolfe (The Johns Hopkins University Press, 2013), p.57.
9 Richmond Lattimore, *Themes in Greek and Latin Epitaphs* (University of Illinois Press, 1962), p.192.
10 Ibid., p.193.
11 Sarah Iles Johnston, *The Restless Dead* (University of California Press, 1999), p.173.

12 *Inanna's Descent to the Nether World*, lines 295–305 (the translation and transliteration are both available on the Electronic Text Corpus of Sumerian Literature (https://etcsl.orinst.ox.ac.uk/section1/tr141. htm). The translation given here is simply 'demon', but the Sumerian shows that the sign 'gal$_5$' is used for these demons – they are Gallus.

13 Ogden, *Dragons, Serpents, and Slayers*, p.99.

14 Apuleius, *Metamorphoses (The Golden Ass), Volume I: Books 1–6*. Edited and translated by J. Arthur Hanson. Loeb Classical Library 44 (Harvard University Press, 1996), p. 224. Confusingly, Hanson has translated 'lamiae' as 'harpies', another mythological monster with very little relationship to the Lamia, except that both could, at one point or another, be used as a way of insulting women.

CHAPTER 3: FOOLISH OLD WOMEN

1 Ignatios the Deacon, *The Life of the Patriarch Tarasios* translated by Stephanos Efthymiadis (Aldershot: Ashgate Variorum, 1998).

2 Karen Hartnup, *On the Beliefs of the Greeks* (Brill, 2004), p.89.

3 Ibid.

4 Ibid.

5 Ibid., p.94.

6 Jeffrey Spier, "Medieval Byzantine Magical Amulets and Their Tradition" *Journal of the Warburg and Courtauld Institutes* Vol. 56 (The Warburg Institute, 1993), p.30.

7 Hartnup, *On the Beliefs of the Greeks*, op. cit., p.144.

8 J. S. Moorey, "A Bronze 'Pazuzu' Statuette from Egypt" *Iraq* Vol. 27 (British Institute for the Study of Iraq, 1965).

9 Frans Wiggermann, "Lamashtu, Daughter of Anu" in M. Stol, *Birth in Babylonia and the Bible* (STYX Publications, 2000), p.229.

10 Hartnup, *On the Beliefs of the Greeks*, op. cit., p.85.

11 Peter Hatlie, "The Religious Lives of Children and Adolescents" in Derek Krueger (ed) *Byzantine Christianity* (Fortress Press, 2010), p.184.

CHAPTER 4: MOST WOMEN ARE SORCERERS

1 James Montgomery, *Aramaic Incantation Texts from Nippur* (Museum of the University of Philadelphia, 1913), p.189.

2 Sanhedrin 67a.

3 Montgomery, *Aramaic Incantation Texts*, op. cit., p.138.

4   Ibid., p.238.
5   Ibid., p.155.
6   Ibid., p.117.
7   Ibid., p.178.
8   See e.g. James Nathan Ford and Matthew Morgenstern, *Aramaic Incantation Bowls In Museum Collections* (Brill, 2019), p. 14 (where you can also find a handy list of all the other bowls bearing this same story).
9   Martin Schwartz, "*Sasm, Sesen, St. Sisinnios, Sesengen Barpharanges and 'Semanglof'" *Bulletin of the Asia Institute* Vol. 10 (Bulletin of the Asia Institute, 1996), p.254.
10 Martin Schwartz, "On Aiiehiia, Afflictress of Childbirth, and Pairika: Two Avestan Demonesses (with an Appendix on the Indo-Iranian Shipwrecked Seaman)", *Bulletin of the Asia Institute* Vol. 22 (Bulletin of the Asia Institute, 2008), p.96.
11 Montgomery, *Aramaic Incantation Texts*, op. cit., p.170.
12 Shabbat 151b.
13 Eruvin 100b.
14 Niddah 24b.
15 Montgomery, *Aramaic Incantation Texts,* op. cit., p.189.
16 All figures taken from Dorit Kedar, *Who Wrote the Incantation Bowls* (unpublished PhD thesis, Berlin, 2018), p.104.
17 Shaul Shaked, James Nathan Ford, Siam Bhayro, *Aramaic Bowl Spells: Jewish Babylonian Aramaic Bowls Volume One* (Brill 2013), p.249.
18 Dorit Kedar, *Who Wrote the Incantation Bowls*, op. cit., p.133.
19 Ibid., p.135.
20 Sanhedrin 67a.

CHAPTER 5: THE OTHER WOMAN

1   Eli Yassif, *Pseudo Ben-Sira: The Text, Its Literary Character and Status in the Hebrew Literature of the Middle Ages* (PhD thesis, the Hebrew University, Jersualem, 1977) p.64–65.
2   Ibid, p.23–24.
3   Raphael Patai, *The Hebrew Goddess* (Wayne State University Press, 1990) p.264.
4   Gershom Schloem, *On the Kabbalah and its Symbolism* (Schocken Books, 1965) p.155.
5   David Biale, *Eros and the Jews: From Biblical Israel to Contemporary America* (University of California Press, 1997) p.101.

CHAPTER 6: SIREN SONG

1   Peter Damian, *Letters 91–120: Fathers of the Church, Mediaeval Continuation* translated by Owen J Blum (CUA Press, 1989) p.276.

2   Ambrose, *Select Words and Letters* (Nicene and Post-Nicene Fathers series 2), translated by Philip Schaff , Vol.10 (Eermans Pub Co., 1984) p.433.

3   Homer, *The Odyssey* translated by Emily Wilson (W. W. Norton & Co., 2017) p.184–191.

4   Philostratus, *Apollonius of Tyana vol. 1* translated by Christopher P. Jones (Harvard University Press, 2005) p.22.

5   Daniel Ogden, *Dragons, Serpents, and Slayers in the Classical and Early Christian Worlds: A Sourcebook* (Oxford University Press 2013), p.103.

6   William J. Travis, "Of Sirens and Onocentaurs: a Romanesque Apocalypse at Montceaux-l'Etoile", *Artibus et Historiae* Vol. 23 (IRSA s.c., 2002) p.59.

7   Thomas of Cantimpré, *Liber de natura rerum*, translated by Helmut Boese (de Gruyter, 1973) iv.5.

8   William of Malmesbury, *The Deeds of the Bishops of England*, translated by David Preest, (Boydell Press, 2002) p.187.

9   Quoted in Susan L'Engle, "Depictions of Chastity: Virtue Made Visible" in *Chastity: A Study in Perception, Ideals, Opposition* (Brill, 2008) p.100.

10 *The Metrical Life of St Hugh of Lincoln* edited and translated by Charles Garton (Honywood Press, 1986) p.16–23.

11 William of Malmesbury, *Saints' Lives*, edited and translated by M. Winterbottom and R. Thompson (Oxford University Press, 2002) p.14–15.

12 Quoted in Roger Boase, "'The Penitents of Love' and the Wild Man in the Storm: A Passage by the Knight of La Tour-Landry", *The Modern Language Review* Vol. 84 (Modern Humanities Research Association, 1989) p.824.

13 Quoted in Roger Boase, "The Siren in the Storm and the Wild Man's Solace", *EHumanista* Vol.32 (Department of Spanish and Portuguese, University of California Santa Barbara, 2016) p.670.

14 Quoted in Ibid., p.671.

CHAPTER 7: MOTHER OF THE LORDS OF LUSIGNAN

1   As quoted in Donald Maddox, Sara Sturm-Maddox, *Melusine of Lusignan* (University of Georgia Press, 1996) p.30.

2   Jean d'Arras, *Melusine; or, The Noble History of Lusignan* translated by Donald Maddox and Sara Sturm-Maddox (The Pennsylvania State University Press, 2012), p.182.

3   Ibid, p.75.

4   Hoffeld, "Adam's Two Wives" *The Metropolitan Museum of Art Bulletin* Vol.26 (The Metropolitan Museum of Art, 1968) p.432.

CHAPTER 8: THE MONSTER OUTSIDE

1   *Burne-Jones Talking: His Conversations 1895–1898 Preserved by his Studio Assistant Thomas Rooke*, edited by Mary Lago (John Murray, 1981) p.11.

2   Quoted in Peter Trippi, *J. W. Waterhouse* (Phaidon Press, 2002), 149. Trippi claims that it is from a clipping from the April 27, 1897 edition of the magazine *Truth*, found in the sketchbook of Herbert Draper.

3   Henry Rider Haggard, *The Complete Works of Henry Rider Haggard* (OK Publishing, 2017) p.4645.

4   John Ruskin, *The Works of John Ruskin vol. XVIII* (George Allen, 1912) p.123.

5   William Makepeace Thackeray, *Vanity Fair* (Wordsworth Editions, 1991) p.607.

6   George Elliot, *Daniel Deronda* (Oxford University Press, 2014) p.8.

7   Coventry Patmore, *The Angel in the House* (George Bell and Son, 1885) p.175.

8   Bram Stoker, *Dracula* (Ignatius Press, 2012) p.287.

9   Rudyard Kipling, *The Works of Rudyard Kipling* (Wordsworth Editions, 1994) p.232.

10 William Tindall, *W. B. Yeats* (Columbia University Press, 1966), p.11.

11 Robert Browning, *The Poetic and Dramatic Works of Robert Browning vol. 1* (Houghton, Mifflin and Company, 1895) p.1.

12 Dante Gabriel Rossetti, *The Collected Works of Dante Gabriel Rossetti vol. 1* (Ellis and Elvey, 1890) p.97.

13 Virginia M. Allen, "'One Strangling Golden Hair': Dante Gabriel Rossetti's Lady Lilith", *The Art Bulletin* Vol.66 (CAA, 1984) p. 290.

14 Rossetti, *The Collected Works,* op. cit., p.312.
15 Christina Rossetti, *Poems* (Roberts, 1888) p.122.
16 Dashiell Hammett, *The Four Great Novels* (Pan Books, 1983) p.567.
17 All quotations in this paragraph taken from Mashey Bernstein, "The Fatal Attraction of Lilith", *Christianity and Literature* Vol. 42 (The Johns Hopkins University Press, 1993) p.457.

CHAPTER 9: LILITH REWRITTEN

1 https://artviewer.org/calida-rawles-at-various-small-fires/
2 Judith Plaskow, *The Coming of Lilith* (Beacon Press, 2005) p.32.
3 Judith Plaskow, *Standing Against Sinai* (Harper Collins, 1991).
4 Lily Rivlin, "Lilith" *Ms Magazine* (1972) p.96.
5 Aviva Cantor Zuckoff, "The Lilith Question", *Lilith Magazine* (1972).
6 Germaine Greer, *The Female Eunuch* (McGraw Hill, 1971) p.261.
7 Aliza Cohen, "Escaping Eden: Finding Lilith in Queerness", *Autostraddle* (2018) (https://www.autostraddle.com/escaping-eden-finding-lilith-in-queerness-428957/).
8 Cantor Zuckoff, "The Lilith Question", op. cit.
9 Octavia E. Butler and Charles Rowell, "An Interview with Octavia Butler" *Callaloo* Vol. 20 (The Johns Hopkins University Press, 1997) p.50.
10 https://www.dw.com/en/transgender-woman-from-pakistan-finds-peace-in-germany/a-50599140.
11 Shana Carroll, "Becoming Lilith" on the blog The Transition Transmission (2018) (https://medium.com/the-transition-transmission/becoming-lilith-e7c1b029ff80).
12 Janet Mock, "Beauty Beyond Binaries: The Mermaid Trend Has an Extra-Special Meaning for Many Trans Women", *Allure* (2017) (https://www.allure.com/story/trans-women-mermaid-trend-meaning).
13 Ibid.

EPILOGUE: SURVIVAL

1 Charles Stewart, *Demons and the Devil: Moral Imagination in Modern Greek Culture* (Princeton University Press, 1991) p.100.
2 Ibid.

APPENDIX

1   Jerome, *In Esaiam*. PL 24.163.

10 per cent of the author advance and author royalties for this book will be donated to the Lilith Fund.

Image Credits

Page 3
(Top left) sailko / Wikimedia Commons
(Top right) © Ashmolean Museum, University of Oxford
(Bottom left) Paul Perdirizet (1870–4 juin 1938) / Wikimedia Commons

Page 4
(Top left) © The Trustees of the British Museum
(Top right) © The Trustees of the British Museum
(Bottom) Photo by Fine Art Images/Heritage Images via Getty Images

Page 5
(Top) The Cloisters Collection, 1955 / The Metropolitan Museum of Art
(Bottom left) Caitriana Nicholson / Wikimedia Commons

Page 6
(Top) Granger / Bridgeman Images
(Bottom) akg-images

Page 7
(Top) Fabio Boccuzzi / Shutterstock
(Bottom) Purchased from the artist, 1896 / Wikimedia Commons

Page 8
The Artchives / Alamy Stock Photo

Index